SpringerBriefs on Pioneers in Science and Practice

Volume 26

Series editor

Hans Günter Brauch, Mosbach, Germany

More information about this series at http://www.springer.com/series/10970
http://www.afes-press-books.de/html/SpringerBriefs_PSP.htm

Betty A. Reardon · Dale T. Snauwaert

Betty A. Reardon: A Pioneer in Education for Peace and Human Rights

Springer

International Institute on Peace Education

The University of Toledo
1872

Betty A. Reardon
International Institute on Peace Education
New York, NY
USA

Dale T. Snauwaert
Educational Foundations and Leadership
The University of Toledo
Toledo, OH
USA

The cover photograph was taken from the personal photo collection of the author. A website on this book with additional information on Betty A. Reardon, including links to videos and a selection of the covers of her major books is at: <http://afes-press-books.de/html/SpringerBriefs_PSP_Reardon.htm>.

ISSN 2194-3125 ISSN 2194-3133 (electronic)
ISBN 978-3-319-08966-9 ISBN 978-3-319-08967-6 (eBook)
DOI 10.1007/978-3-319-08967-6

Library of Congress Control Number: 2014944325

Springer Cham Heidelberg New York Dordrecht London

Copyediting: PD Dr. Hans Günter Brauch, AFES-PRESS e.V., Mosbach, Germany

Printed on acid-free paper

Springer is part of Springer Science+Business Media (www.springer.com)

One of the most personally and professionally rewarding collaborations of my years in peace education has been that with Dale Snauwaert, Tony Jenkins and Janet Gerson, especially in the on-going development of the International Institute on Peace Education that gives me a healthy hope for the future of peace education. So, I dedicate this book to this "collaborative," and to the hundreds of peace educators, students and citizen supporters, peacelearners all, linked together in the world-wide network of solidarity and cooperation that energizes the Global Campaign for Peace Education, an initiative made possible by Cora Weiss, President of the Hague Appeal for Peace, to Larry Metcalf who taught me the imperative of reflective learning for effective social education, to Willard Jacobson who saw the need for teacher preparation in field, and to Valentina Mitina whose cooperation proved that even national antagonisms could be transcended when addressed through learning; and to all from whom I have continually learned as I endeavored to understand and to confront the many challenges of educating for peace. All in this world wide network of possibilities for peace through learning have my deepest appreciation and admiration.

Betty A. Reardon
May, 2014

Preface

Dr. Betty A. Reardon is a pioneering and world-renowned leader of peace education and human rights.[1] Her groundbreaking work has laid the foundation for an inspiring new cross-disciplinary field that integrates peace education and the quest for international human rights within a gender-conscious, global perspective. In recognition of her internationally acclaimed contributions, achievements and awards as a teacher, activist, researcher, author, and consultant spanning five decades, she was nominated by the International Peace Bureau (Geneva, Switzerland) for the Nobel Peace Prize in 2013.

My association with Betty Reardon as a colleague and friend has spanned over two decades, and began with our first and auspicious faculty meeting together at Colgate University in 1990. Our mutual interest and dedication to the formulation of global peace and international human rights education have given rise to meaningful collaboration over the years. For example, as founding director of The University of Toledo's Center for Democratic Education and Non-Violence, my colleagues and I were honored to organize the "Betty A. Reardon Collection," an archive of her published and unpublished works, which opened in 2009 in the Ward M. Canady Center for Special Collections at The University of Toledo.

Given the wide range and complexity of Reardon's work, this short commentary will highlight what I perceive as her core ideas, acknowledging that my summary is not exhaustive. These ideas include universal human dignity and universal moral inclusion; violence as dehumanization and the core problematic of peace education; a human rights ethical framework; a transformational paradigm of peace; and peace learning and reflective inquiry.

Central to Reardon's conception of peace and peace education are two fundamental normative assertions: universal human dignity and universal moral inclusion. These two claims are normative, not empirical, in the sense that they

---

[1] The author is very grateful to Mary M. Darbes for helpful and insightful feedback on this preface. A website on this book with additional information on Betty A. Reardon, including links to videos and a selection of the covers of her major books is at: <http://afes-press-books.de/html/SpringerBriefs_PSP_Reardon.htm>.

ethically assert what *should* be. These related core conceptions constitute the ethical foundations of Reardon's overarching philosophy.

Universal human dignity and moral inclusion are logically interrelated. Universal human dignity is the normative claim that all human beings possess an equal intrinsic value that *should* be respected. In turn, this equal inherent dignity bestows upon each person standing in the human moral community. That is, each person is seen to be an equal member of the human moral community and thus each person has a right to equal moral consideration. This moral inclusion is universal in scope; it pertains to all human beings. These interrelated, normative assertions are the basis of Reardon's value-based conceptions of peace and violence.

In making these two fundamental ethical assertions, Reardon is a part of the long tradition of cosmopolitanism. Cosmopolitanism has many dimensions—epistemological, social, political, and ethical. The cosmopolitan ethical imperative mandates that we see the other as a person; it demands that we transcend the longstanding human patterns of violence, dehumanization, and objectification of persons in favor of the recognition of their humanity, and thereby embrace their standing in the human moral community.[2]

Violence is that which dehumanizes, which tears and erodes human dignity, and so being, it is the core problematic of peace and peace education. As Reardon states:

> I identify violence as the central problematic of peace education. All violence degrades and/or denies human dignity. This is why I assert that the substance of the field should comprise an inquiry into violence as a phenomenon and a system, its multiple and pervasive forms, the interrelationships among the various forms, its sources and purposes, how it functions and potential alternatives for achieving the legally sanctioned, socially accepted, or politically tolerated purposes commonly pursued through violence.[3]

This conception is a similar to Johan Galtung's understanding of violence as that which impedes and delimits human potential. Galtung writes:

> … *violence is present when human beings are being influenced so that their actual somatic and mental realizations are below their potential realization … Violence is here defined as the cause of the difference between the potential and actual*, between what could have been and what is. Violence is that which increases the distance between the potential and the actual, and that which impedes the decrease of this distance.[4]

---

[2] Chris Brown, 1992: *International Relations Theory: New Normative Approaches* (New York: Columbia University Press); Immanuel Kant, [1795] 1983: *Perpetual Peace and Other Essays*, trans. Ted Humphrey. (Cambridge: Hackett); Martha Nussbaum, 1997: "Kant and Cosmopolitanism," in: James Bohman, Matthias Lutz-Bachmann (Eds.): *Perpetual Peace: Essays on Kant's Cosmopolitan Ideal* (Cambridge: MIT Press).

[3] Betty A. Reardon, 2010: *Human Rights Learning: Pedagogies and Politics of Peace* (San Juan, Puerto Rico: UNESCO Chair for Peace Education, University of Puerto Rico), 55; see Chap. 11 in this volume.

[4] Johan Galtung, 1969: "Violence, Peace, and Peace Research," in: *Journal of Peace Research* 6, 3: 168.

Paulo Freire also conceptualizes violence as dehumanization; he writes:

> Any situation in which 'A' objectively exploits 'B' or hinders his and her pursuit of self-affirmation as a responsible person is one of oppression. Such a situation in itself constitutes violence … because it interferes with the individual's ontological and historical vocation to be more fully human. With the establishment of a relationship of oppression, violence has already begun …[5]

Freire maintains that it is our ontological and historical vocation to become fully human, to strive for and actualize our potential as human beings. We have a human right to the actualization of our humanity. All forms of coercive political, economic, and social interference, both direct and structural, with our human completion dehumanize and oppress, and are thereby unjust.[6]

Reardon identifies a number of social structures and modes of thought that violate human dignity. They constitute what Galtung refers to as direct, structural, and cultural violence.[7] These violent structures constitute a system of control, domination, and oppression, including ways of thinking and believing that justify and normalize these structures. In Reardon's view, militarism (the war system), patriarchy/sexism, and a technocratic-managerial economic hierarchy, and its concomitant knowledge industry and social philosophy, constitute the basic structure of a violent society.[8]

For Reardon the transformation needed for the ongoing pursuit of peace, and thereby, a reduction in violence, requires a fundamental paradigm shift in social values and worldviews—a shift from a paradigm of war toward a paradigm of peace.[9] This value shift was expressed early on in her work through the assertion of the following "world order values": "minimization of violence, war prevention; maximizing of economic welfare … increasing of social justice by relieving discrimination and oppression; broadening of the democratic base of public policy … restoration of ecological balance."[10]

---

[5] Paulo Freire, 1970: *Pedagogy of the Oppressed* (New York: Continuum).

[6] For further discussions see Dale T. Snauwaert, 2011: "Social justice and the philosophical foundations of critical peace education: Exploring nussbaum, Sen, and Freire," in *Journal of Peace Education* 8, 3; David Ragland, 2012: "Theorizing Justice in Betty Reardon's Philosophy of Peace Education: A Gender and Feminist Political Conception" (The University of Toledo).

[7] Galtung, 1990: "Violence, peace, and peace research; "cultural violence," in: *Journal of Peace Research* 27, 3.

[8] See Reardon's bibliography of publications in this volume as well as 1.2, 1.3, 1.4, and Epilogue.

[9] Betty A. Reardon, 1989: "Toward a Paradigm of Peace," in: Linda Rennie Farcey (Ed.): *Peace: Meanings, Politics, Strategies* (New York: Praeger); " Learning Our Way to a Human Future," in: Betty A. Reardon, Eva Nordland (Eds.): *Learning Peace: The Promise of Ecological and Cooperative Education* (Albany, NY: State University of New York Press, 1994).

[10] "Transformations into Peace and Survival: Programs for the 1970s," in: George Henderson (Ed.): *Education for Peace: Focus on Mankind* (Alexandria, VA: Association for Supervision and Curriculum Development, 1973), 133–34; see Chap. 5 in this volume.

In subsequent work, the value shift is articulated within a human rights framework. A human rights framework is the *lingua franca* of cosmopolitan ethics.[11] Human rights are a way of expressing what one must do or can never do to another human being who possesses an equal inherent dignity.[12] The language of rights thus can be understood to constitute the principles of a cosmopolitan ethic of human dignity, and thus a counter-point to violence. As Reardon maintains: "Human rights study provides us with tools of definition and diagnosis of what comprises violence, experientially as well as conceptually …"[13]

There are a number of logically consistent ways of conceiving "rights," all of which follow from the value of human dignity. One way to conceive a right is what a human being is due. From this perspective, "rights" constitute what each and every human being is owed by virtue of their humanity. Rights are also justified demands for the enjoyment of social goods.[14] Rights are also conceived as protections against coercion, deprivation, and inhumane treatment. Rights protect the powerless from the powerful. In this sense, rights are political in that they are a means of adjudicating conflict as well as protecting the individual from harm.[15]

Rights thus define what the individual as one who possesses equal inherent dignity is due, is justified in demanding, and/or is protected from. In this way rights are devices, which define what moral choices can never be made or those that must be made.[16] As Reardon asserts, human rights function as "tools for the realization of the conditions necessary to human dignity."[17]

In turn, rights logically entail correlative duties:

1. Duties to *avoid* depriving another the right.
2. Duties to *protect* the other from deprivation of the right.
3. Duties to *aid* the deprived.[18]

The duty to *avoid* deprivation entails restraint: the obligation to refrain from destructive action and/or interference. The duty to *protect* entails the responsibility for establishment of norms, social practices, and institutions that enforce the duty to avoid deprivation. The duty to *aid* is positive in the sense that it is an obligation

[11] Norberto Bobbio, [1990] 1996: *The Age of Rights* (Cambridge, UK: Polity Press); R.J. Vincent, 1986: *Human Rights and International Relations* (Cambridge: Cambridge University Press).

[12] Michael J. Perry, 1998: *The Idea of Rights: Four Inquiries* (New York: Oxford University Press).

[13] Reardon, *Human Rights Learning: Pedagogies and Politics of Peace*, 13.

[14] Henry Shue, 1980: *Basic Rights: Subsistence, Affluence, and U.S. Foreign Policy* (Princeton: Princeton University Press).

[15] Michael Ignatieff, 2001: *Human Rights as Politics and Idolatry*, in: Amy Gutmann (Ed.) (Princeton, NJ: Princeton University Press).

[16] Perry, *The Idea of Rights: Four Inquiries*.

[17] Reardon, *Human Rights Learning: Pedagogies and Politics of Peace*, 46.

[18] Shue, *Basic Rights: Subsistence, Affluence, and U.S. Foreign Policy*, 52–53.

to *provide* for those in need. These duties comprise the obligation of social responsibility inherent in human rights. As Reardon suggests: "Human rights learning, at its core, is the cultivation of ethical reflection and assessment for the exercise of social responsibility."[19]

In turn, Reardon conceives peace in terms of the realization of human rights and duties: "A sustainable world peace can only be assured through the universal actualization of human dignity."[20] She maintains that: "Human rights standards are the specific indicators and particular measures of progress toward and the realization of peace. Human rights puts flesh on the bones of the abstraction of peace and provide the details of how to bring the flesh to life."[21] A society, both national and global, that secures the human dignity of all citizens through the realization of their rights is the standard for "authentic peace." Reardon writes:

> As a political framework for the actualization of human dignity, human rights are the ethical core of peace education; not a complement, or a particular component, and certainly not an alternative or an educationally equivalent substitute for peace education. Human rights are integral to peace education, that is, without human rights peace education lacks a primary component of its core and essential substance. Human rights are the essence and the arbiter of peace, the antithesis of violence, touching on multiple and complex aspects of the human experience, illuminating the necessity of holism to the field. The potential of human rights as the means to cultivate transformational thinking lies in viewing all human rights norms and standards as a whole, an integrated ethical system.[22]

This value-oriented, human rights conception of peace integrates the ideas of negative and positive peace.

Reardon defines negative peace "as the absence of war, achieved by the prevention and/or the general reduction and eventual elimination of armed conflict."[23] She argues that a fully actualized state of negative peace would entail the abolition of war as an institution ("the war system"), including complete and general disarmament.[24]

Positive peace includes but transcends negative peace. It entails not only the elimination of armed aggression but also the positive establishment of justice. It constitutes a social order free of all forms of violence, including structural and cultural violence, as well as the establishment and sustainability of fundamental and wide spread social fairness. Positive peace can be understood as the realization of the complete range of human rights: civil and political *and* economic, cultural, and social. She writes:

---

[19] Reardon, *Human Rights Learning: Pedagogies and Politics of Peace*, 55.

[20] *Human Rights Learning: Pedagogies and Politics of Peace*, 46

[21] *Human Rights Learning: Pedagogies and Politics of Peace*, 47.

[22] Ibid.

[23] *Comprehensive Peace Education: Educating for Global Responsibility* (New York: Teachers College Press, 1988), 6.

[24] "Disarmament and Peace Education," *Prospects: Quarterly Review of Education* 8, 4 (1978); *Comprehensive Peace Education: Educating for Global Responsibility.*

> The major areas of concern in the domain of positive peace are the problems of economic deprivation and development; environment and resources; and universal human rights and social justice. Peace education seems to have subsumed all of these areas into the general concept of global justice . . . "justice," in the sense of the full enjoyment of the entire range of human rights by all people, is what constitutes positive peace.[25]

On the basis of both negative and positive peace, Reardon posits the notion of "authentic peace." Reardon conceives authentic peace as the abolition of the war system and the establishment of global justice and a global civic community. Peace, so conceived, is therefore an ethical imperative, a fundamental human right.[26]

In addition to ethical reflection within a human rights framework as a core element of a shift to a paradigm of peace, there are at least two other elements of this shift in worldview. Reardon's conception of peace and her understanding of the integral elements of a paradigm of peace are profoundly influenced by feminism and holism.[27] This constitutes an ontological perspective, which generates an understanding of life that is interrelated and interdependent: life is understood as an interdependent web of relationships within which respecting and caring for the inherent dignity of life, human and non-human, is imperative. This view is a perspective of deep equality. This holistic ontology in turn leads to the inclusion of all life in the moral community, thereby bringing the moral consideration of the natural world and ecological balance under the umbrella of authentic peace. She writes for example: "Clearly, peace studies must begin to pursue wholism as the framework, process as the primary method, and peace in its widest sense as the goal, if it is to energize the intellectual transformation necessary to a paradigm of peace."[28] In addition, "Holism and critical reflection are essential and necessary to the transformation of thinking (and transformational thinking) conducive to the political processes requisite to the realization of human rights as the basis of a peaceful world order ..."[29]

Based upon her conception of authentic peace Reardon defines the educational task in holistic and transformational terms:

> . . . the general purpose of peace education, as I understand it, is to promote the development of an authentic planetary consciousness that will enable us to function as global citizens and to transform the present human condition by changing the social structures and the patterns of thought that have created it. This transformational imperative must, in my view, be at the center of peace education. It is important to emphasize that transformation, in this context, means a profound global cultural change that affects ways of thinking, world views, values, behaviors, relationships, and the structures that make up our

---

[25] *Comprehensive Peace Education: Educating for Global Responsibility*, 26.

[26] Note that this conception of peace as an ethical imperative is part of the cosmopolitan tradition; see for example, Kant, *Perpetual Peace and Other Essays*.

[27] Her feminism, including her analysis of the relationship between sexism and militarism, is the subject of Volume 27 in this series.

[28] Reardon, "Toward a Paradigm of Peace," 25.

[29] "Learning Our Way to a Human Future," 46.

> public order. It implies a change in the human consciousness and in human society of a dimension far greater than any other that has taken place since the emergence of the nation-state system, and perhaps since the emergence of human settlement.[30]

One of Reardon's core insights is that peace requires and is constituted by learning, and learning is reflective and dialogical, and thus, transformative. Her approach to peace education is thereby transformational. The transformational approach transcends but includes the two other prominent traditions in peace education: the reform and reconstruction traditions.[31] The reform approach is devoted to the prevention of war, including the control and balance of arms. The reconstructive approach seeks to reconstruct international systems, to abolish war, and to achieve total disarmament. Its primary objective is structural and institutional change and the establishment of global conflict-resolution, peacekeeping, and peace-building institutions. The transformational approach aims at the rejection of all forms of violence, direct, structural, and cultural; its goal is a shift to a paradigm of peace, including the development of the human capacities and ways of thought necessary to sustain it.

The transformational approach employs a pedagogy that elicits learning. Reardon describes this approach as follows:

> [transformational] peace educators … describe their goal as eliciting (not imposing or inculcating) positive responses, recognizing that education is not so much a process of imparting knowledge as it is "drawing out" the capacity to learn … In eliciting awareness, the intent is to strengthen capacity to care, to develop a sincere concern for those who suffer because of the problems and a commitment to resolving them through action. Awareness infused by caring becomes concern that can lead to such commitment when one action is followed by other actions, and when action for peace becomes a sustained behavioral pattern, part of the learner's way of life. The objective is to elicit an ongoing and active response to the problems of peace and a commitment to their resolution. … this cycle of care, concern, and commitment is the core of the peace learning process.[32]

Reardon maintains that a transformational peace education should draw out "a new mode of thinking that is life-affirming, oriented toward the fulfillment of the human potential, and directed to the achievement of maturation as the ultimate goal of … positive peace."[33] More specifically, peace education should be

---

[30] *Comprehensive Peace Education: Educating for Global Responsibility* (New York: Teachers College Press, 1988), x.

[31] Betty A. Reardon, 2000: "Peace Education: A Review and Projection," in: Robert Moon, Miriam Ben-Peretz, and Sally Brown (Eds.) *Routledge International Companion to Education* (London: Routledge).

[32] Reardon, *Comprehensive Peace Education: Educating for Global Responsibility*, 21–22.

[33] *Comprehensive Peace Education: Educating for Global Responsibility*, 53.

fundamentally concerned with the development of the *political efficacy* of future citizens—the capacity to engage in transformative political action.[34]

Political efficacy involves "complex learning that requires pedagogies of multiple forms of reflective inquiry." Peace learning and thus reflective inquiry is both critical and ethical; it involves both the analysis of politics and value-based ethical assessment.

Reardon articulates three forms of reflective inquiry: critical/analytic; moral/ ethical; and contemplative/ruminative. Critical/analytic reflection pertains to the discernment of power, an understanding and critique of social institutions, analysis of the structural dimensions of social life, and a critical consciousness (in a Freirian sense) of the political–economic origins of violence. Moral/ethical reflection addresses questions of justice, and thereby structural and cultural violence, guided by the principles of a human rights framework. Contemplative reflection is conceived as self-examination of internal moral motivation and commitment. It pertains to a reflection on what is meaningful and valuable. It also involves the exercise of imagination to envision alternative realities necessary for transformative action.[35]

The central method of facilitating reflective inquiry is not only the posing of questions, but more deeply the posing of *queries*. Reardon writes:

> Reflective inquiry initiated by the posing of questions is deepened through the consideration of queries. In that it is in essence a process of thinking by interrogation, it is thus essentially dialogic, beginning with focusing on and encountering the subject of the inquiry as the entry point into the process of examination of what is to be further explored. In this respect, reflective inquiry begins with an inner process of confronting and questioning toward a basic understanding of the subject or issue. While it is possible for the process to remain inward and still be productive of learning, the practice of reflective inquiry as peace education—learning toward social and political change—must become outwardly dialogic in the form of a learning discourse through posing queries to elicit the individual reflections of all who comprise the learning community (or class).[36]

While questions elicit definitive, descriptive factual answers, queries call for conditional, speculative responses. Queries require reflection rather than recollection or deduction, which in turn produces group dialog and inquiry. "Queries are a way of putting the "quest" into questions and the "search" into research … It is the questing and the search that "opens" an inquiry."[37] Queries open inquiry to deeper reflection and critical analysis.

---

[34] Betty A. Reardon, Dale T Snauwaert, 2011: "Reflective pedagogy, cosmopolitanism, and critical peace education for political efficacy: a discussion of Betty A. Reardon's assessment of the field," in: *In Factis Pax: Journal of Peace Education and Social Justice* 5, 1; see Chap. 13 in this volume.

[35] Ibid.

[36] "Reflective Pedagogy, Cosmopolitanism, and Critical Peace Education for Political Efficacy: A Discussion of Betty A. Reardon's Assessment of the Field," 7.

[37] "Reflective Pedagogy, Cosmopolitanism, and Critical Peace Education for Political Efficacy: A Discussion of Betty A. Reardon's Assessment of the Field," 12.

This conception of a pedagogy of reflective inquiry is deeply influenced by Paulo Freire's critical pedagogy:

> Critical pedagogy is the methodology most consistent with the transformative goals of peace education and human rights learning… I have argued that the theories and practices we have learned from Paulo Freire are the conceptual and methodological heart of the most effective peace learning and peace politics. I so argue largely because I see his work as the primary model of a process in which learning is politics and politics can be learning …[38]

Paulo Freire posits the general historical existence of a social reality dominated by oppression.[39] In response he points us toward the possibility of a society constituted by authentic subjects co-existing in dialogical solidarity seeking to fulfill their ontological vocation to become more fully human. The core problematic is how to move from oppression to liberation and empowerment, which entails both the transformation of the structures of consciousness *and* the transformation of the social structure. The Freirean means to this end is cultural action—dialogical and problem-posing educational interventions (critical pedagogy) to facilitate critical consciousness and authentic subjectivity. Within this theoretical framework Freire conceives hope as "untested feasibility." Freire maintains that there is a strong tendency to perceive social reality as reified, as fixed. This perception locks the individual in a reality that is hopeless, leading to a disempowered self-concept. Freire maintains, however, that it is possible to understand social realities as fluid *limit situations* that are social constructions subject to critique and transformation. Critical pedagogy is a method that engages in *problem-posing* activities that *re-present* taken-for-granted social assumptions into problems to be critically explored and understood. It constitutes a method that empowers and liberates the consciousness of the student. This approach significantly shapes Reardon's idea of critical reflective inquiry.

It is also apparent that Reardon's pedagogy is significantly influenced by John Dewey. Dewey defines education as "that reconstruction or reorganization of experience which adds to the meaning of experience, and which increases ability to direct the course of subsequent experience."[40] Dewey conceives the reconstruction of experience in terms of the development of human capacities and powers. Learning is fundamentally about capacity building: knowledge is power. The reconstruction of experience, entailing the growth of capacity, is facilitated by various modes of reflective experimental inquiry and esthetic experience connected to the conjoint activity of social life. From this perspective, peace is a basic conjoint, communal activity, and peace education a process of the reconstruction of experience facilitated by reflective inquiry connected to that activity. Both Dewey and Reardon emphasize the development of the student's internal capacities and powers through active reflective inquiry as the essence of education.

---

[38] Reardon, *Human Rights Learning*, 66.

[39] Freire, *Pedagogy of the Oppressed.*

[40] John Dewey, 1916: *Democracy and Education: An Introduction to the Philosophy of Education*, Text-Book Series in Education (New York: The Macmillan company), 74.

In summary, Reardon's transformational pedagogy addresses the core problematic of how to promote authentic planetary consciousness in the movement from oppression to empowerment. She argues that this pedagogy, and its reflective, dialogical inquiry, must be critical, ethical, and contemplative, which will cultivate the human capacities necessary for the political empowerment and efficacy of citizens, the core goal of peace education.

In conclusion, this book is a rich collection of reflective inquiry and ongoing learning by one of the great pioneers of peace education. This commentary introduces Dr. Reardon's core ideas, which are elucidated consistently from the beginning of her work to the present. In addition to being a leading world figure in the field of peace, disarmament, and human rights education, Dr. Reardon has also been a major contributor to the development of a feminist analysis of peace issues within the context of a global, ethical perspective. Her major writings on peace, disarmament and human security from a gender perspective will be the subject of another volume in this series (volume 27). Betty Reardon has powerfully shaped the theory and practice of peace and human rights education over five decades. Her work is truly path breaking, both enlightening and inspiring to me and to many others. May the publication of these collections of her work serve to challenge and inspire peace builders and learners everywhere.

Toledo, April 2014 Dale T. Snauwaert

Acknowledgments

As it has often been with the most meaningful of my endeavors, this book is the product of collegial cooperation that initiated it, delineated its form, chose the selections included, searched out photos, and brought the manuscript to completion.

First among these collaborators is Hans Günter Brauch, primary editor of the *Pioneers in Science and in Practice* series whom I thank for the invitation to put together this manuscript. So, too, I am grateful for his hours of often tedious work of converting the texts into publishable form. I am profoundly honored to be among the other authors in this series who have conceived, developed, and applied to education and action the rich and promising intellectual terrain of peace knowledge. Thank you, Hans Günter.

My deep and abiding gratitude goes to Dale Snauwaert, who supported, facilitated, and carried out all phases of the project from its inception. How fortunate I was to have such an able scholar, outstanding peace educator, respected colleague, and very dear friend as the editor of this book and its companion volume. There was no end to the tasks and details he so gracefully undertook throughout the process. His skill, patience, and care made completion possible. Thank you, Dale.

I am deeply appreciative of Tony Jenkins', Director of the *International Institute on Peace Education* (IIPE), technical contributions, particularly for searching and preparing for publication all of the photos that appear in both volumes. He was very generous with his time during a period when he carried an extra heavy academic and program load in his work as one of the prime movers of this generation of peace educators. Thank you, Tony.

New York, May 2014 Betty A. Reardon

Contents

Part I About the Author and the Framework of the Book

1 Professional Biography of the Author: A Life in Peace Learning . . . 3

2 Reardon's Publications Archived in the Canady Center for Special Collections, The University of Toledo . . . 15

3 Organization and Rationale for the Selection of the Texts in This Volume . . . 25

Part II Generations of Reardon's Professional Formation and Practice as Reflected in Selected Essays: First Generation—The Foundations 1963–1985

4 The World Law Fund: World Approach to International Education . . . 29
4.1 National Interest and Curriculum . . . 31
4.2 The Ambiguities of Understanding . . . 33
4.3 World Order in the Curriculum . . . 34
4.4 Origin of the Fund . . . 35
4.5 Law as a Universal Experience . . . 36
4.6 The "Models Project" . . . 37
4.7 An "Emerging Discipline" . . . 37
4.8 Training the Teachers . . . 38
4.9 Summer Institutes . . . 39
4.10 Need for Readers . . . 40
4.11 An International Colloquium . . . 41
4.12 World Order Seminars . . . 41
4.13 LAWS and the Teacher . . . 42

4.14 Manuscripts and Syllabi 43
4.15 The World Order Reader 44

5 Transformations into Peace and Survival: Programs for the 1970s 47
5.1 Introduction 49
5.2 Meeting the Crises: A Revolution in Education 52
5.3 World-Order Studies as Survival Curriculums 53
5.4 Personal Identity and World Civilization 56
5.5 Language Facility for a Multicultural Community 57
5.6 Decolonializing Education 59
5.7 Systems Approach and Survival Skills 61
5.8 Human Values and Moral Development 62
5.9 Dialogues for Moral Decision Making 65
5.10 Professional Responsibilities 67

6 Conclusions from "The Knowledge Industry" 71
6.1 Introduction 73
6.2 Conclusions and Recommendations 73
6.2.1 Effects upon Development Ideology 73
6.2.2 Working Within the System 75
6.2.3 Entry Points for Change 76
6.2.4 Approaches to Change 77

7 Disarmament and Peace Education 81
7.1 Emotions or Politics? 83
7.1.1 Public Values 87
7.2 Global Interdependence 88

Part III Generations of Reardon's Professional Formation and Practice as Reflected in Selected Essays: Second Generation—The Formation 1985–2000

8 The Fundamental Purposes of a Pedagogy of Peace 93
8.1 Introduction 97
8.2 Teaching Toward the Development of Peacemaking Capacities 102
8.3 Transformational Approaches to Learning 106

9 Toward a Paradigm of Peace 109
9.1 Preface 110
9.2 Taming the Lion Within 111
9.3 Peace as a Dynamic, Organic Process 114

9.4 Peace Education as Life Enhancement 116
9.5 Metaphors of Birth and Life 118
9.6 Learning: Merger of Personal and Political, Means and Ends 119

10 Learning Our Way to a Human Future 121
10.1 Introduction 123
10.2 The New Moment: The Educational Challenges and Opportunities 125
10.3 What the New Moment Means for Learning: The Responsibilities of Educators 125
10.4 The Particular Responsibilities of the United States and the Countries of the Former USSR for New Learning 127
10.5 An Emerging Paradigm for Security and Community: Learning for a Transformed World Order 128
10.6 The Project on Ecological and Cooperative Education: A Response to the Challenge of Learning to Transform 129
10.7 The Task and the Goal for the North American Educational Community 129
10.8 An Ecological Framework 130
10.9 The Meaning and Promise of Cooperative Learning 131
10.10 Toward Global Cooperation and Social Responsibility: Learning for Responsible Citizenship in a Pluralistic World 134
10.11 Our Vision of a Democratic World Society: The Observation of Comprehensive, Universal Human Rights 135
10.12 From Domination to Mutuality: Power as Synergy, a Cooperative Learning Task 136
10.13 Education for a Healthy Planet, Healthy Society: A Future Worth Hoping for, A Goal Worth Struggling for, A Task Worth Learning. 138
10.14 Learning to Care: The Basis of Responsibility 139
10.15 Teaching Toward the Future in the Present 140

Part IV Generations of Reardon's Professional Formation and Practice as Reflected in Selected Essays: Third Generation—Framing for Futures 2001–2014

11 Human Rights Learning: Pedagogies and Politics of Peace. 145
11.1 Proposition 1: Human Rights Are Integral and Essential to Peace and Peace Education 147

11.2 Proposition 2: Human Rights Learning Is a Contemporary Form of Freirean Political Pedagogy . . . 149
11.3 Proposition 3: The Violence and Vulnerabilities of the Global System Frame Ethical Issues for Human Rights Learning and a Politics of Peace . . . 150
11.4 Proposition 5: We Need to Devise a Pedagogy for Hidebound Institutions . . . 157
11.5 Proposition 6: Critical Pedagogy Is the Methodology Most Consistent with the Transformative Goals of Peace Education and Human Rights Learning . . . 158
11.6 Proposition 7: Inquiry Is the Teaching Mode Most Consistent with the Principles and Purposes of Critical Learning . . . 160
11.7 Concluding Summary Proposition: Holistic Frame-Works and Critical Reflection Are Consistent with and Contribute to Transformation Toward the Actualization of Human Dignity . . . 162
References . . . 163

12 Human Rights and the Renewal of the University . . . 165
12.1 Human Rights: a Response to the Problematic of Contemporary Universities . . . 168
12.2 The University as Learning Community . . . 169
12.3 Purpose and Mission of the University Articulated Within the Human Rights Framework . . . 173
12.4 Human Rights Education, Human Rights Learning and Human Rights Training: Contrasts and Complementarities . . . 174
12.5 Human Rights Education as the Substance of the Scholarly Components . . . 178
12.6 Human Rights Learning: A Process of Ethical and Intellectual Formation, Sharpening the Mind While Strengthening the Heart . . . 178
12.7 Human Rights Training: Providing Non-Academic Social Justice Learning Opportunities . . . 179
12.8 Reclaiming the Moral High Ground: Renewing the University to Transform the Society . . . 180

13 Reflective Pedagogy, Cosmopolitanism, and Critical Peace Education for Political Efficacy . . . 181
13.1 Dale Snauwaert's Reflections . . . 184
13.2 Reardon's Responses to Snauwaert's Queries on Reflective Inquiry . . . 189
13.2.1 Methodological Orientation: A Purposeful Interrogatory Process . . . 189

13.2.2 The Place of Dialogue: Communal Reflection Building Learning Communities 190
13.2.3 Conceptual Frameworks: Tools for Shaping and Plotting the Inquiry 191
13.2.4 Background Knowledge: Substance Is Constitutive to Reflective Inquiry 194
13.2.5 Justice and Peace: Defining Concepts, Describing Conditions, Honing Conceptual Tools . . . 195
13.2.6 Open Inquiry: Formulation of Cogent Questions; Expectations for Replies 196
13.2.7 The Moral and Political Philosophies of Open Reflective Inquiry 197
13.3 Snauwaert's Concluding Reflections 198

14 Epilogue: The First Day of Hope 199

About the Author 213

About the Book 215

Part I
About the Author and the Framework of the Book

Chapter 1
Professional Biography of the Author: A Life in Peace Learning

What follows here is a subjective account of my personal memory of the experiences that were influential to the teacher-learner I became and the efforts I have made to contribute to the evolution and development of the field of peace education. I have spent most my life as a teacher-activist who determined where I would spend my energies by what I believed might contribute to the field. I did not seek a life of scholarship so much as to take up whatever opportunities became available me to advance that primary purpose. The writings that appear in this collection, some of them 'scholarly' and some of them not, were almost entirely undertaken to advance the field, to refine and make our modes of teaching more effective to achieving our guiding social and political norms.

I was born in New York City on June 12th, 1929 (the same day that Anne Frank was born in Frankfurt) the first of two daughters born to Julie Burke Reardon and Michael August Reardon who soon thereafter moved the family to Rye, New York, my father's birth place and childhood home. My sister, Barbara (1932–2008) and I grew up and attended public schools in this small village that grew into an upper income suburb by the end of World War II. Most middle class families in our section of town knew most others.

B.A. Reardon and D.T. Snauwaert, *Betty A. Reardon: A Pioneer in Education for Peace and Human Rights*, SpringerBriefs on Pioneers in Science and Practice 26,
DOI 10.1007/978-3-319-08967-6_1

Showing second grade art work with life-long friend Peggy Park 1938. *Source* Personal photo collection of the author

A number of the teachers who taught me and my peers also had taught our parents. It was in most respects a community, but it also reflected the social strata of the society with residents in estates and up-scale housing areas, middle class business and trades people, house workers and laboring people, largely recent Italian immigrants and a very few African American families among the latter. The public schools served mainly the middle and working classes. We were taught the basic learning skills, a bit of American history that included some Native American culture, but nothing about the fate of those peoples at the hands of our European ancestors. We learned that the slaves had been freed by Abraham Lincoln, but nothing about the lot of the slaves' descendants in our own time. We also learned about the "right of revolution," the Declaration of Independence and the Bill of Rights, the first ten amendments of the US Constitution. Whether it was intended as an affective learning objective or not, I internalized "the self-evident truths" and took their realization to be the work of my society. At the same time, young as we were, through subtle and sometimes blatant messages in our environment we became aware of the class and race differences and intuited their importance to our lives, and, as I continued to learn, the impediments they raised to the self-evident truths.

I attended high school in Rye, as well, where I began to have some intentional education on issues of social and economic justice that shed greater light on American racial injustice. Of the many fine teachers who introduced me to foreign languages, history, the sciences and made a noble but benighted attempt at teaching me math, one who had the greatest effect on the development of my social consciousness and world awareness was Frances Hamilton in a class that was called something like "Modern Problems" or "American Issues." What mattered was her introduction to critical thinking and to the United Nation where some of us students accompanied her, sitting among the NGOs as early as its first days in 1946 and 1947 in Flushing Meadows before the world organization was installed in the "big glass house on the East River."

1942 Rye Grammar School Graduation Class, Betty is in second row, second from left. *Source* Personal photo collection of the author

Another significant formative aspect of my childhood and adolescence was World War II that our family became more acutely aware of somewhat earlier than other American families because of my father being in the military. This fact was a worry shared by all my family, but the others in the family were not so convinced as I, first from the perspective of a 10 year old, at what I thought of as "the stupidity" of war. Surely, I thought there had to be another way to deal with the problems. I still do. Such thinking led me to become interested as a teen-ager in the United Nations and the newly forming movement of world federalism which seemed to my young mind to be an imminently sensible idea.

Our mother, a housewife and community activist instructed us in what we might now call "counter culture," to the prevailing norms, assuring us that race and class differences were not what determined human worth, that all should be treated fairly and with respect. She was a no-nonsense parent, but we knew without a doubt that we had her unconditional love. Our father, an army officer and a criminal investigator who served several times with other branches of government, gave us the notion that we should behave with dignity and responsibility. He was often sorely disappointed in our response to these instructions, but always loving and delighted by us. He also instructed me in his own counter culture message that, gender notwithstanding, I could be and do whatever I hoped for. I do wonder if the message would have been the same, had he had a son. It was his expectation, not one for most middle class girls of the time, that we should receive higher education. With some significant sacrifice from my parents—mainly my mother who did the managing and worrying over money in those days following the Great Depression and the Second World War, that I began undergraduate education.

High school year book graduation portrait, 1947. *Source* Personal photo collection of the author

I graduated in 1951 with a BA in history from Wheaton College, one of the "Heavenly Seven" undergraduate colleges for women in New England that educated the daughters of the elite and a few of the bright young scholarship students of other classes. In this very WASP environment there was one Chinese student from Hong Kong, only a few Jewish and Catholic students, one African American student, and some African American maids who cleaned the dormitories. My on-going lessons on race and class and now ethnicity (and only much later, on reflection, gender) were imbedded with the fine academic education we young women were offered, as we were told in our freshman orientation, to prepare us to be suitable wives for successful men. I learned much at Wheaton and am still a 'loyal' if aware alumna who is glad to say that the college now welcomes many scholarship students of all ethnic backgrounds and both men and women students of all classes from many countries.

Although I had thought of teaching as the 'work,' women graduates expected to be an interim short pre-marriage career, I opted instead to find some type of professional work in New York City, for though I knew it well, New York still had the attractions of big cities that lured the young from the suburbs and the countryside. I tried for work in publishing and what was then called "race relations"—some few years later to blossom into the civil rights movement. Foiled by lack of typing skills, through the next 3 years I occupied my days at the Rockefeller Foundation summarizing and devising categories for 'declinations,' i.e. refused grant requests. Working in "the files" with other recently graduated young white women, our work delivered to our desk by equally educated young black men, provided further learning about social stratification by gender and race. (Years later I was to return to the foundation offices to discuss a writing assignment on arms spending and found that some of the young men had risen above the level of delivering the files. All the young women were long gone.) While I enjoyed socializing with my peers during lunch hours, and certainly reveled in what city evenings offered in entertainment and meeting young men, I felt a deep need to do something with my days that might serve my evolving social and political values, and address issues such as those that had led me earlier to seek work in promoting racial justice.

Goaded by friends I took up teaching and spent the first year teaching at an elite girls boarding school, Miss Halls in New England, and the next 9 years on the faculty of the Rye Country Day School, another private school, teaching history and social issues to middle or "junior high school" students ages 12–15. I found teaching challenging, rewarding and full of joy. Making direct connections with young and curious minds and coaxing the not so curious to find something relevant that would interest them in learning was a very rewarding way to spend my days. I certainly had failures in any number of my efforts, but on the whole I found satisfaction as I began the learning about learning and the development of the citizen that was to become the core of my life's work in what some years later I came to identify as peace education.

It is not without some importance, I think, that I began this work in the intense years of the Cold War that produced fears of nuclear attack. The fears, however, did not significantly affect my school. We had perhaps one or two drills to prepare for a warning, but I never had to get students to "duck and cover," as apparently was happening in many other schools in the 1950s. There was among the school staff a sensible notion that were an attack to actually occur, all these precautions would mean naught. None-the less the adversarial, bi-polar thinking that prevailed affected the environment in which I taught, as did the emerging awareness of the "Third World." During these school teaching years, I earned a master's degree in history from New York University, granted the year in which I made the second of now countless visits to Europe 1959, the beginning years of travels that ultimately took me throughout the ever fascinating and instructive world.

In my last several years at Rye Country Day, I developed a world affairs study program largely focused on understanding the post-colonial countries of the Global South. The program was complemented by summer study tours for which I prepared students and conducted them to the Middle East, Latin America, Eastern Europe and the Soviet Union, attempting to introduce the students to the realities of the world outside their own privileged North American environment. The school element of the program funded by Leadership and World Society (LAWS) lead to my being invited to manage LAWS for a few years and to initiate and direct The Schools Program of the World Law Fund, later to become the Institute for World Order (IWO).

At IWO I worked on curriculum development, teacher training and networking in world order studies in the United States, linking with and learning from similar efforts in other countries. In the US I worked with teachers, mainly through professional associations, and in some cases university departments of education. It was a time when there was growing interest in developing global awareness, but not necessarily in cultivating concerns for global justice. Some efforts seemed to be directed primarily at building support for US involvement in the world on the basis of national interest, educating for support of US foreign policy.

Portrait for 1962 yearbook of The Rye Country Day School dedicated to her by the graduating class. *Source* Personal photo collection of the author

I found quite a different perspective to characterize global awareness education in Europe where teachers I worked with were focusing on the structural violence of the world economic system that systematically disadvantaged the Global South. But there were some peace and justice minded educators in the US, so I was able to build a national network of teachers who were committed to teaching toward the realization of what IWO identified as world order values: peace, economic equity, social justice, political participation and ecological balance. With their help teaching materials, participatory instructional methodologies and techniques for the development of critical and creative thinking about problems of global violence and injustice were developed and disseminated as I conducted IWO sponsored teacher training workshops throughout the US and in parts of Canada. The predecessor to the International Institute on Peace Education was conducted during three successive summers during the early 1970s running as a residential training session at Stanstead College in Quebec, Canada.

After 13 years (1963–1976) at IWO during which I had become deeply involved in the international network of peace educators that comprised the Peace Education Commission (PEC) of the International Peace Research Association (1972–present) who profoundly influenced my views of peace education, I left the Institute. Differences about my insistence on the primacy of teacher empowerment and education as opposed to relying solely on the publication of curricula based on their research as a means to introduce questions of war prevention into secondary schools made it impossible for me to effectively pursue the goals IWO had assigned to me. The materials were already appearing, but not the requisite teacher preparation courses. A number of my publications archived in the Ward M. Canaday Center for Special Collections at the University of Toledo Library of are such materials, and others were also producing relevant curricula, but no systematic efforts were being made to establish the growing field of peace education in teacher education institutions.

Believing strongly as I do that the most significant component of education is teaching and the professionals who do it, I wanted to find a situation in which I could pursue this goal of teacher education and continue to collaborate with colleagues in the PEC network on the development of our common field. While working in the Teachers College Columbia University based office of the World Council for Curriculum and Instruction I met Professor Willard Jacobson, nationally known as a science educator, who shared my concerns and goals. In 1982, together with an assist from Professor Douglas Sloan, a philosopher and historian, we began the seminar that evolved into a graduate peace education specialization in international and comparative education. As the program was developing, at the urging of Willard Jacobson who guided me through the process, I earned a doctorate in education from Teachers College, awarded in 1986.

The Peace Education Program at Teachers College evolved from one seminar in 1982 to a four core course specialization, offered as we developed it till 2003, after which I no longer taught at Teachers College in New York. I continued, however, for a few years to offer intensive certificate courses at Teachers College Tokyo campus, and teach as a visiting professor in various universities in Japan where a vibrant peace education movement was taking hold and continues to this day. I had begun to accept such visiting professorships in the early 1990s to earn income to supplement the regular consultant fee I received from United Ministries in Education, an ecumenical initiative to assist them promoting peace education, to allow me to continue to develop the program at Teachers College where adjunct honoraria were minimal. During my time there the college gave little financial or other support to the program, an experience common to many American pioneers in peace studies and peace education. Minimal but sufficient outside funding and a growing volume of enrollments kept the specialization alive through many ups and downs, including the formation of a Peace Education Center intended to offer in-service education and manage the annual International Institute on Peace Education.

The visiting professorships were rewarding and rich learning experiences, especially those in Japan where I never learned the language. Though the learning would have been far richer, had I known the language, I gained invaluable understanding of the position of the outsider, the recent immigrant to a new culture and the daunting task of meeting daily needs and performing fundamental tasks in a cultural framework distinctly different from the one through which you had formed your views of life and the world. I came ultimately to feel at home in spite of the communication barrier and to love the country, the culture and the people among whom I have made close and lasting friendships. I remember vividly a sense of homecoming on returning to Japan from China after the Fourth World Conference on Women in China in 1995, a feeling experienced on every landing in Narita Airport. I find that my deepest feelings are for the places of most significant learning. Fortunate to be able to teach and have professional interactions in English, I learned to listen in a more nuanced way and to continue to pursue learning exchanges often in situations with little clarity I continued to work for, an insight into the ambiguous conditions under which the politics of peace are often conducted. But teacher-student learning was evident, giving support to my notion of the advantages of pursuing politics as learning.

Leaving IWO and regularly paid employment for adjunct status and a working base at Teachers College, I found the limits of economic security were well compensated by the opportunity to pursue new approaches and develop my own perspectives. Free of the tasks of churning our curricula (which I had done not only in the publications such as the Random House series, but also in the quarterly publication of the teaching aid "Ways and Means of Teaching about World Order") and promoting the world order approach, I was also able to enter more fully into reflection on my pedagogical practice than was possible in the earlier training workshops. The workshops had taught me much in terms of how to demonstrate methods and engage the interest of the teacher-learners, and even offered opportunities for post workshop debriefing with colleagues to refine and try to improve our procedures. I found that while I often missed the "shop talk" with classroom teachers, reflecting on my own made me more conscious of my own teaching behaviors and the unfolding of the teaching-learning process. Unfortunately, the fruits of these reflections while making my teaching more personally satisfying and—I certainly hope—more effective, did not make their way into my published theoretical work. They have, however, to this day a meaningful place in my conceptualization of institutional and normative issues of peace and in my ideas about pedagogy, particularly that which may prove helpful to aspiring peace educators. Some of these pedagogical insights made their way into the methodology of the curricula published in the 1970s. But until the publications of the 21st century dealing specifically with teaching process (i.e. *Education for a Culture of Peace in a Gender Perspective*, *A Manual on the Rights to Freedom of Religion and Belief and* "Meditating on the Barricades" that addresses the pedagogy of reflective inquiry) were not in print. However, I do hope that these teaching behaviors "rubbed off" on students who may have adapted and further refined them, now publishing their own theories, and, I hope, will move on to "how to do its" so as to further develop techniques of cultivating peace learning. Nor have I completely abandoned the normative and systemic world order perspectives that have to this day a meaningful place in my conceptualization of peace. So, too, I still find some of the earlier pedagogy, particularly that relevant, to consideration of alternative security systems to be relevant to current challenges. As I write this, we are facing possibilities of multiple armed conflicts and the need for the capacity to think in terms of demilitarized security systems was never greater.

In the years after ending my formal association with Teachers College (2003–present), I continue to work in the building of and learning from international networks in peace education and women's movements for human rights and peace, among them the Feminist Scholar-Activist Network on Demilitarization (FeDem) and the International Institute on Peace Education (IIPE). I consider IIPE to be the major accomplishment in my work in international cooperation in the development of peace education, an endeavor that was recognized in the Special Honorable Mention awarded by the UNESCO Prize for Peace Education (2001). I have called IIPE, now my sole institutional affiliation, "a moveable feast" as it is convened each year in a different part of the world, hosted by a local university or peace organization. Beginning in 1982 on the occasion of the UN Second Special Session on Disarmament as a traditional summer program in new curricular content, it has evolved into an intense, residential learning experience in the philosophy and practice of peace education in which we "walk the walk" as well as "talk the talk." It has become the core of an international, multicultural, intergenerational learning community of peace educators, working in formal, non-formal and informal education. It embodies the combined, cooperative learning of the organizers and the participants, all of whom contribute to the learning of all. A short term learning community, fully and authentically participatory, it has seen the birthing of practical long-term collaboration in the further development and dissemination of the field.

Those who have over the past decade taken on its management, Tony Jenkins, and its program design, Janet Gerson (former students and now colleagues) have made it a model of peace education as peace action with focus on learning as the main mechanism for social change and community as the natural environment of authentic, intentional learning. This team, now including Dale Snauwaert (a colleague since serving as visiting professors in the same 1990 academic year at Colgate University) is, as well, continuing to develop the theoretical bases and refine the pedagogical practices of the field.

Through all the years of professional work, I have, as well, been active in citizen movements for peace and human rights and a participant in the civil society activities centered on the United Nations as the institutional body through which global peace and justice might most effectively be sought. My work with the UN itself was in the areas of disarmament, human rights, gender equality and peace education, taking action with those CSOs who encouraged UNESCO's work in disarmament education, initiated the UN Decades for Human Rights Education and Learning, and drafting and lobbying of Security Council Resolution 1325 on Women, Peace and Security. I worked, as well, on UNESCO's World Congress on Disarmament Education, preparing its main working paper and the education aspect of the World Disarmament Campaign run by the UN Department for Disarmament Affairs in the late 1970s. I have enjoyed a long, cooperative relationship with UNESCO, participating in experts meetings and collaborating with staff in editing *Towards a Women's Agenda for a Culture of Peace*, undertaken with colleague-friends Ingeborg Breines of UNESCO and Dorota Gierycz of the UN Division for the Advancement of Women and in producing curriculum materials *Tolerance the Threshold of Peace* and *Education for Culture of Peace in a Gender Perspective,* as requested by Kaisa Savolainen, author of the definitive work on the pivotal 1974 recommendation on peace education.

Celebrating 80th birthday with colleagues in Tokyo in 2009. *Source* Personal photo collection of the author

It was through involvement in these essentially intergovernmental projects as well as the observation of national politics that I began to see even more positive possibilities in shifting the paradigm of politics from a framework of conflictual power struggles to one of learning toward more effective exercise of responsibility for management of the public good; a shift I believe to be integrally related to the transformation of the global patriarchal order toward one of human equality and universal human dignity. Both of these closely interrelated paradigm shifts should be on the agenda for the further development of peace education, and are likely to figure in my future work.

So, too, my present work on seeking to illuminate the connections between violence against women and the militarized security system ("Statement on Military Violence against Women" drafted for the 2013 session of the UN Commission on the Status of Women) will strive to bring reflective inquiry to the public discourse on such issues as rape in the military, military sex trafficking and the resistance to the empowerment of women in peace and security policy making as mandated by UNSCR 1325. Underlying these concerns is the argument that Asha Hans and I put forward in *The Gender Imperative*: *Human Security versus State Security* that absent a monumental effort to confront and overcome patriarchy peace is not possible.

All of these efforts come forth from identification as a feminist peace educator as documented in Volume 27 of this series. More precisely, I identify as a teacher and consider the most important aspect of my personal journey through peace education to be the opportunities I had had to learn by teaching, to enter into the wonder of connecting with other learners—at first students, later colleagues as well—around a common task of illuminating as much as our collaborative efforts could the various and complex issues and obstacles to working toward a global society in which universal dignity is the assumed norm. Human dignity is the norm which has guided my efforts to learn to be a teacher in respectful relationship with all learners, and which I have tried to articulate in my writing. I will continue to pursue its realization.

I am blessed in this pursuit by the professional and personal companionship of the many colleagues and students with whom I have engaged in peace learning throughout my years in the field. I am confident that those of the present and coming generations will carry the field forward with ever more relevant learnings. I hope those who come after me will find what I and my generation have done useful. Whether they do or not, I have learned much through these efforts, and I have enjoyed strong solidarity and built deep friendships with many with whom I have shared this life of learning. No professional career could reap greater human rewards than these relationships.

Betty A. Reardon
New York, March, 2014

Chapter 2
Reardon's Publications: Archived in the Ward M. Canaday Center for Special Collections, The University of Toledo

Reardon, Betty A. (1967). The World Law Fund: World Approach to International Education. *Teachers College Record*, *68*(6), 453–465.

Reardon, Betty A, & Mendlovitz, Saul. (1968). World Law and Models of World Order. In J. Becker & H. Mehlinger (Eds.), *International Dimensions in the Social Studies* (Vol. 38th Yearbook). New York: National Council for the Social Studies.

Griffith, Priscilla, & Reardon, Betty A (Eds.). (1968). *Let Us Examine Our Attitude Toward Peace: An Inquiry Into Some of the Political and Psychological Barriers to World Peace*. New York: World Law Fund.

Reardon, Betty A. (1968). World Order Education. *World Law Fund Progress Report*, *1*(2).

Reardon, Betty A. (1969). Prologue, A Unit on Peace and World Order. *Media and Methods*, *10*(10), 33–36.

Reardon, Betty A. (1969). War is ...? *Ways and Means of Teaching About World Order*, *1*(Fall).

Reardon, Betty A. (1969). The World Law Fund. *News and Views, Pennsylvania Council for Social Studies*, *16*(1).

Reardon, Betty A, & Thorpe, Gerald. (1970). Peace Games. *AAUW Journal*, *May*, 192–195. Reardon, Betty A. (1970). Teaching About Arms Policy. *Ways and Means of Teaching About World Order*, *2*(Winter).

Reardon, Betty A. (1970). Who Speaks for Man? *Ways and Means of Teaching About World Order*, *3*(Spring), 1–2.

Reardon, Betty A. (1970). Who Speaks for Man? The 25th Anniversary of the United Nations. *Ways and Means of Teaching About World Order*, *4*(Fall).

Thorpe, Gerald, & Reardon, Betty A. (1971). World Order and Simulation. *The High School Journal*, *55*(2), 53–62.

Reardon, Betty A. (1971). A Case for Futurism in the Social Studies. *Social Science Record, April*.

B.A. Reardon and D.T. Snauwaert, *Betty A. Reardon: A Pioneer in Education for Peace and Human Rights*, SpringerBriefs on Pioneers in Science and Practice 26,
DOI 10.1007/978-3-319-08967-6_2

Reardon, Betty A. (1971). Futurism. *Ways and Means of Teaching About World Order*, *7*(Fall), 1–2.

Reardon, Betty A. (1971). Introduction, The Human Person and the War System. *Intercom, 13*(1), 21–28.

Reardon, Betty A. (1971). Michael Scott: An Individual and the International System. *Intercom, 13*(1), 66–72.

Reardon, Betty A. (1971). The World Law Fund. *Intercom, 13*(2).

Reardon, Betty A. (1971). World Law: What Does it Mean? What Could It Do For the World? *Vital Issues*, *20*(10).

Reardon, Betty A, & Thorpe, Gerald. (1972). Futurism in the Classroom. *California Council for the Social Studies Review*, *11*(4), 3–6.

Fraenkel, Jack R, Carter, Margaret, & Reardon, Betty A. (1973). *Peacekeeping*. New York: Random House.

Reardon, Betty A, Fraenkel, Jack R, & Carter, Margaret. (1973). *Struggle for Human Rights*. New York: Random House.

Reardon, Betty A, & Carter, Margaret. (1973). Procedures for Analyzing and Clarifying Values Related to Human Rights. *Pennsylvania Council for Social Studies*, *1*(2), 7–12.

Reardon, Betty A. (1973). Legal Education from the Global Perspective. *Law in American Society*, *2*(3).

Reardon, Betty A. (1973). Model Building and Systems Inquiry. *Ways and Means of Teaching About World Order*, *12*(June), 1–2.

Reardon, Betty A. (1973). Peace is Possible … Who Can Make It Probable? *Today's Catholic Teacher*, *6*(7).

Reardon, Betty A. (1973). Transformations Into Peace and Survival: Programs for the 1970s. In G. Henderson (Ed.), *Education for Peace*: *Focus on Mankind* (pp. 127–151). Alexandria, VA: Association for Supervision and Curriculum Development.

Reardon, Betty A, & Colby, Curtis. (1974). *Beyond the Cold War*. New York: Random House.

Reardon, Betty A, & Colby, Curtis. (1974). *War Criminals, War Victims*. New York: Random House.

Reardon, Betty A. (1974). The Aims of Education for Peace. *Peace and the Sciences*, 74–76.

Reardon, Betty A. (1974). Beyond Nationalism: Education and Survival. In D. W. Allen (Ed.), *Controversies in Education* (pp. 57–64). Philadelphia: W. B. Saunders Company.

Reardon, Betty A. (1974). Beyond Nationalism: Education and Survival. *The New Era*, *54*(7), 168–174.

Reardon, Betty A. (1974). Education for Peace and Social Justice. *Geographical Perspective*, *34*(Fall).

Reardon, Betty A. (1974). Report of the WCCI Transnational Committee for Constitutional Review. In M. Haavelsrud (Ed.), *Education for Peace*: *Reflection and Action*. Norway: IDC, Science and Technology Press.

Reardon, Betty A. (1974). The Role of Women in Future Studies. *Earthrise*, *2*(5), 181, 188–189.

Fraenkel, Jack R, Carter, Margaret, & Reardon, Betty A. (1975). *The Struggle for Human Rights*. New York: Random House.

Reardon, Betty A. (1975). International Women's Year. *Earthrise*, *3*(4).

Reardon, Betty A. (1975). Women's Movements and Human Futures. *Convergence*, *8*(3), 41–52.

Reardon, Betty A. (1975). Comments on State of the Globe Report. *Alternatives: A Journal of World Policy*, *1*(4), 561–565.

Reardon, Betty A. (1975). A Social Education for Human Survival: A Synthesis of Practices in International Education and Peace Studies. *Social Studies Review*, *15*(1), 42–48.

Reardon, Betty A. (1975). Women and Structural Violence: A Crucial Issue for Peace Education. *Journal of Peace Education, India*.

Reardon, Betty A. (1975). Women's Movements and Human Futures. *Convergence*, *8*(3), 41–52.

Reardon, Betty A. (1976). Designing a New World Order. In B. Stanford (Ed.), *Peacemaking: A Guide to Conflict Resolution for Individuals, Groups, and Nations*. New York: Bantam Books.

Reardon, Betty A. (1976). Disarmament: A Key Concept for Peace Education. *Journal of World Education*, *7*(4), 1, 10.

Reardon, Betty A. (1976). Woman and Food: Personal Perspectives on a Global Problem. *Ways and Means of Teaching About World Order*, *20*(January), 1–4.

Reardon, Betty A. (1976). World Law and International Institutions. In T. W. A. C. o. Philadelphia (Ed.), *The INTERdependence Curriculum Aid* (pp. 101–111). Philadelphia: The World Affairs Council of Philadelphia in Cooperation with the School District of Philadelphia.

Reardon, Betty A. (1977). *Discrimination: The Cycle of Injustice*. Sydney, Australia: Holt-Saunders.

Reardon, Betty A. (1977). Human Rights and Education Reform. *Bulletin on Peace Proposals*, *8*(3), 247–250.

Reardon, Betty A. (1977). A Teacher's Guide to *World Military and Social Expenditures*. New York: Rockefeller Foundation Educational Publishing Program.

Reardon, Betty A. (1977). Teaching About Arms and Security. *Ways and Means of Teaching About World Order*, *23*(May), 1–4.

Reardon, Betty A. (1977). Using World Order Models to Teach Global Law. *Law in American Society*, *6*(4).

Reardon, Betty A. (1978). Disarmament and Peace Education. *Prospects: Quarterly Review of Education*, *8*(4), 395–408.

Reardon, Betty A. (1978). The Human Person and the War System. In I. W. Charny (Ed.), *Strategies Against Violence: Design for Non-Violent Change*. Boulder, CO: Westview Press.

Reardon, Betty A. (1978). Human Rights. Philadelphia: School District of Philadelphia, World Affairs Council of Philadelphia.

Reardon, Betty A. (1978). Peace as an Educational End and Process. In B. Weston, S. Schwenninger & D. Shamis (Eds.), *Peace and World Order studies*. New York: Transnational Academic Program, Institute of World Order.

Reardon, Betty A. (1978). A Preliminary Study of the Obstacles to, the Status of, and Potential for Education for the Promotion of Disarmament (SS/78) Conf. 603/13. Paris: UNESCO.

Reardon, Betty A. (1978). *Reflections on a Task: Increasing the Volume and Effectiveness of Women's Political Participation.* Background paper for COPRED/UNESCO, International Colloquium on Women's Political Participation.

Reardon, Betty A. (1978). Teaching About Disarmament: The Process, Conversion and Citizen Action. *Ways and Means of Teaching About World Order, 25*(May), 1–4.

Reardon, Betty A. (1978). Teaching About the Arms Race: Its Dynamic, The Costs, and the Consequences. *Ways and Means of Teaching About World Order, 24*(February), 1–4.

Reardon, Betty A. (1979). The Child and World Order. *The Whole Earth Papers, Global Education Associates* (11), 1–10.

Reardon, Betty A. (1979). Obstacles to Disarmament Education. *Bulletin on Peace Proposals, 10*(4), 356–367.

Reardon, Betty A. (1979). Organizer's Report on COPRED International Symposium on Women's Political Participation: COPRED.

Reardon, Betty A. (1980). Commitments to Principles: A Review of Progessional and Political Statements on Education for International Understanding, Cooperation and Peace. *World Studies Journal, 1*(4), 12–20.

Reardon, Betty A. (1980). Debating the Future. *Network, 8*(3), 17–20.

Reardon, Betty A. (1980). Disarmament Education in American Universities. *Peace and the Sciences*, 33–41.

Reardon, Betty A. (1980). Equivalents for Equity: New Dimensions of Security. *Planet Earth, Fall*, 18–19.

Reardon, Betty A. (1980). Moving to the Future. *Network, 8*(1), 14–21.

Reardon, Betty A. (1980). Report on a Study of the Plan for the University for Peace, Costa Rica: UNESCO Sector/Bureau Ref. 3139-HRS/31 BOC Ref. 270457.

Reardon, Betty A. (1980). A Report on UNESCO's World Congress on Disarmament Education. *The Peace Chroncile, Fall.*

Reardon, Betty A. (1980). Secondary School and Teacher Training Curricula for Disarmament Education: Problems, Needs, and Priorities (SS/80), Conf. 603 (pp. 1–21). Paris: UNESCO.

Reardon, Betty A. (1980). The Status of Disarmament Education and Recommendations for Its Further Development (SS/80) Conf. 603. Paris: UNESCO.

Reardon, Betty A. (1980). UNESCO's Focuses on Disarmament Education: Educators Gathering in Paris. *Disarmament Times, 3*(3).

Reardon, Betty A. (1980). Women and Disarmament: Traditional Values in a Transnational World. In S. McClean (Ed.), *Women's Contribution to Peace*. Paris: UNESCO.

Reardon, Betty A. (1980). Women Show Skills Despite Limited Roles in Peace. *The Church Woman, December*, 13–14.

Reardon, Betty A. (1980). World Disarmament Education Congress: A Report. *COPRED Proceedings, August*, 7–10.

Reardon, Betty A. (1981). The Challenge of Disarmament Education *Educators Supplement Institute for Global Education.*

Reardon, Betty A. (1981). Education for Peace and Disarmament: A Suggested Sequence of Learning Objectives. In M. Haavelsrud (Ed.), *Approaching Disarmament Education* (pp. 238–252). England: Westbury House.

Reardon, Betty A. (1981). Militarism and Sexism: Influences on Eduction for War. *Connexion, 9*(3), 6–10.

Reardon, Betty A. (1981). *Militarization, Security, and Peace Education: A Study of Action Programme for Concerned Citizens.* Valley Forge: United Ministries in Education.

Reardon, Betty A. (1981). The New Myth: Educating for Global Transformation. *Planet Earth, Fall, 1981.*(Fall).

Reardon, Betty A. (1981). The Status of and Recommendations for Disarmament Education. In M. Haavelsrud (Ed.), *Approaching Disarmament Education* (pp. 114–128). England: Westbury House.

Reardon, Betty A. (1982). Disarmament Education as World Order Inquiry. *Teachers College Record, 84*(1), 137–149.

Reardon, Betty A. (1982). The First Day of Hope. *Teachers College Record, 84*(1), 255–265.

Reardon, Betty A. (1982). *Militarism, Security, and Peace Education.* Valley Forge, PA: United Ministries in Education.

Reardon, Betty A. (1982). Presentation to the Preparatory Committee for UN Second Special Session on Disarmament. *International Peace Research Newsletter, 20*(3).

Reardon, Betty A. (1982). Response: Needs in Peace Education Development Identified by Glass. *Teachers College Record, 84*(1), 237–239.

Reardon, Betty A. (1982). Teaching Unit: UN Special Session on Disarmament. *Macroscope, 11*(Spring), 7–10.

Jacobson, Willard, Reardon, Betty A, & Sloan, Douglas. (1983). A Conceptual Framework for Teaching About Nuclear Weapons. *Social Education, 47*(7), 476–479.

Reardon, Betty A, Scott, John Anthony, & Totten, Sam (1983). Nuclear Weapons: Concepts, Issues, and Controversies Introduction. *Social Education, November/December*, 474–479.

Reardon, Betty A. (1983). A Gender Analysis of Militarism and Sexist Repression: A Suggested Research Agenda. *International Peace Research Newsletter, 21*(2).

Reardon, Betty A. (1983). International Colloquium on Disarmament Education in Institutions of Higher Learning. *International Peace Research Newsletter, 21*(2).

Reardon, Betty A. (1983). Review of *In a Different Voice*. *Teachers College Record*, *84*(4), 966–969.

Reardon, Betty A. (1984). Adult Education for Disarmament and Peace in a North American Christian Context. *Gandhi Marg*, *July/August*, 344–356.

Reardon, Betty A. (1984). International Education and Teacher Preparation. *Higher Education in Europe*, *UNESCO*, *Fall*.

Reardon, Betty A. (1984). Principles and Standards for Curriculum Development and Teacher Preparation. In M. Haavelsrud (Ed.), *Handbook on Disarmament*. Paris: UNESCO.

Reardon, Betty A. (1985). Civic Responsibility for a World Community. In D. Conrad & T. M. Thomas (Eds.), *Images of an Emerging World*: *From a War System to a Peace System*. Katyam, India: Prakasam Publications.

Reardon, Betty A. (1985). Recent Developments in Peace Education in the United States. In D. Ray (Ed.), *Peace Education*: *Canadian and World Perspectives* (pp. 203–215). London, Ontario: Third Eye.

Reardon, Betty A. (1986). An Experiment in Education for World Peace. *Education in Asia*, *6*(2).

Reardon, Betty A. (1987). Excellence in Education Through Peace-Making. *Breakthrough*, *Spring/Summer*, 18–21.

Reardon, Betty A. (1988). *Address on Behalf of the International Jury for the UNESCO Prize for Peace Education*. Paris.

Reardon, Betty A. (1988). *Comprehensive Peace Education*: *Educating for Global Responsibility*. New York: Teachers College Press.

Reardon, Betty A. (1988). *Educating for Global Responsibility*: *Teacher-Designed Curricula for Peace Education*, *K-12*. New York: Teachers College Press.

Reardon, Betty A. (1988). Introduction *UNESCO Yearbook on Peace and Conflict Studies*. Paris: UNESCO.

Reardon, Betty A. (1988). *The Teacher's Responsibility for Our Common Future*. Paper presented at the Second Meeting of International Teachers for Peace, Bonn, West Germany.

Reardon, Betty A. (1988). Women, Peace and Development, Development Education Kit 4. Geneva: United Nations.

Reardon, Betty A. (1989). Feminist Concepts of Peace and Security. In P. Smoker (Ed.), *Global Studies Handbook for A Level Examinations*.

Reardon, Betty A. (1989). A Feminist Perspective on World Constitutional Order. *WCCI Forum*: *Journal of the World Council for Curriculum and Instruction*, *3*(2), 16–28.

Reardon, Betty A. (1989). Getting from Here to There: An Educator's Response to Thomas Berry's "The American College in the Ecological Age". *Religion and Intellectual Life*, *Winter*.

Reardon, Betty A. (1989). Pedagogical Approaches to Peace Studies. In M. T. Klare & D. C. Thomas (Eds.), *Peace and World Order Studies Guide* (5th ed., pp. 20–27). Boulder, CO: Westview Press.

Reardon, Betty A. (1989). Toward a Paradigm of Peace. In L. R. Farcey (Ed.), *Peace: Meanings, Politics, Strategies*. New York: Praeger.

Reardon, Betty A. (1989). Women and Peace: Development Education Kit #4. Geneva: JUNIC/NGO, United Nations.

Reardon, Betty A, & Tierney, James F. (1990). Teaching Peace: A Study Guide to *The Conquest of War*. Scarsdale, NY: Alternative Defense Project.

Reardon, Betty A. (1990). Feminist Concepts of Peace and Security. In P. Smoker, R. Davies & B. Munske (Eds.), *A Reader in Peace Studies*. New York: Pergamon Press.

Reardon, Betty A. (1990). A Memorial Tribute to Lawrence E. Metcalf. *Social Education*, *54*, 107–108.

Aziz, Unku Abdul, & Reardon, Betty A. (1991). The UNESCO Prize for Peace Education: The Ten Years of Learning for Peace. *Peace Education Miniprints* (19), 1–12. Malmo, Sweden.

Reardon, Betty A. (1991). Challenges for Peace Studies in a Dramatically Changing World. *Peace Studies Bulletin*, *1*(1).

Reardon, Betty A. (1991). Feminism and Authentic Globalism: Toward an Inclusive Constitutional Order. *CSWS Review*, 28–31.

Reardon, Betty A. (1991). Feminist Pedagogy and Peace Studies. *Benedictines*, *XLV*(I), 11–26.

Reardon, Betty A. (1991). Forward. In T. Swee-hin (Ed.), *Journeys of Peace Education*. Sydney: Earth.

Reardon, Betty A. (1991). Ou est la vraie Securite? Pour une Securite Globale. *Journal de la Movement de la Paix*, *383*(June).

Reardon, Betty A. (1991). Review of *Societies of Peace: Anthropological Perspectives*. *New Ideas In Psychology*, *9*(3), 409–410.

Reardon, Betty A. (1991). Review of Societies of Peace: Anthropological Perspectives. *Peace & Change*, *January*, 116–118.

Reardon, Betty A. (1993). Challenges and Opportunities of Disarmament Education. In M. Haavelsrud (Ed.), *Disarming: Discourse on Violence and Peace*. Tromso, Norway: Arena.

Reardon, Betty A. (1993). A Feminist Perspective on World Constitutional Order. In R. A. Falk, R. C. Johansen & S. S. Kim (Eds.), *The Constitutional Foundations of World Order* (pp. 227–243). Albany, NY: State University of New York Press.

Reardon, Betty A. (1993). Foward. D. T. Snauwaert, *Democracy, Education, and Governance: A Developmental Conception*. Albany, NY: State University of New York Press.

Reardon, Betty A. (1993). Pedagogy as Purpose: Peace Education in the Context of Violence. In P. Cremin (Ed.), *Education for Peace*. Limerick, Ireland: Educational Studies Association of Ireland.

Reardon, Betty A. (1993). *Women and Peace: Feminist Visions of Global Security*. Albany, NY: State University of New York Press.

Reardon, Betty A, & Nordland, Eva (Eds.). (1994). *Learning Peace: The Promise of Ecological and Cooperative Education*. Albany, NY: State University of New York Press.

Reardon, Betty A. (1994). A Feminist Critique of "An Agenda for Peace": United Nations, Division of the Advancement of Women GAP/1994/WP.2.

Reardon, Betty A. (1994). Human Rights and Values Education: Using the International Standards. *Social Education, 58*(7), 427–429.

Reardon, Betty A. (1994). Learning Our Way to a Human Future. In B. A. Reardon & E. Nordland (Eds.), *Learning Peace: The Promise of Ecological and Cooperative Education*. Albany, NY: State University of New York Press.

Reardon, Betty A. (1995). *Educating for human dignity : learning about rights and responsibilities*. Philadelphia: University of Pennsylvania Press.

Reardon, Betty A. (1996). Responding to a Major Problem of Adolescent Intolerance: Bullying *Peace Education Miniprints* (Vol. 82). Malmo, Sweden: Peace Education Miniprints.

Reardon, Betty A. (1996). Review of *Teaching About International Conflict and Peace. Teachers College Record, 97.*

Reardon, Betty A. (1996). Women or Weapons? *Peace Review, 8*(3), 315–321.

Reardon, Betty A. (1996). Women's Vision of Peace: Images of Global Security. In J. Turpin & L. A. Lorentaen (Eds.), *The Gendered World Order: Militarism, Development, and the Environment*. New York: Routledge.

Reardon, Betty A. (1996 [1985]). *Sexism and the War System*. Syracuse, NY: Syracuse University Press.

Reardon, Betty A. (1997). Human Rights as Education for Peace. In G. J. Andreopoulos & R. P. Claude (Eds.), *Human Rights Education for the 21st Century*. Philadelphia: University of Pennsylvania Press.

Reardon, Betty A. (1997). The Role of Women in the Struggle for World Peace. *Journal of Hokusei Jr. College, 33*, 1–8.

Reardon, Betty A. (1997). *Tolerance: The Threshold of Peace*. Paris: UNESCO.

Osseiran, Sanaaa, & Reardon, Betty A. (1998). The United Nations' Role in Peace Education. In C. Alger, F (Ed.), *The Future of the United Nations Systems: Potential for the Twenty-first Century*. Tokyo: The United Nations University Press.

Reardon, Betty A. (1998). Gender and Global Security: A Feminist Challenge to the United Nations and Peace Research. *Journal of International Cooperation Studies, 6*(1), 1–28.

Reardon, Betty A. (1998). The Pedagogical Challenges of Peace Education: The Good News and the Bad News. *Peace Studies Newsletter, Peace Studies Association of Japan, 17.*

Reardon, Betty A. (1998). Women or Weapons. In L. A. Lorentaen & J. Turpin (Eds.), *The Women and War Reader*. New York: New York University Press.

Breines, Ingeborg, Gierycz, Dorota, & Reardon, Betty A (Eds.). (1999). *Toward's a Women's Agenda for a Culture of Peace*. Paris: UNESCO Publishing.

Reardon, Betty A. (1999). Educating the Educators: The Preparation of Teachers for a Culture of Peace (Vol. 99). Malmo, Sweden: Peace Education Miniprints.

Reardon, Betty A. (1999). Women or Weapons: The Militarist Sexist Symbios. In I. Breines, D. Gierycz & B. A. Reardon (Eds.), *Towards a Women's Agenda for a Culture of Peace*. Paris: UNESCO Publishing.

Reardon, Betty A. (2000). The Role of Teachers in the Global Campaign for Peace Education. *Education International*, *4*(4).

Reardon, Betty A. (2000). Peace Education: A Review and Projection. In R. Moon, M. Ben-Peretz & S. Brown (Eds.), *Routledge International Companion to Education*. London: Routledge.

Reardon, Betty A. (2001). *Education for a culture of peace in a gender perspective*. Paris: UNESCO.

Reardon, Betty A, & Speigler, Mado. (2001). *Passport to Dignity*. New York: People's Movement for Human Rights Education.

Reardon, Betty A, & Cabezudo, Alicia. (2001). *Learning to Abolish War*. New York: Hague Appeal for Peace.

Reardon, Betty A. (2002). Human Rights and the Global Campaign for Peace Education. *International Review of Education*, *48*(3–4), 283–284.

Reardon, Betty A. (2003). Toward Human Security: A Gender Approach to Demilitarization. *Women in Asia*, *33*.

Reardon, Betty A. (2003). Women's Organizations Working for Human Rights and Peace. *Social Education*, *67*(1), 58–61.

Reardon, Betty A. (2006). Peace Education, An Invaluable Tool for Progress. In I. Breines & H. d'Orville (Eds.), *60 Women Contributing to the 60 Years of UNESCO: Constructing the Foundations of Peace*. Paris: UNESCO.

Jenkins, Anthony & Reardon, Betty A. (2007). Gender and Peace: Towards a Gender Inclusive, Holistic Perspective. In J. Galtung & C. Webel (Eds.), *Handbook of Peace and Conflict Studies* (pp. 209–231). New York: Routledge.

Reardon, Betty A. (2007). Review of *Educating for a Culture of Social and Ecological Peace*. *Journal of Peace Education*, *4*(1), 115–117.

Reardon, Betty A. (2008). The Eradication of Torture: The Imperatives of Gender and Education. *New York City Law Review*, *11*(2), 265–279.

Reardon, Betty A. (2008). It Doesn't Have to Be That Way: An Interview with Betty Reardon. *SGI Quarterly*, *52*(April), 12–13.

Reardon, Betty A. (2008). Peace Education: Current Challenges and Opportunities. *The Ritsumeikan Journal of Peace Studies*, *9*(March).

Reardon, Betty A. (2009). *Human Rights Learning: Pedagogies and Politics of Peace*. Paper presented at the UNESCO Chair for Peace Education Master Conference, University of Puerto Rico. Reardon, Betty A., & Hans, Asha (Eds.). (2010). *The Gender Imperative: Human Security vs. State Security*. New Delhi, India: Routledge.

Reardon, Betty A. (2010). Women and Human Security: A Feminist Framework and Critique of the Prevailing Patriarchal Security System. In B. A. Reardon & A. Hans (Eds.), *The Gender Imperative: Human Security vs. State Security*. New Delhi, India: Routledge.

Reardon, Betty A. (2010). *Human Rights Learning: Pedagogies and Politics of Peace*. San Juan, Puerto Rico: UNESCO Chair for Peace Education, University of Puerto Rico.

Reardon, Betty A. (2010). The Patriarchy Problematic. In M. D. J. Elena & M. S. Romero (Eds.), *Genero y Paz*. Barcelona: Icaria.

Reardon, Betty A. (2011). Introduction to *Sexism and the War System*. In S. Christine (Ed.), *Feminist International Relations: Critical Concepts in International Relations* (Vol. 1). New York: Routledge.

Reardon, Betty A, & Snauwaert, Dale T. (2011). Reflective Pedagogy, Cosmopolitanism, and Critical Peace Education for Political Efficacy: A Discussion of Betty A. Reardon's Assessment of the Field. *In Factis Pax: Journal of Peace Education and Social Justice*, *5*(1), 1–14.

Reardon, Betty A. (2012). Education for Sustainable Peace: Practices, Problems and Possibilities. In P. T. Coleman & M. Deutsch (Eds.), *Psychological Components for Sustainable Peace*. New York: Springer.

Reardon, Betty A. (2012). Human Rights and the Renewal of the University. In C. Brunner & J. Scherling (Eds.), *Bildung, Menschenrecht, Universitat*. Klagenfurt, Austria: Drava Verla.

Reardon, Betty A. (2013). Criminalizing War and Those Who Make It. *Global Campaign for Peace Education Newsletter* (105).

Reardon, Betty A. (2013). Meditating on the Barricades: Concerns, Cautions, and Possibilities for Peace Education for Political Efficacy. In P. P. Trifonas & B. L. Wright (Eds.), *Critical Peace Education: Difficult Dialogues*. New York: Springer.

Chapter 3
Organization and Rationale for the Selection of the Texts in This Volume

This volume is organized in two parts, the first offers my brief autobiographical notes and my publications; the second part is divided into three generations of the formation of and reflection on my learning over the length of my professional life in peace education. The selections in each part represent not so much what I might consider the best of my work, as those pieces which most encapsulate the learning that the respective generation of experience provided me. I chose this conceptualization and organization in hope that it might be instructive and encouraging, especially to young educators taking up the field. I hope to demonstrate a life's experience of learning that was meaningful to me in my quest to better understand the problematic of peace and develop approaches to learn and to guide others in learning how to confront it. I hope also to illustrate the evolution of a field within the context of the education of a peace educator whose learning is said to have been helpful to others in the field. Usefulness to others following a similar quest is the most significant satisfaction I have had from having published these reflections on and arguments about peace education.

In that same spirit of offering my experience to other peace educators, each selection is preceded by a retrospective reflection, giving the professional and political context in which it was written and providing some of my present views and perspectives on the themes and issues. These reflections are, as well, instruments of reflective inquiry into the learning that the piece represented for me that may reveal particular aspects of the evolution of peace education. Throughout the emphasis is on learning, a process of becoming in which persons and societies come to embody and to strive for the values that inform their world views. In the case of peace education the process is one in which learners become conscious of their respective capacities and motivated to act toward the realization of the values of peace and justice in the single living system that is this fragile Planet Earth.

The selections in each section span a chronological period that represents what I recall of the professional and political environments in which a generation of peace education came to maturity and made way for the next generation, just as it

B.A. Reardon and D.T. Snauwaert, *Betty A. Reardon: A Pioneer in Education for Peace and Human Rights*, SpringerBriefs on Pioneers in Science and Practice 26,
DOI 10.1007/978-3-319-08967-6_3

did in the individual learning that formed my evolving approach to peace learning, a generational, engaged process of personal and social change toward achieving the goals stated above.

The first of these three generations (1967–1985) is the foundations of learning about the substance of the problematic of peace as it was conceptualized by world order research and values. World order studies provided the framework for this generation of my experience in the field as I sought to introduce this perspective and approach to teachers and teacher educators.

Through the second generation (1985–2000), I developed my own distinct approach to the field, not discarding the world order framework, but integrating it into what I was learning from the many educators approaching the problematic from the base of various and differing concerns and disciplines into a holistic comprehensive and critical framework for the organization of the field.

The third and most mature generation (2000–2013) produced a more nuanced political view and a more complex approach to critical pedagogy, so favored by those who had taken up the concept of comprehensive-critical peace education. Reaching back to what I had learned of reflective teaching in the first generation, I began to see the need to refine reflective inquiry into the multiple forms that cultivated thinking best suited to the nature of the problematic addressed. I had always believed that pedagogy should be designed so as to produce the most relevant mode of thinking in which to address the substance under study.

A potential fourth generation lies in the realization that I have actually been practicing varying forms of reflective inquiry, that those forms should be identified and illuminated for pedagogical purposes and ultimately transformed into replicable teaching methods, inquiry questions and queries suited to each particular problematic issue on which learning is centered. This task is what I see as the learning vehicle that could take my practice, and perhaps through the current work of colleagues in the field now developing their own approaches to reflective inquiry (Janet Gerson, Tony Jenkins, and Dale Snauwaert in particular), into a next generation of the evolution of peace education. All practicing peace educators have a potential contribution to make to the evolution of the field, be it in this or another area of inquiry and learning. I look forward to learning from and with them.

Betty A. Reardon
New York, April, 2014

Part II
Generations of Reardon's Professional Formation and Practice as Reflected in Selected Essays: First Generation—The Foundations 1963–1985

Chapter 4
The World Law Fund: World Approach to International Education

Retrospective Reflection on "The World Law Fund" (1967)

This article from The Teachers College Record *was the first of the professional publications archived in the Ward M. Canaday Center for Special Collections at the University of Toledo Library.*[1] *Only a few years away from my days as a lower secondary school teacher, it was written by default when I was unable to get any of the high profile academics associated with "The Fund" to respond to the editor of the Record to draft a piece on The Schools Program, a decision the professors may have been glad of when the project it described was denounced in an editorial in the Wall Street Journal. I was, however, given an opportunity to publish a response, and so began such interactions with the skeptics that have continued through all my years in peace education.*

In these early years my primary learning was focused on the concept of war prevention within a problematic of the requisite changes in the international system as the frame within which to inquire and learn toward this political goal, a valid subject, we contended, for citizenship education. From this came several elements of the pedagogy that informed the teachers workshops, curriculum design and writing on the nature and purposes of this new field from 1964 to 1975 toward the development and dissemination of a world order approach to what I came to conceptualize in broader terms as peace education as it was to be taught to teachers and in elementary and secondary schools.

The focus of my programmatic and developmental work for the next decade or so was on encouraging and facilitating the introduction this world order approach

---

[1] This chapter was first published as: "The World Law Fund," *Teachers College Record*, 68(6), 453–465. The permission to republish this text was granted by Gary Natriello, Executive Editor, Teachers College Record on 8 March 2014.

B.A. Reardon and D.T. Snauwaert, *Betty A. Reardon: A Pioneer in Education for Peace and Human Rights*, SpringerBriefs on Pioneers in Science and Practice 26,
DOI 10.1007/978-3-319-08967-6_4

to international and social education into secondary schools. Efforts at dissemination brought me into close and collaborative relationships with talented classroom teachers whose teaching techniques and conceptual approaches to the subject added a great deal to the pedagogical repertoire that I had acquired in my own classroom years. These were the exciting years of "the new social studies" when the social sciences were being integrated into the curricula of citizenship education or social studies as an appropriate means to prepare students for political efficacy in a rapidly evolving world order as citizens of a nation that played a major role in its evolution. Much of my networking and dissemination efforts were done through the National Council for the Social Studies through which I came to know and collaborate with outstanding educators in the field, professors of education as well as classroom teachers; Lawrence Metcalf, Jack Fraenkel, Margaret Carter with whom I produced the first published curricula in the field.

The observation of Earl Johnson, one of the most distinguished social educators of the day with whom I had the privilege to work, that the Fund's primary emphasis on the substance of the problematic as defined in what they described as "the emerging discipline of world order" was not, in the form in which the academic researchers presented it, suited to the concerns of teachers charged with educating those who would become (if there ever was such a being) "the average citizen." The scholars involved in the "ground breaking" scholarly work of the World Order Models Project called only for that substance to be introduced into general education without the slightest interest in or understanding of the development of a pedagogy that would make this possible or consideration of the contradiction between the structures and practices of the schools and the 'transformative' values they advocated. It was this disconnection between the needs of schools and the priorities of "critical peace research," I was to learn pervaded the entire field, globally, producing tensions in the emerging professional organizations, such as those that nearly a decade later lead to my departure from the World Law Fund.

None-the-less, I learned a great deal from the ways and the perspectives from which the international team of scholars such as Saul Mendlovitz, Richard Falk, Rajni Kothari, Ali Mazrui, Gustavo Lagos and others associated with the Fund engaged in their common work. In addition to the methodology of comparing and imaging alternative security systems, there were the normative and critical perspectives that became central to the field of peace education as it has evolved internationally through the ensuing decades. "The world order approach" was the very foundation of all my conceptual work. I hope the subsequent selections in this work will help to illuminate that evolution and my own efforts to be a part of it.

Betty A. Reardon
New York, March, 2014

> Pupils study many wars without learning very much about war. History courses still give major attention to war and politics without casting much light on either. The reason for this failure may be found in the fact that the instructional materials are almost entirely descriptive in nature, and the teaching method is inappropriate.... The material does not encourage [them] to theorize about war, or to reflect upon alternative theories of war.[2]

Professor Metcalf here raises the issue which growing numbers of educators believe should be the foremost concern of all international education. If curriculum is to be relevant to the lives of the students, the problem of war must be included in our high school social studies courses, for many of them who are presently in classrooms may be waging war in the jungles in the near future. They have a right to understand the phenomenon, which might be taking over their lives.

One of the functions of education is to equip students to understand the world in which they live. It is a world in which internationalism is a fact of the everyday life of all Americans and in which international conflict may claim the lives of many or all of us. Given these circumstances, the study of war and the means of its prevention should form a major part of any curriculum for international education.

During the past several years there has been a concerted movement toward education for "international understanding." Dr. James Becker (Foreign Policy Association, formerly of the North Central Association Foreign Relations Project) has raised some challenging questions about that approach to the problem in an article on international understanding: "What is to be understood? By whom?[3] For what purpose?"[4] In reviewing the most widespread practices in education for international understanding one may respond that curriculum planners believe most students should be given two types of understanding—that of other cultures and that of the decision making process in U. S. foreign policy—in order to act more effectively in the national interest. The United States' position of world responsibility demands at least this much and more.

4.1 National Interest and Curriculum

Although the *world responsibility* of the United States has been a significant motivating factor in the growing emphasis on international education, *national interest* has been the most influential factor in the formation of curriculum materials. It is possible, however, to discern situations in which world responsibility seems to conflict with national interest. Curriculum materials tend to handle

---

[2] Metcalf, Lawrence. Statement to the United States Office of Education on Curricular and Instructional Needs in International Education, 1966.

[3] Becker, James; Porter, Martha, 1966: "What is Education for International Understanding?" in: *Social Education*.

[4] Mendlovitz, Saul, 1964: "Teaching War Prevention". *Bulletin of Atomic Scientists*.

this problem by presenting the conflict as two sides of a foreign policy question. Students who have gained some real understanding of another culture or cultures with different world views and, consequently, different concepts of world responsibility, will see other dimensions to the conflict which are not reflected in most study materials currently available.

With Professor Earl Johnson at the 1973 annual conference of the Wisconsin Council for the Social Studies. *Source* Personal photo collection of the author

Some educators have assumed that education on American foreign policy is the best approach to international education. Since the goal of the United States is peace, it is assumed teaching students to make world affairs judgments on the basis of American national interest would be a real contribution toward the achievement of peace. Yet today students are called upon to take a position on whether or not it is sometimes necessary to wage war in order to achieve peace. Few curriculum materials raise questions relevant to this issue, nor do they provide the exercises in evaluation so necessary to forming an opinion about or assuming a position on the question. Are our current practices in international education truly contributing to peace if they fail to offer this kind of intellectual training?

At Stanstead 3 in 1973 with Saul Mendlovits *left*, World Order Models Project, Duncan Graham, co-organizer to the summer program for teachers; and Franklin Wallin, then President of the Institute for World Order. *Source* Personal photo collection of the author

In looking at foreign policy questions, students are generally presented with a picture of the United States as it operates within the present international system and are led to evaluate policy within the present system. But because they are practically never being asked to evaluate the system itself, they never face the question of whether the system is more conducive to war or peace, nor are they able to consider ways in which the system could be improved. Yet today students are expressing concern about major public issues, especially on the national scene, and we find them raising very fundamental questions about political and social systems. Should not curriculum be preparing students to debate these issues intelligently? Do not educators have a responsibility to enable students to confront these questions in ways more constructive than the emotional outbursts of demonstrations and riots?

4.2 The Ambiguities of Understanding

Another assumption underlying current practices in education for international understanding is that the fostering of international friendship through world affairs education will produce peace among nations. Thus, if we each study the history, culture and values of the other, nations will 'understand' each other, become 'friends' and refrain from organized mayhem against each other. The historical fact of so many intra-cultural wars is too obvious a refutation of this thesis. Indeed, to truly understand another culture may emphasize conflicting values and interests rather than resolve them.

More fundamental in terms of curriculum is the factor of conflict itself. International education must come to deal with the many complex aspects of conflict and its resolution. The World Law Fund, and those educators associated with it, assert that the curriculum of international education should include materials which produce an analytical study of war, conflict and system change and that these aspects of curriculum should be added to inter-cultural and foreign policy study to form a new area of curriculum known as *world order.* The Fund advocates training in all three of these areas of international education in order to prepare students adequately for responsible world citizenship. Its program has been directed at the introduction of the subject of world order into the curricula of universities, colleges and secondary schools throughout the world. This is an admittedly ambitious goal, and those who have had experience with curriculum revision would doubtless add one that is quixotic if not foolhardy. Yet the Fund's experience over the past 4 years indicates that the goal is both reasonable and attainable.

4.3 World Order in the Curriculum

The success of the program to date can be attributed to four main factors: (1) the world-wide concern among scholars and educators about the damaging and potentially disastrous system by which relations among nations are now conducted; (2) a program based on the question: "Applying rigorous but conventional intellectual and academic standards for existing courses, is it possible to construct a course which directly confronts the problem of war prevention;" (3) the unusual structure of the program, which operates at all levels of institutional education and in a sense in all stages of curriculum development at one time; and (4) (at least in the United States) the wide movement within the social studies, seeking to incorporate more substantive material into the high school curriculum and to reshape teaching methods in the direction of inquiry and analysis.

In general the Fund seeks to define basic concepts, to develop appropriate teaching materials, to train teachers in the subject matter and the use of the materials and to relate these developments to the most important advances made by other curriculum projects. Many of the methodological aspects of the Fund's program originated in these projects. The work of Donald Oliver (Harvard Graduate School of Education) on the analysis of controversy, that of Edwin Fenton (Carnegie Institute of Technology) on inquiry and the writings of Michael Scriven (The Social Science Consortium) on evaluation have profoundly affected the pedagogical direction of the development of world order programs for high schools.

The Fund's high school program emerged in 1963 out of its university program, the latter having been initiated the previous year as the result of a survey of universities and colleges to determine to what extent world order issues were included in the curriculum. The survey was conducted by Professor Saul Mendlovitz (Rutgers Law School, Consultant to the World Law Fund), who discovered that although specific issues of world order were treated within the context of various courses in political science and international relations, few of these courses dealt with all the interrelated factors with a view toward war prevention. Shortly thereafter Professor Mendlovitz was commissioned by the Fund to take the first step toward the solution of the problem, the preparation of the first materials to initiate academic study of war prevention. The resulting Reader, *Legal and Political Problems of World Order,* became the first in a series of Fund publications for use in universities, high schools and adult education *courses* and discussion groups.[5]

4.4 Origin of the Fund

It is perhaps appropriate to mention here the origin of the World Law Fund and the basic premise on which its program has been developed. In 1958, Grenville Clark, noted lawyer and distinguished public servant, together with Professor Louis B. Sohn of the Harvard Law School, published an extensively detailed plan for war prevention based on a revised United Nations Charter entitled *World Peace Through World Law.* The elimination of war as an instrument of national policy had long been a concern of Mr. Clark, a man who had also devoted much time to the solution of community problems. Clark and Sohn put forth their Plan, not as *the* solution to the problem but as *a* contribution toward a solution. One might, in fact, consider Mr. Clark a kind of pioneer of the inquiry method. A strong believer in the educative effectiveness of prolonged, analytic discussion, he wished to initiate such discussion of war-peace problems. It was his conviction that the establishment of a peaceful international system could result only from identifying the major issues, carefully analyzing related problems and weighing the merits of various solutions. The Plan was put forth, therefore, as a first step in such a process.

Despite the fact that Clark and Sohn were themselves totally without messianic intent in the publication of their book, it was realized that the initiation of worldwide, public discussion on the basis of nothing more than one plan could be considered indoctrination and would likely result in the emergence of little more than a dialogue between the adherents and opponents of the Plan. Such a limited dialogue could not possibly bring about a discussion of the breadth and depth necessary to the desired educative process. Professor Mendlovitz took this

---

[5] A catalogue describing all these publications is available on request from the Fund.

circumstance into consideration in the preparation of *Legal and Political Problems of World Order* and conceived of his task as one of avoiding the potentially propagandistic dialogue in favor of valid scholarly discourse. He made what he conceived to be the only legitimate academic use of *World Peace Through World Law*, a model of one *possible* world system for the control of organized international violence. Thus the materials in the Reader are employed to examine the model's ability to stand up to the tests of feasibility, workability and justice. The Clark-Sohn Plan is used similarly in the four volumes of *The Strategy of World Order*, a revised, expanded version of the original Reader edited by Professor Mendlovitz in collaboration with Professor Richard Falk of Princeton and published by the Fund in 1966.

4.5 Law as a Universal Experience

In adopting the Plan as a study material, the World Law Fund defined its first basic assumption: "... in all modem states legal institutions are used to control and regulate violence... law is almost a universal experience and can be appealed to as a rational method, for achieving order and even justice."[6]

The use of the Mendlovitz materials in several disciplines and the variety of problem foci selected by the instructors led to the conclusion that the subject of world order, while maintaining its basic adherence to law as a source of control and justice, must give careful attention to the analysis of many interrelated problems and must extend itself far beyond the substance of disarmament and conflict resolution. These circumstances reinforced the conclusions derived from contacts with scholars and teachers in other countries.

Not unmindful of the complexities and conflicts inherent in the first basic assumption, Harry B. Hollins, Managing Director of the World Law Fund, began his task of launching a world-wide educational effort by testing its validity. During a trip to present translations of *World Peace Through World Law* to leaders and scholars of many countries and to elicit their reactions to it, he learned two significant lessons which profoundly influenced the guidelines for the operation of the Fund: first, that law as a conceptual basis for order does have some degree of universal meaning; and second, that no one plan and no single perspective on the problem of war will produce a workable solution for a complex, multi-cultural world in which the hierarchy of critical problems varies from nation to nation.

The recognition of these conditions led to the internationalization of the operation from the earliest stages. Scholars and educators from all areas of the world were enlisted to assist in the formulation and evaluation of programs and encouraged and assisted with the initiation of similar operations in their own

6 Oliver, Donald. Report to the World Law Fund on 1963 summer course.

countries. The exchange of course outlines and course syllabi among educators of several nations has enriched the resources for world order education while moving it further toward its goal.

4.6 The "Models Project"

The Fund has recently launched a project which has tremendous potential as the basis and vehicle for world-wide public discussion and offers the opportunity for academic examination of world order issues. The "Models Project," which began as an attempt to overcome the limitations imposed by the existence of a single war prevention plan, may prove to be the single most important development since the publication of *World Peace Through World Law*. Six teams of scholars are now being assembled in Eastern and Western Europe, Latin America, Africa, the Middle East and Asia. Each team viewing world order from the perspective of their own community of nations will draft a plan for a world system of the same degree of specificity as that of Clark and Sohn—that is, the plans will provide for the control of violence, the peaceful settlement of disputes and the necessary means for economic development and the achievement of human rights. The current schedule for the completion of these draft plans is 1969 at which time the Fund proposes to integrate them into its total materials program and to offer thereby the legitimate alternatives required for scholarly discourse.

4.7 An "Emerging Discipline"

The Fund has interpreted its experiences with this new dimension in international education as the basis of the emergence of world order as a new academic discipline with very special relevance to the contemporary world and to the personal concerns of university and high school students.

The characteristics of the "emerging discipline" of world order, as it has been defined by Professor Mendlovitz, demonstrate the degree to which the subject matter is responsive to the new academic requirements of international education.[7] The control of international violence is the central problem of all world order studies and accounts for the problem solving orientation of the discipline. Emphasis is placed on analysis and evaluation of actual and potential institutions to deal with the problem through the examination of alternative systems and proposals or 'models.' Since the solution of the central problem requires a drastic change in the international system, world order is developing as a discipline which

[7] Mendlovitz, S., 1961: "The Emerging Discipline of World Order," an address, November, 1961.

emphasizes *process* and encourages an analytic approach to change and the factors which influence it. The variety of substantive specializations required to analyze the problems have resulted in a subject matter which is interdisciplinary and relies upon the insights and methodological tools of law, economics, political science, history, the behavioral sciences and philosophy. The most unique attributes of the discipline are its global and futuristic aspects. One of its primary aims is the development of a world perspective on world problems. It also directs itself toward the restructuring of the present system in terms of a preferred system for the next decade or century. In so doing, it attempts to free the minds of its students from the ideological and nationalistic limitations imposed by present world conditions. Because it is so catholic in its concerns, world order might well form the substantive basis for an entire curriculum in the social studies. It holds, therefore, greater potential for the adequate training of future world citizens than any other single discipline within the social studies.

4.8 Training the Teachers

If this new discipline is to take its place in the high school curriculum among the other substantive specializations of the social sciences, it must become part of the education of all social studies teachers. The training of secondary school teachers is the largest and without question the most costly area of operation of the World Law Fund. It is also an area of such strategic importance to the success of the entire program that every resource and effort expended on it is more than merited, for perhaps no other professional group has more influence over the formation of public attitudes and acquisition of background for the making of public decisions than do high school teachers.

As yet there are very few professors of education who are familiar with the field, and therefore there are no regular courses offered in graduate schools of education and only a minimum number of courses in the undergraduate institutions which prepare so many of our teachers. Within the disciplines of political science and international law, however, the situation is quite different. More and more professors are adopting the Fund's publications so that the number of substantive courses related to world order are growing. What has been accomplished to date in the education of in-service teachers has been for the most part the result of the efforts of professors in departments of political science at such institutions as the University of Florida, University of South Carolina, University of Southern California and the University of California at Riverside. (One notable exception to this pattern was a 1965 summer program at the University of the State of New York at Buffalo where two educationists conducted an interdisciplinary seminar for teachers which relied for its substantive coverage on lectures by scholars in such subjects as political science, psychology and history.)

Reactions to these experiences on the part of both in-service teachers and political scientists have been positive and enthusiastic. There is no question that although difficulties were faced on both sides, the instructors and the students in these courses were especially motivated in their efforts by the urgent and interesting nature of the subject under study. Even the most able high school teachers found extensive theoretical reading in the latest works on the legal and political aspects of international relations tough going because their training had provided them with little or no background in political science and law. But almost without exception they responded well to the challenge and to the acknowledgment that teachers could handle the highest level of substantive, graduate work. For their part the political scientists found, in spite of all the ground work that had to be done, that the high school teachers were stimulating students who would use the efforts of their instructors in a very concrete and constructive manner.

4.9 Summer Institutes

In the majority of cases in-service teachers have been introduced to world order through these substantive courses, but the Fund has also sponsored three significant full-scale summer institutes conducted by teaching teams of educationists and political scientists and/or international lawyers. The first of these teams, Professor Donald Oliver and Professor Saul Mendlovitz, conducted an institute as a special offering in Social Studies and Curriculum Methods during the regular 6 weeks Harvard summer session in 1963. The students at the institute were selected from classroom teachers, curriculum coordinators and instructors in education from all over the United States and received double graduate credit for successful completion of the program. In substance, the course explored and evaluated the use of several conceptual systems or 'models' through which the problem of maintaining world order might be viewed, and then examined the political feasibility of developing more effective institutions for handling international conflict. In dealing with these topics, the students also worked on developing materials and instructional methods for the high school level through the case method. Each student researched a specific incident of international conflict, including its historical background and consequences and indications of future implications, and from this body of information wrote up a case to be used as a teaching unit.

As Professor Oliver observed, "… having a curriculum development specialist and a specialist in international relations working together…proved to be quite successful…both gained insights into the use of the case method approach for teaching this material."[8]

The case method and construction of the models as a means of examining alternative solutions to the problems raised in the cases proved to be a significant contribution to the Fund's program. These techniques were introduced into the world program in June 1965 when Professors Oliver and Mendlovitz moderated a

[8] Oliver, Donald. Report to the World Law Fund on 1963 summer course.

colloquium on international conflict control and world law for professors of education and curriculum development experts from the United States and five other countries.

This team approach has twice been employed under the direction of Professor Earl S. Johnson (School of Education, University of Wisconsin, Milwaukee). Professor Johnson has served as coordinator and methodology expert for two summer institutes organized along the lines of the Harvard prototype. In one case his teammate was from the field of international law and in the other from political science, thereby providing Professor Johnson with opportunities to weld his pedagogical skills to the two primary substantive disciplines of world order. The results constitute a major contribution to world order education, a complete and profoundly analytical guide to pedagogy and a syllabus which adapts the publications of the Fund as well as selections from the general literature of world order to the needs of high school social studies teachers.

4.10 Need for Readers

Professor Johnson's analysis of these two institutes has been an important contribution to the projection of future directions in the teacher training program. He experienced problems similar to those encountered by the political scientists, i.e. the teachers' limited acquaintance with political and behavioral sciences. He noted also that the tremendous effort of covering so much new, highly complex substantive material detracted from efforts in the area of pedagogy. He urged, therefore, that future institutes extend sessions from 6 to 8 weeks. Professor Johnson cautioned that the use of models may easily lend itself to the kind of methodological gimmickry that has recently afflicted other innovations in the social studies. His recommendation for a series of readers aimed at various reading levels to provide appropriate and properly edited selections from the most responsible scholarly literature in the field is already part of the Fund's publication plan. All of the participants in these teams agreed that the interaction of the team members contributed a great deal to the communication of the importance of inquiry and the examination of alternatives. It is interesting to note that both Professors Johnson and Oliver emphasize an analytic approach to content and show a methodological preference for the dialectic. Each of them has made a significant contribution to the pedagogical characteristics of the new discipline, Professor Johnson through a new adaptation of his educational philosophy, and Professor Oliver through the introduction of the concept of public controversy as the core of his new social studies curriculum.

4.11 An International Colloquium

These contributions became part of the development of international curriculum through the colloquium on international conflict control and world law co-sponsored by the World Law Fund and the Harvard Social Studies Project in 1965. The purposes of the colloquium, in addition to acquainting leading educators with the substantive issues and the teaching materials currently available, were to bring together an international group of scholars who would attempt to view the problems and the materials from a world perspective and to project ways in which such a perspective could be integrated into future study materials. Another significant purpose of the colloquium was to test the educational validity of the World Law Fund's secondary school program by raising such questions as how and where the issues of world order should be treated in the secondary curriculum and whether appropriate methods for instruction in these matters could be developed simultaneously with the curriculum materials.

The colloquium produced an international team which continues to work for the improvement of instruction in world order and for the introduction of the topic at the secondary level of their respective educational systems. There was general agreement that the World Law Fund's program was academically sound and that the approach of the Harvard Social Studies Project of the analysis through case studies of issues of public controversy was an appropriate medium for the teaching of world order.

Having agreed to continue as an informal committee-of-the-whole, the group determined to work toward fulfilling the most acute need in this area of education—the production of materials of appropriate substance and teaching approach. The first project is now under way—the production of a case book on international conflict which is being designed for use in all countries at the senior high school level.

4.12 World Order Seminars

Among the participants in the colloquium, four were involved in the organization of world order seminars in other parts of the world. One pre-dated the colloquium and resulted in the representation of India at the 1965 meeting. The University of Delhi planned and executed a 10-day intensive seminar for Indian political scientists in the fall of 1964. One of the Indian scholars who had a special interest in secondary education established a seminar program on international organization for high school students after his participation in the colloquium.

A similar program was inaugurated for eleven high schools in Bogota by the Colombian participant who also assisted members of the faculty of the University of Bogota in organizing a seminar held in September, 1966 for forty teachers of international law from various Colombian institutions. In August the English colloquium participant acted as a visiting lecturer on world studies at a special summer course for secondary school and university instructors organized under the auspices of the University of London. He is a member of the University faculty and has established there a world studies teaching and resource center.

Earlier in the summer Professor Mendlovitz had formed part of a team of American, African and European scholars who conducted a seminar at the University of East Africa in Tanzania for a group similar to those who attended the English summer course.

It should be noted as a manifestation of the Fund's internationalization of programs that all of these seminars were internationally staffed, as were the participant groups.

Among the faculty and the participants of these seminars there is a constant exchange of project reports and materials. Efforts are being made to integrate materials from one country into the curricula of other countries. Although limited, attempts are being made to use some materials in the original language wherever possible. In this way, foreign language study may be practically and programmatically linked to world order studies, giving students an opportunity to use their language skills while experiencing in a primary sense the views of another nation on world problems.

4.13 LAWS and the Teacher

One of the primary agencies in the initiation of innovative programs within the schools of the other countries has been Leadership and World Society. Since 1958, LAWS has supported innovations in world affairs education in high schools in the United States and in 1965 began to offer the same support to schools throughout the world. The basic assumption in the LAWS operation is that teachers are the persons most directly involved in curriculum and most capable of designing and carrying out effective teaching plans. With the assistance of small grants from LAWS, programs on world order have been introduced by individual teachers into more than two hundred high schools in the United States and some two dozen schools in other countries. So, in spite of the fact that packaged units and specially devised high school materials are not as yet available, world order is entering the curriculum of our schools. LAWS has been largely responsible for this development.[9]

The greatest problem the Fund has so far encountered is in this very area of the production of suitable materials, a factor which is attributable to two conditions; first, the emerging, evolving nature of the basic discipline; and second, the lack of appropriate background among authors of high school texts. The second factor, of

---

[9] A booklet, "LAWS, The Story of a Partnership in International Studies" by David Mallery, is available on request.

course, has been faced by all agencies producing world affairs materials for secondary schools. University professors of the related disciplines have been commissioned to write units which are then edited or virtually 'translated' by educationists who have produced secondary level social studies materials into language understandable to high school students. There is, as well, the auxiliary problem of convincing the commercial publishers that there is a market for world order materials.

4.14 Manuscripts and Syllabi

The Fund has two documents in the 'translation' stage which are scheduled for publication and classroom testing in the very near future. One of them deals with constitutional process and its potential application to the world community; the other describes a world law 'model' and examines some of the problems involved in the establishment of such a system. Among other materials in preparation are two readers which when completed will make a significant contribution to the solution of the materials problem. Although each reader is being produced in a different fashion, both are planned to be adaptable to the same types of courses at the 11th and 12th grade level. The differences in production stem from the origins of the proposed readers.

Some high school teachers have made use of university materials, adapting them to the special purposes of their own courses, as many teachers have for years in history and social studies courses. One such teacher, Mrs. Priscilla Griffith (head of the Social Studies Department at Melbourne High School, Melbourne, Florida), had devised her own syllabus based on the adaptation of such materials to a junior-senior international relations course. The course, which includes a variety of audiovisual materials as well as selected readings from diverse sources, is now in its 4th year. Mrs. Griffith, therefore, has had sufficient experience with the materials to determine which readings are most effective. She is currently bringing together the best of these readings with her own introductory comments and discussion questions as a basic world order reader for high schools along the lines suggested by Professor Earl Johnson. In this way one teacher's extensive preparatory work and classroom experience can be put into shape for the use of other teachers who know full well the high cost in time and thought that goes into the preparation of such a syllabus.

It is extremely costly to put together such a unit. Few schools can provide source materials in such quantity as has been necessary in the teaching of the Melbourne course. The course was one made possible by a grant from LAWS. Among other materials resulting from LAWS projects are an entire social studies curriculum based on the concept of change and problems of transition in the emerging nations; a unit on international law; a syllabus for a one semester course on world problems; and a great variety of plans for extracurricular activities of a truly academic nature. (One of the outstanding characteristics of LAWS projects is their demonstration of the degree to which high school students are willing and able to invest intense intellectual effort in the confrontation of major public issues which are personally important to them.)

4.15 The World Order Reader

The World Order Reader, which grew out of the Harvard Colloquium, is probably the most exciting study unit projected by the Fund, for it may well be the first truly international curriculum material. It is being internationally produced and tested and plans are being made for international distribution in at least six languages.

This Reader, as noted earlier, will consist of a series of cases of international conflict and a suggested conceptual framework which will enable students to examine the nature of conflict, to evaluate systems for the resolution of international disputes and to assess the peace-keeping requirements for world order. The cases are being contributed by authors from various countries and will be edited by Dr. James Henderson (Institute of Education, London University), Dr. Hartmut von Hentig (Pedagogical Seminar, Gottingen University) and Dr. Lawrence Metcalf. The editors met recently in London and projected the publication date for mid 1968.

The testing of this Reader is another project which will be facilitated by LAWS which since the awarding of its first grants outside the United States in 1965 has added to the hundreds of participating American schools several dozen counterpart schools in Germany, England, India, Colombia, Canada, the Netherlands and Swaziland.

Among other projected study units is a series being prepared by Robert Hanvey of the *Anthropology Curriculum Project* dealing with the maintenance in various social units from primitive tribes up to and including the community of nations. A series based on an area studies approach is also being planned with the intention of presenting problems of world order as viewed from other geo-political areas. These units will be produced by scholars from the various areas for use in their own secondary schools and translated for use in other countries. Frank Njenga, instructor in law at the University of East Africa in Tanzania, is currently working on the first unit, representing an African view of world order problems.

The materials, therefore, are generating from two sources, one within the high school classroom itself and the other from the substantive theoreticians. But unfortunately, the rate is not fast enough to feed the growing demands from teachers and teacher educators.

Although world order units and materials have yet to be packaged, the Fund has gathered evidence which indicates that there is a place for them within most social studies courses. Meeting this demand has become the Fund's first priority for the high school program.

The Fund has refrained from setting up its own machinery but rather has pursued its goals by acting as a catalytic agent to initiate appropriate programs within the established channels of curriculum revision. If, as has been repeated so often, war is too important to be left to the generals, teaching about it is too broad and too complex to be left to any single educational agency or institution. Teaching about world order is more than an obligation of educators; it also offers an advantage to them. We cannot expect General Bourgoyne to have as much pedagogical payoff with today's students as Ho Chi Minh, nor can we expect the issues and goals involved in the Mexican War to engage the minds of our students to the same degree as those related to the Vietnam conflict. Although the Bourgoynes and the wars of our national history must be part of secondary education, the events of our own times are of more interest and more significance to today's students. This point was made in terms more pertinent to curriculum development by Dr. Byron Massialis at the last convention of the National Council for the Social Studies when, in response to a question about content, he answered that it must concern itself with the leading issues of our time, among them war.

Chapter 5
Transformations into Peace and Survival: Programs for the 1970s

Retrospective Reflection on "Transformations for Peace and Survival: Programs for the 70s" (1973)

I read this piece as a summary of what I had learned in the first 10 years of full professional commitment to a field I had not yet come to think of as peace education; and a forecast of many of the normative principles and pedagogical inclinations that would inform most of my future work. It was a decade in which I was actively involved in curriculum development and theoretical collaboration with the some of the most influential American social educators of the day, many of whom are referenced here. Yet to come were the years of close working relationships with peace educators from various other countries whose exchanges and cooperative endeavors produced the international peace education movement of the last quarter of the 20th century. While the piece reflects American efforts to conceptualize a more global approach, it is deeply imbued with the critiques of American education that sprung from the observations of American educators, particularly those of the survival education (closely akin to peace education) movement represented in the volume in which 'Transformations…' was published. The emerging internationalization of the field is evident here with references to the ideas of the Mexican based education critic, Ivan Illich and the Brazilian philosopher and pedagogue, Paulo Freire. I learned of Freire in these same years when a friend, knowing of how I was starting to view the politics of pedagogy, passed on a piece from the Harvard Education Review. *Freirean critiques became more widely known with the publication of* The Pedagogy of the Oppressed, *a foundational work on the field of critical pedagogy that came to have a significant effect on peace education. Their critiques found education, especially public schooling—even in democratic societies—to be a reflection of an unequal class*

B.A. Reardon and D.T. Snauwaert, *Betty A. Reardon: A Pioneer in Education for Peace and Human Rights*, SpringerBriefs on Pioneers in Science and Practice 26,
DOI 10.1007/978-3-319-08967-6_5

system and the hierarchical social structures that sought to educate for self-replication, avoiding if not repressing challenge by emphasis on content mastery over critical thinking, an issue that still remains unresolved.

As I undertook more international work through the newly formed Peace Education Commission of the International Peace Research Association (1972) and the World Council for Curriculum and Instruction that held its first world conference in England in 1974, I found similar critiques being expressed by European educators who likened the structures and processes of state sponsored education to those that mediated the neocolonial structures of the world economy. It was these critiques which produced the strong emphasis on social and economic justice as the essential foundation of peace that became a hallmark of the international peace education movement. In these waning years of the Vietnam War that many peace educators saw as a colonial war, war began to be interpreted as a means not only to pursue national interest and 'security,' but also to maintain the global power hierarchy. The curricular concepts contained in this volume on survival education were infused with critical analysis of that structure. Needless to say such curricula were not welcomed by most of mainstream education. Yet as reflected here, peace educators were hopeful of affecting change, while fully aware of the obstacles thereto. Most of the essays in the volume in which 'Transformations…' appeared were imbued with hope that recognition of structural injustice could make possible it's remediation with education as significant agent in the process. That belief rings throughout this selection.

While the education establishment was far from accommodating to these ideas, we had some encouragement from the work of UNESCO that validated the field with the 1974 Recommendation on International Understanding, Cooperation and Peace; and Education concerning Fundamental Human Rights and Freedoms that was approved by the agency's General Conference. Little known in the United States, it was in the spirit of other UNESCO initiatives such as the Associated Schools Project that supported education for world citizenship. But neither did it, as an interstate agency, yet embrace education regarding issues of structural injustice.

So, too, in this piece I see some of the very obstacles to the full recognition of the nature and significance of those unjust structures that continued to remain invisible even to numbers of peace educators in spite of our enthusiasm for "speaking truth to power." Clearly, there was much sorely needed learning yet to come on my part and in the evolution of the field. A genuine sense of chagrin is raised by reading some of the blatantly sexist language that was common, even among the progressives of the day. The use of male pronouns to refer to the abstract 'genderless' persons who were the subjects of concern in the essay—students, among other oppressed, and among which I had developed at least that level of gender consciousness that lead me to include women—makes me wince.

The terminology of 'man' and 'mankind' for which I would later use such words as 'persons' and 'humanity' were not, I must emphasize, used here without reflection. I recall a conversation with the wonderful, most human of social educators, Earl Johnson in which I queried him about the distinctions between the terms as applied in his work to speak of all humans as a group. His reply was that 'man' referred only to the species as such, but 'mankind' inferred the moral, reflective nature of the species, that which carried the human responsibility for the rest of what was soon to be called the "planetary system" or "the living Earth". These were instructive and clarifying normative ideas that—while the language may have been sexist—fed my hunger to develop means to integrate ethics into what I practiced still as "world order studies." They gave a flesh and blood, living dimension to the otherwise abstract world order values that were so central to the pedagogies that the social educators with whom I was working were developing. This was the great decade of "values analysis" and "moral decision making" as the methods and goals of social education for democratic citizenship.

As my learning continued I became aware, not only of gender injustice, but also of the many destructive, un-reflected assumptions people hold without questioning, crucial ethical issues and the severe conceptual obstacles to teaching and learning for the achievement of the very changes we worked for. I did not 'unlearn' these sexist concepts, but rather learned to better understand them and their significance, and came to perceive gender to be a main element in the peace problematic. It also cultivated two other ideas that inform my approach to education, what it comprises and how pedagogy and the teacher-learner relationship are the most crucial elements in the entire process. They are first and foremost, that most people are capable of learning, and that fixed ideas can change through learning to understand how we came to hold them, to reconsider how those ideas affect how we view the world and its problems, and to develop other ideas that may refute or complement the old ones—never 'undo' them—preserving the insights they give us that enable us, among other things, to understand and respect those who hold notions similar to our "old ideas." These thoughts incubated the pedagogic concept of civil disputation, and the norm of honoring human dignity through the mediation of difficult differences.

Another point of interest in this essay is the reaching toward, but not yet grasping the essential holism that was required in the field. It would take nearly another decade before I comprehended what I came to see as comprehensive peace education and the integral interrelationship between sexism and the war system. So within this piece are glimmers of two of the most essential conceptual lenses through which I have sought to shed light on the problems and processes of peace learning.

Betty A. Reardon
March, 2014

5.1 Introduction

From a vantage point early in the 1970s it seems a bit futile to forecast proposals for the decade.[1] Programs for the 1970s should have as their long-range targets not this decade but the next century. Perhaps farsighted programs will help avoid the

[1] This article was originally published in *Education for Peace: Focus on Mankind*, edited by George Henderson, 127–51. Alexandria, VA: Association for Supervision and Curriculum Development, 1973.

fruitless kinds of incremental and fragmented change that has characterized the past two decades of American education. Given the current trend projections, educational needs, and various other societal problems, it is evident that drastic changes in educational policy are required. Without such changes we cannot expect the school system itself to survive, much less make any significant contribution to the change of any other system or, indeed, to the survival of mankind. It is that *survival crisis* which programs for the 1970s must face as the key issue in goal formation and strategy planning. It is therefore imperative that survival education become the core of all programs.

The first requisite of survival is peace, a state of order in which tensions and conflicts can be resolved without destruction or lethal violence. (Note: peace need *not* be the absence of tension or conflict but only the nonviolent management of these phenomena.) Educational programs must therefore be concerned with defining and achieving such an order to assure survival in all realms of human experience—as part of a species, or mankind; as members of groups and subgroups, or societies; and as human beings, or individuals.

As we inquire into the definitions and strategies for achievement of the desired order, we must recognize not only the interrelationships among these realms of experience but also the uniqueness of each and the distinctions among them. We cannot, for example, expect world peace to provide "inner peace" for every human being (the ability to handle personal and internal conflicts) any more than we can expect to achieve world peace by gradually bringing "peace of soul" to each member of the human species. Nor can we expect a nonviolent or even a 'just' order among nations to resolve all the varied and complex tensions existing within and among other levels of human social organization. We should, however, recognize that some of these domestic and personal tensions do in fact result from the stresses imposed by the "war system" which characterizes present world politics and that any attempt to eliminate them must include efforts to replace that system with a "peace system," a form of politics which reduces and attempts to eliminate organized violence.

Helping to bring such a system into existence should be a primary goal of educational programs in the 1970s. Anything less would be an inadequate response to the petitions of the young reflected in the data in Chap. 4, "Let's Listen to Our Children and Youth." Such a goal requires an education that inquires into three realms of human experience: into social and political structures and processes, with an eye toward understanding and managing institutions and deriving strategies for nonviolent change needed for species survival; into modes to express ideas, feelings, and interpretations of proposed changes, aiming at the kind of exchange among and within groups that will result in intelligent policy formation; and into individual moral growth, intellectual development, and ways of making both personal and political choices on the basis of sound value judgments.

A more comprehensive description of these goals was presented in the Asilomar "Statement of Objectives and Approaches for Improvement of the Social Studies." For the purposes of this chapter, as you read the statement, reproduced below, simply substitute 'education' at each mention of "social studies".

> The purpose of the social studies is to educate students toward the development of a world in which all human beings may live in dignity. The goals of learning should be construction of a future world system in which all human persons enjoy material well-being, the benefits of education, access to information, freedom from oppression and violence, participation in making the decisions which affect their lives, and a respectful, nourishing, and fulfilling relationship with all forms of life and their environment.
>
> Learning experiences should be designed to help students understand the processes and causes of change through the careful analysis of all available data. It is imperative that learning experiences equip the learner with the ability to participate effectively in the process of change. This approach should foster the development of a value system which accords human dignity to all persons and produces empathy with and compassion for other humans of diverse cultures, both in their own countries and in other parts of the world.
>
> The social studies, through social and behavioral sciences and the humanities, should introduce several basic concepts to students of all nations and all cultures. These concepts include the notion that mankind is a single species with basic common needs and that the world is a global system incorporating many human cultures and subsystems. Human and cultural differences should be studied and appreciated as varieties of the total human experience.
>
> Students should be able to recognize and define problems, to gather and apply data in order to understand problems, to conceptualize and plan solutions, to evaluate various plans according to a value system which encourages commitment to action. Students possessing such skills may use them to build a world system in which human life is valued above institutions, freedom as valued above political ideology, and justice is valued above order.
>
> Learning experiences should provide the child with opportunities to select subjects and modes of study and encourage his personal participation in the learning process. Children must be helped to understand themselves and others and permitted to discuss and reflect upon the nature of self and of other selves, such reflections being vital to the child's ability to build his own learning structures and to become a reflective evaluator of his own learning. Content should be based upon the realities of the life of the child, his community, and world society. Controversy, conflict, and serious problems must be as much a part of the child's in-school learning as they are of his out-of-school learning.
>
> Such education implies the need to overcome unnecessary barriers among the disciplines and to create and use knowledge in a way which will contribute to the realization of the desired future world system. The creation and use of such knowledge should encourage the development of the highest levels of cognition, which can produce the kind of affective learning experiences which lead to changes in behavior and to desired social change.[2]

[2] Alice Miel and Louise Berman, editors. "Educating the Young People of the World". Washington, DC. Association for Supervision and Curriculum Development, 1970, pp. 107–108.

5.2 Meeting the Crises: A Revolution in Education

The question for educators proceeding from the statement above is: What kinds of projects and programs can carry out its purposes? Fortunately there are many possibilities within the growing survival-curriculum movement and also in projects dealing with social issues and human development. Many of these projects have an admitted crisis orientation, an orientation which, far from being a hysterical approach, is a pragmatic one. The common orientation is crisis-centered rather than problem-centered because there is a general recognition that our present structures and processes for problem solution are inadequate to meet the current situation. In fact, what differentiates a 'crisis' from a 'problem' is the inability of the established institutions to deal with the former. A second common characteristic of this growing group of 'survivalists' is the search for unprecedented solutions and the concomitant assumption that such solutions will probably require new and radically different institutions, an idea described by Michael Scriven as "survival through revolution."[3]

Scriven was, in fact, the first to put forth a suggestive outline for a survival curriculum which must be developed to replace the "war curriculum" described by Thornton B. Monez in Chap. 2 of this book. Other notable contributions on the relationship between education and survival, together with suggestions for curricular and pedagogical approaches, have been made by William H. Boyer, of the University of Hawaii,[4] and Fannie R. Shaftel, of Stanford University.[5] Although these researchers carry out their work in the tradition of social reconstruction, their writings call for an activist commitment and, indeed, tend to be more revolutionary than reformist in that they document the need for immediate and drastic changes in educational organization and practice.

It is the thesis of this chapter that, while there is a general recognition of the need for educational change of revolutionary proportions, there has been no systematic general diagnosis from which we may project a comprehensive vision of change and design strategies for bringing the vision into reality. Criticism and problems are dealt with separately (if at all), and consequently little or no headway is made toward meeting the real needs of the schools. We must recognize that education is in a systems crisis and requires a drastic system change, a revolutionary approach to meet that crisis.

When we try to sum up all that has been said in the critiques and studies of the schools, the problem of reaching a diagnosis is not so difficult to resolve. Let me posit one possible general diagnosis as a basis for some of the programs to be recommended for the 1970s. The schools are a barometer of the society, revealing the stresses it suffers, demonstrating the gap it exhibits between articulated and

---

[3] Michael Sciven "Education for Survival." In: G. Kanley, editor. The Meal School. Wilmette, Illinois: The Kagg Press, 1969.

[4] William Boyer. "Education for Survival." *Phi Delta Kappan* 52(5):258–62; January 1971.

[5] Fannie Shaftel. "A Survival Curriculum in the Social Studies." Address to the Southern California Social Studies Council, October 1970.

manifested values, and shaking with the trauma of recognizing the need for change but having no clear and comprehensive vision of what form that change should take. In short, the schools, like most other aspects of society, are oppressive in their atmosphere, product-oriented in their processes, past- and content-oriented in their teaching methods, and hierarchical and elitist in their organization.

For example, the tendency to classify and categorize young people not only in age groups but also in so-called ability groups, and thereby to separate some groups from other groups, undoubtedly contributes to the polarization which afflicts our society. (It is easy enough for the educators to decry the attacks of hard-hat hawkish laborers on the dove demonstrations of students, but they might well recognize that the world view and value system of that group of hard hats were profoundly influenced when they were separated into a 'nonacademic' course in secondary school or, even worse, were consigned at a young age to groups with reading or language difficulties, which we know now to be in large part culturally determined.)

At best, the schools' mode of organization and operation is inefficient, and at worst, it is inhumane. Ranging from Silberman, to Denisson, to Leonard, to Rossman, to Goodman, to Firestone, and the feminists, the charge is pretty well documented that delight, exuberance, excitement at the adventure of life, and joy in learning have no place in most American schools.

5.3 World-Order Studies as Survival Curriculums

A prescription that would follow from such a diagnosis would include a new school system which is anti-elitist, person-oriented, inquiry-centered, process-concerned, and future-directed and, God willing, would function in a happy environment in which students could prepare to work toward the survival of mankind on planet earth. In short, a set of conditions should prevail m the schools which peace researchers now refer to as "positive peace," in which peace can be maintained—that is, "a state of assured justice."[6]

Without such an environment no curriculum, even one based on survival criteria, will serve the purpose. Let us keep the goals implied in this prescription in mind as we seek out substantive bases for survival curriculums. Such goals, I believe, are implicit in programs now being devised to deal with the issues of environment, population, human rights, economic development and welfare, social justice, and war and peace. One particular area of study which combines elements of such issues and works toward a goal similar to that advocated in the foregoing prescription is "world order." After more than 10 years of research and development, this topic offers techniques of problem definition, modes of inquiry, and value analysis, as well as particular teaching-learning strategies.

---

[6] Bert V. A. Roling. "The Contents of Peace Research." Paper prepared for the 1971 meeting of the International Peace Research Association, held in Bled, Yugoslavia.

The central concern of the world-order inquiry is peace, a goal described by the discipline as the elimination of organized violence among nations. This central concern with violence has led researchers in the field to see the potential for organized violence arising out of those very problems which individually threaten the survival of man. Working separately in their own regions of the world, but coordinating their efforts through such programs as the World Order Models Project, they have come to see these problems as so closely interrelated that they would be more effectively resolved by integrated programs organized at a world-system level rather than being dealt with as distinct phenomena approached individually by national systems.

World order, therefore, is a comprehensive, integrated, multidisciplinary subject. Researchers have assumed the responsibility of suggesting modes to bring about changes in the world political system to attain the goals of world order. As a result, world order is not merely an academic inquiry into problems of war or peace and survival. It is also a policy science directed at finding viable solutions to those problems. This policy science orientation makes it a highly appropriate substantive base for educational programs designed to equip and motivate students to act for change.

The basic concern for world peace gives rise to the assumption that the most urgently required change—perhaps, in fact, a prerequisite to changes at other levels of human organization—is that which would radically transform the world political structure by replacing the war system with adequate world institutions to make nonviolent resolution of conflicts among nations both possible and probable. Thus supporters of world-order studies advocate that students inquire into the structures and processes of the world political system with a view toward transforming it into a true peace system. World order is, therefore, political education for world citizenship. It is a conscious attempt to politicize students responsibly with regard to world problems in much the same manner as Edmund W. Gordon advocated in regard to national problems of race and social justice and student power in the cogent and moving paper he delivered at Asilomar.[7]

Programs such as those advocated by Gordon and world order educators should have top priorities for the 1970s, not only because of their concern for peace but also because of the related goals espoused as essential to peace—social justice and economic welfare. Such programs would make operational Earl S. Johnson's definition of the "politicization of social knowledge," which is "the purposeful turning of thought and action, collectively and individually, toward the realities of our time—war, the rape of nature, racism, hunger."[8]

World order seeks not only nonviolent solutions to conflicts but, even more important, *just* solutions to conflicts. It is a normative, value-centered discipline

---

[7] Edmund W. Gordon. "Building a Socially Supportive Environment" In: Alice Miel and Louise Berman, editors *Educating the Young People of the World*. Washington, D.C.: Association for Supervision and Curriculum Development, 1970. pp. 59–70.

[8] Earl S. Johnson. "Commentary on Social Studies Curriculum Guidelines" *Social Education* 36(3). 258ff; March 1972.

which aspires to more than the elimination of war, aiming also at relieving human suffering resulting from drastically disparate distribution of the world's wealth; from the prejudices, discrimination, and oppression which deprive far too many human beings of their rights and dignity; and from the wanton exploitation of the earth's resources by that powerful minority which controls and uses them without regard to the interests of the people of this and succeeding generations. The search for just solutions is expressed by world order as an attempt to achieve five goals:

1. The minimization of violence, or *war prevention*
2. The maximizing of *economic welfare*, or the providing of better standards of living for more people
3. The increasing of *social justice* by relieving discrimination and oppression
4. The broadening of the democratic base of public policy making by increasing the *participation* of minorities and individuals in decision-making processes
5. The improving of the quality of life through restoration of *ecological balance*.

> World order examines these goals by asking some significant questions: What is the present state of the world with regard to peace, economic welfare, social justice, political participation, and ecological balance? If we make no significant changes in the international system, what is the state likely to be in the next generation? If that state is, as most trend analyses indicate, not one likely to achieve peace and the other related world order goals, what changes in the system would be most likely to do so? How can we bring about those changes?
> The methodology of world order encompasses many techniques of inquiry and active learning which offer some hope for improving education on values and public issues. There are five basic steps to this methodology. The first is the *diagnosis*: a summary and analysis of world problems, their causes and their relationship to the... values. The second step is a *prognosis* or a projection of the evolution of these problems and the potential for the emergence of other problems over a 20–30 year period. These two are preliminary to a third step which actually attempts to deal with the future in the *positing of several alternative international systems* designed to resolve the problems defined in the first step. This projection is followed by the *evaluation* of the alternatives and the *selection* of a *preferred system*—the alternative which emerges from the evaluation as the one most likely to achieve peace, economic welfare, and social justice in the world community. The final step, *transition*, plots the strategies and policies needed to transform the present world system into the "preferred world."[9]

It is these processes and questions which should be addressed to all students in every school in terms appropriate to their age and environment. It is the goals implicit in these questions which should form the central purposes of education not only *at all levels* but also *in all subjects*. They are raised in only a few of our schools now; if they are not raised in most schools long before the end of this decade, the schools will have made no contribution to survival or to peace. For these reasons the contributors to this Yearbook assert that these issues and problems should provide the main content of curriculums in the 1970s.

[9] Betty A. Reardon. "Prologue." *Media & Methods. Exploration in Education*. 6(2):35; October 1969.

While the central concerns of world order studies are suitable for programs addressing themselves to the problems of survival, the researchers have not yet directed themselves specifically to problems of personal identity and individual fulfillment. These problems have been treated only to the degree to which they affect or are affected by systems and institutions (granted that the degree is arguable and the argument should be an integral part of the general survival inquiry).

5.4 Personal Identity and World Civilization

The personal realm is a major focus of the rapidly developing human potential movement, which is another important area of survival programs and one which could well serve to complement world order studies in programs for the 1970s. In its efforts to help people regain or develop a sense of self, to cultivate, manage, and enjoy emotional responses and aesthetic experiences, the human-potential movement offers much promise of turning us away from some of the dehumanizing aspects of a complex technological society. Certainly the threads of such a movement should be woven into educational programs for survival. Both Shaftel and Scriven argue in favor of such content; Shaftel in terms of reuniting the affective with the cognitive, and Scriven in terms of the potential usefulness of such techniques as encounter groups and Synanon games.

I would, however, while recognizing their promise, recommend the inclusion of such techniques as complements to world order rather than as primary program components, because they have less to offer in terms of immediate crises management and institution building. While learning from these fields may help assure that new institutions may avoid the antihuman elements of the old and encourage the institutions' designers to include the possibilities of human fulfillment as criteria for the desirability of proposed institutions, it does not contribute directly to the design of the structures. That is clearly a systems problem, and systems change is our most immediate survival problem, the crucial component in establishing peace, and the main focus of world order studies. So, while giving consideration to other program components and full value to all survival levels, the world-systems crisis should be our starting point. Unless some resolutions or new institutions are devised rapidly, there may be no issues of survival in the personal or the social realms.

Another resource for program development in the personal and social realms lies in the field of world cultures and the emerging world civilization. This field has special potential for fulfilling the goals enunciated in the Asilomar Statement, cited earlier in this chapter. Theodore Brameld, for instance, has advocated the establishment of a center for inquiry and study aimed at bringing forth a "world civilization" (a network of common values and human institutions mixed with a plurality of cultures and life styles), the purpose being to aid in the deliberate synergizing of such elements to formulate a community of mankind. Programs such as this will offer us opportunities to study the various philosophies, interpretations of life, and definitions of man which have been devised in diverse cultures and at different periods of human history.

With such a rich variety of resources to call upon, human beings may be better able to develop identities, giving each one full personhood while enabling him to relate fully to his species. A person so identified may be better able to survive crises in the other realms and to adapt and expand his or her identity as his or her community grows. Schools therefore should teach world cultures with this purpose in mind, *not simply as they relate to American culture or compare to each other but as the infinite variety of human qualities, values, and life styles which form the total pool of human resources, the heritage of all mankind.*

If the schools are going to provide this culture pool and permit persons to select from it, they must break out of the tightly structured organization that many now find so oppressive, an organization in which individuals are identified by the system and expected to conform to identities, be they 'students,' 'teachers,' or 'administrators.' Schools must not only tolerate alternative cultures and life styles (those within our own country, as well as those from other countries) but also teach about them, permit students to select freely from among them, and help them develop the skills for making those selections. Certainly such education is required to deal with the antecedents of violence. As Chap. 3 points out, by impositions of roles and behavior the schools themselves can be perceived as perpetrators of violence. And further, since "violence is a solution" resulting from decisions, skills for decision making and for evaluating alternatives are made an even more urgent requirement of survival.

5.5 Language Facility for a Multicultural Community

One of the prime requisites for peace is full and accurate communication among peoples. The study of other cultures, therefore, should include immersion in another language, one in which the logic, structure, and harmonies connote thought patterns, sensitivities, and values vastly different from the native culture of the learner. For generations, educated Asians and Africans have learned about the cultures of their conquerors by gaining fluency in French, Dutch, Portuguese, or English. Westerners should become equally fluent in languages, not to command another tool for exploitation but to gain a key to a wider portion of their own human heritage, to come to understand more deeply other members of their species, and thereby gaining a wider sphere of identification as part of mankind.

The contrast in the language proficiency of Europeans and Americans has long been cited as an indication of the degree of Americans' culture-bound view of the world. Few Europeans, however, speak Asian or African languages, and their need to learn other European languages was a pragmatic survival mechanism required by a small multicultural geographic region.

The United States, though no small region, without question is multicultural, and therefore the need for us to learn the languages of those who share our region is just as vital to our survival. Societal survival also requires communication. The various black subcultures must learn standard English to protect their interests, but they must also be encouraged to maintain and develop their own modes of expression to preserve their cultural identity. Middle class white Americans should be familiar with this other American language, and both blacks and whites have as much responsibility to learn the third American language—Spanish—as Puerto Ricans and Chicanos have to learn English. Native Americans must be not only permitted but encouraged to learn and to express themselves in their Indian languages. Many more members of the immigrant cultures, from the descendants of the *Mayflower* to recent arrivals from Hong Kong, should have opportunities to study these first American languages.

There is no more effective way to understand our fellow human beings nor a better index of respect than learning their languages. Mutual respect and human dignity for all can only exist in a polyglot global society. Enforcement of one language for instruction and for the economic and political life of a society is a phenomenon of the age of nationalism. If peace and human community building are major goals of education, then the development of multiple language facility should be one of the chief strategies in achieving that goal. If human fulfillment is also one of the goals, there is further need for teaching and learning in various languages, including the nonverbal ones.

The inhibitions on learning, such as those imposed by denying children the right to learn in their mother tongues, have also been imposed through the restrictions on physical activities by which children normally express themselves. Sitting to learn is clearly not the natural order of things. Human expression often attains its most exquisite form in dance and in other art forms freely conceived and executed. The natural and universally human expression of joy is mostly physical—tactile and visual. If learning is to be joyous, these modes of expression must be rekindled and nurtured in our schools, especially if we are seeking to develop some sense of, universal human identity. If art is the truly universal language of man, then the humanities must play a vital role in survival education. In the "three grand divisions" of knowledge identified by Earl S. Johnson, such education would fall within "the realm of *poetics* [where] are to be found the myths… those things… whose endless pursuit has given direction and purpose to… lives."[10] Would not the formulation and pursuit of new myths for a mankind community provide a fruitful theme for such programs?

The ability of persons from various cultures, political systems, and ideologies to communicate clearly and accurately will be absolutely essential to formulating new mankind myths, to deriving universal values, and to establishing new world

[10] Johnson, *op. cit.*, p. 262.

institutions which will permit survival *on an equal basis* of the many societies and persons to be served by those institutions. It is not efficient in a survival crisis to say everything twice (especially when translations do not always issue identical statements). Nor is it fair for discourse to be conducted in one language rather than another simply because the power and technology of one nation have spread its idiom farther. World institution builders should be able to shift from one language to another, with the same ease and full appreciation of the medium being used as an accomplished musician displays in shifting from one musical mode of composition to another. Multilingual persons are more fully able to enjoy and contribute to varieties of human experience and to expand their identities to include still more groups. Certainly such proficiency should be a major aim of educational programs for human development.

There are also important aspects of individual survival to be benefited by polyglotism. The human rights of minorities have often been violated by states and societies in which power is applied and justice rendered in the language of the governing elites. There should be no room in a human community for such scenes as are now witnessed—persons being tried in court procedures of which they do not understand a word, in which they are charged with violations of laws imposed on them by an alien culture in a language which to them is utterly 'foreign.' If the individual is to play an effective role in the world community, he or she must not be limited by the lack of language facility.

5.6 Decolonializing Education

Planning and implementing such a program will involve other activities which will be enormously helpful in building the human community. Languages are best learned from persons at ease in the language to be mastered and through interactions and experiences in that language. This means that more people are going to have to spend more time living in cultures other than their own. Ideally such an exchange of persons of various cultures will increase in volume and change in character. A change may be expected in the nature of exchange between the 'developed' and the 'developing' nations. Heretofore students, scholars, and scientists from Asian and African countries have come to the industrialized countries to 'receive' expertise and command of technology in much the same way that our young have come to schools to 'receive' education. In this way, as Ivan Illich points out, education ceases to be an 'activity' and becomes a 'commodity,' a commodity controlled by specialists and 'marketed' to the advantage of the specialists—the professional and technical elites.[11] It is to the advantage of the specialists to maintain this specialization, and the institutions of education and

[11] Ivan Illich. *De-Schooling Society*. New York: Harper & Row, Publishers, 1971.

[12] Paulo Freire. *The Pedagogy of the Oppressed*. New York: Herder & Herder, Inc, 1970.

science thus become the bastions of elitism, or, in the terms of Paulo Freire, "the instruments of oppression."[12]

Some of the antidemocratic consequences of specialization and secrecy are brought into focus in the chapter, in which Theresa L. Held calls for more adequate political education. To continue to keep most information about these specialties in the hands of a few persons or in only a few Western languages helps to maintain global elitism and to make language another tool of oppression. Such a market economy of education does not offer much promise of producing a democratic human community. We need to shift to something more like bartering or, even better, 'sharing.' Transfer of technology to the languages of the third world not only would make the benefits thereof available to that part of the globe, but also would make it possible for the first world to understand better the perspectives of the third world on technology and development. Most important, it could break the present technological monopoly of the forces of industry, as well as of the military and scientific elites of the northern tier of nations.

This present 'marketing,' as defined by Illich, may be termed 'training,' or initiation into certain levels of specialization. But it cannot be considered education, especially not education for peace or survival. For if peace is a state of order in which conflicts can be resolved without violence, it is also a state which aspires to justice. Injustice and alienation, so characteristic of this kind of schooling, probably nurture more organized violence—that is, warfare—than any other circumstances, and assuredly exemplify the kind of intrasocietal and structural violence George Henderson deals with in Chap. 9. If education is to be an instrument of peace and survival, then it must be a means to overcome injustice and alienation. It must consciously strive toward equal rights for all, including human dignity and equal value of persons. Language facility, therefore, can no longer be the exclusive prerogative of the elites; nor can crucial forms of education, such as the sciences and technology, be formulated and transmitted only in the languages of the powerful.

If the educational system is to respond adequately to the criticisms of Freire and Illich and if justice is to become a goal, then there will have to be a drastic reorganization of the structure of education. It can no longer be merely a conduit for passing on specialization from the initiated to the uninitiated. It must become a fair exchange among equals, or what Michael Rossman[13] calls the 'conversation,' a sharing of the riches of ability, knowledge, and inquisitiveness, a matching of needs to resources on the basis of justice. Sharing of language and culture is one way of beginning that conversation, that fair exchange. "You teach me your language and I will teach you mine (be it Swahili or nuclear physics). You may learn my perceptions and problems and I will try to learn yours. Together we may find a new perception, and help each other toward solutions."

[13] Michael Rossman "Learning and Social Change." Paper distributed by the National Student Association in 1968, to be reprinted in a forthcoming book under the same title.

Such an approach might help to, in Freire's terms, "humanize education"; that is, make it an instrument of freedom. It would at least be a step toward 'decolonializing' the schools, a step which is, I believe, a more urgent need for survival than 'de-schooling' society, as Illich advocates.[14] For, in shifting from interactions between the autonomous and the dependent to an exchange among equals, the colonial relationship would be ended. It would, too, I am convinced, remove the 'neocolonial' aspects between the developed and the developing from the educational relationship. It might even help overcome the alienation which Illich attributes in large part to the mystique of specialization.

It is interesting to note that Buckminster Fuller shares Illich's antispecialization convictions.[15] Fuller believes not only that specialization has been a means of permitting the few to exercise, often unjustly, power over the many, but also that it is a major obstacle to survival. I agree with his conclusions that we need more generalists and that therefore *all* students should receive a basic 'general' education. This goal would be one means of combating the social and political polarization currently plaguing our society, a condition which has been reinforced by giving one kind of education to the elites and another to the masses.

5.7 Systems Approach and Survival Skills

Fuller also advocates a 'systems' approach to the study of phenomena and problems. In fact, the demystification of specialties may be achieved through the study of systems. If programs incorporate such studies, including inquiry into what systems are, how they came into being, how they operate, and what purposes they serve, we may better come to understand the phenomenon of elitism and work toward the kind of egalitarian and participatory society which many believe would be more conducive to peace and survival. Fuller also tells us that synergism and cooperative and sharing processes are more productive than competitive ones—another factor to consider in education for the establishment of a just and peaceful human community on a planet even now stretching its resources beyond their ability to meet the needs of all its inhabitants.

Even though we grant some validity to the criticism of a systems approach which holds it to be antihuman and amoral, it is nonetheless a highly efficient tool for the study of institutions and processes. It should also be noted that this criticism can be partly answered by much of the work being done in natural rather than man-made systems, which are, in fact, the models for Fuller's work. An adequate systems approach would include inquiry into ecosystems and biosystems, emphasizing the life-sustaining aspect and changing nature of systems. It would

---

[14] Ivan Illich. "The Alternative to Schooling." *Saturday Review* 54(25): 44–48, 59–60; June 19, 1971.

[15] R. Buckminster Fuller. *Operating Manual for Spaceship Earth*. Carbondale: Southern Illinois University Press, 1969.

also demand that all students be given full opportunity for acquaintance with the life sciences. Mathematics and the sciences, like languages, must become agents for equalizing educational experience, rather than means of producing elites. A sufficient variety of teaching-learning strategies must be devised so that no one need be deprived of this essential part of a general education.

We must recognize too that the study of systems, if it is to contribute to survival, must include an inquiry into the human and moral effects of systems. It is in this specific area of inquiry that Scriven has some useful contributions to make to peace and survival programs. He insists that a survival curriculum should raise the fundamental questions of law and ethics, among them, "Why should those who suffer under a system tolerate it?"[16]

Since groups who find a system intolerable may turn to violence to alter or overthrow the system, this should indeed be a core question in the curricula of the 1970s, as should these parallel questions: How can we change systems? How can we establish justice without violence? When legal recourses are inhumanly slow or stacked against the oppressed, what other alternatives can be projected to ameliorate their lot?

Scriven raises his question about systems in his list of recommendations for "survival skills." He also lists as a skill (because he asserts that in part it can be learned) that quality called 'creativity,' a skill I would refer to as "constructive imagination" or utopianism at its most pragmatic. Unless we can learn to create practical alternatives to violence, there can be no peace and little chance of long-range survival.

The schools of the 1970s should be preparing students to conceive and put into effect alternative systems which are human, moral, and practical. They should be encouraging disciplined speculation on alternative life styles, forms of government, and social orders. They should as well be developing skills of evaluation to aid the young to select from various alternatives their preferences for modes of survival. Further, they should be helping the young to formulate strategies for change, and should be making it possible for them to test their strategies in practical action programs, such as the Omega program, which was born in a Jesuit high school in New York in the late 1960s and is now spreading to schools in other areas. (Omega students plan and carry out community-development projects, some in their own city, some going as far as Appalachia. They determine their own success by what they accomplish, and they are given academic credit for their work.)

5.8 Human Values and Moral Development

The Omega program takes its philosophy from the ecumenism of Pope John, with special reference to his encyclical, *Pacem in Terris*, a document which has a

[16] Scriven, *op. cit.*, p. 35.

mankind focus. Much of the program strategy derives from Paulo Freire's concept of 'conscientization,' the process of becoming aware of the social and political structure, or 'system,' of which each individual is a part, and of striving to motivate and equip individuals not to 'adapt' to the structures but to 'use' them and, where necessary, to change them to meet their own needs. There is a frank and well conceived moral element to the program, one which might well be emulated by 'secular' schools; for, as Scriven asserts, "The survival curriculum is largely about morality in practice."[17]

The late 1960s and early 1970s have heard much about "the new morality," the erosion of "good, old-fashioned virtue," and very serious, if limited, public debate about the morality of foreign policy and the values implicit in a system which uses more resources on weapons than on education, hospitals, and public works combined; spends more of its wealth in pursuit of "national prestige" in the space program than it does on attempts to remove the "national shame" of those dehumanizing social Siamese twins, poverty and racism; and seems more concerned with "law and order" as a goal in itself rather than as a means to justice.

The moral issues imbedded in our survival crises raise questions about the decision-making ability of the American public and consequently about the role of public education in developing a moral basis for such decision making. Justice is clearly a moral issue, as well as a guideline for the evaluation of political and social systems. One of the primary purported functions of our governmental system is to "ensure justice." Indeed, Scriven points out that the Constitution is a kind of moral contract to guarantee equal justice to all citizens, though few recognize it as such. If preparing the public to deal with such issues is part of the job of the schools, then they can no longer avoid the responsibility of education for moral development.

Although moral education is controversial, schools have never hesitated to 'moralize.' The young have been fed to the teeth with the prevailing kind of moral instruction. "Obey the rules whatever they are!" "Be loyal to your country regardless of its policies!" "Learn about sex, but do not try it!" "Do not take drugs!" "Adjust to reality!" Bright children may or may not be taking drugs, but most do not want to adjust to reality as defined by adults. What they want is to adjust reality to human needs, and that is a sound moral judgment. If, indeed, as the pragmatists tell us, "morality is the intelligent foresight of consequences," much of the demand for revolution is a sign of a rapidly maturing moral sense among many of our young people and growing numbers of educators. There is now a clear and urgent need to respond to that sense and to help such persons develop moral judgment as one of the major skills of change.

There must be in our survival inquiry a careful investigation of the relationship between means and ends. We may at bottom agree with some of the young, and even with some radical educators who see violent revolution as the only means to relieve oppression, and we may want to implement Scriven's recommendation that

[17] *Ibid.*, p. 52.

"curricula at the *moment* should be organized around studying and *creating* the great revolutions of the past, present, and future."[18]

Yet most of us, educators and/or liberals, are caught in the most acute moral dilemma of our time, the tension between the unacceptability of deliberate violence and the intolerability of gross injustice. Discussion of this dilemma should be an integral part of the survival curriculum. Its resolution cannot be left either to those who will act without reflection or to those who reflect without action. To avoid this moral issue would be the greatest cop-out of education, and indeed failure to confront it may make survival impossible.

Much work has already been done in the area of moral development on which suitable programs can be based for all age levels, and also for cross-generational and community inquiries into moral issues. In a speech before the California Council for the Social Studies, Fannie Shaftel eloquently raised the issue in her reference to the morality of a society that permitted the occurrence of the Genovese incident, a murder witnessed by many "law-abiding citizens" who did not want to become involved. In her speech on survival curriculum she made two telling points on a subject which should serve as a significant guideline in formulating programs "Our problem," she stated, "is not so much the result of a lack of available knowledge as it is first of all a *crisis in values.*"[19]

> The priorities … essential to survival demand a new ordering based upon the valuing of human progress rather than material progress. … What will it take to shift the priorities in our economic system from the gross national product to serving the needs of all people in the ecosphere? Knowing and caring is the necessary condition for achieving the results of a survival curriculum. … They are crucial aspects of one process. … The cognitive and the affective are inseparable.[20]

I suspect that a good deal of the confusion over moral education can be traced to the functional separation of the two domains by many current curriculum programs. If values education is limited to abstract analysis of value conflicts, it may gain the acceptance of those who believe that schools should be apolitical and non-activist. But it must be recognized that, unless the continuum of analyzing-knowing-feeling-acting is observed, education will have no effect on raising the level of moral behavior and decision making in our society.

Note especially Shaftel's response to the question of approach to social, or, if you will, public, moral issues:

> I see the values component as a product of an affective-cognitive mode of study designed to cultivate feelings and values based on continual exploration, through problem-solving processes, of the consequences of choices.[21]

---

[18] *Ibid.,* Italics added—and please note that the 'moment' was dated 1969.

[19] Shaftel, *op. cit*, p. 5.

[20] *Ibid.*, p. 12. Note the similarity of these ideas to those expressed in the Asilomar Statement quoted earlier in this chapter.

[21] *Ibid.*, Italics added.

In this statement Shaftel nicely ties together several inseparable elements of the survival curriculum: the thought-feeling or valuing-analyzing element with the process of selection from among alternatives; an ongoing process, part of life itself, continued exploration, implying that there will always be social-moral problems and that survival will always depend upon minds developed to function accordingly. A nice case, I think, for the usefulness of a key technique of world-order studies, using Utopia not as an end but rather as an intellectual tool for constantly reshaping the present in search of a preferred future and also for the utility of the normative perspective which world-order studies bring to that search.

The study of possibilities for a communally preferred future requires that analysis of controversy, value clarification, priority setting, and moral-judgment making become major objectives of the survival curriculum. Many schools are already doing significant work in these areas, basing it on such offerings as those of Hunt and Metcalf, Oliver and Shaver, and Kohlberg.[22]

At the core of Hunt and Metcalf's work is the belief that reflective thinking is the capacity which education should most strive to develop so that values may be clarified and certain areas formerly 'closed' to classroom scrutiny or public debate may be opened and fully reviewed in the general interest. Obviously, a survival curriculum could not tolerate the closing of any issues in the three realms of human experience. Full and open inquiry must prevail, and few, if any, taboos can be imposed. Scriven notes that to some people a survival curriculum will seem to emphasize 'shock' elements, and he asserts that it is not the content per se which makes it shocking but its unfamiliarity. I would contend that this unfamiliarity is also what makes the "closed areas" so dangerous. (I suggest that readers review Hunt and Metcalf's list of closed areas. War is among them.) Nothing human should be alien or unfamiliar to a graduate of the survival curriculum. One who has mastered skills for analysis of controversy, value clarification, and moral judgment through the examination of formerly closed areas is more likely to be a constructive citizen of a peaceful world community.

5.9 Dialogues for Moral Decision Making

If *nothing* human is to be alien to our graduates, then 'humanizing' society and its institutions, including the schools, as Freire asserts, should be an aim of education. The method he proposes to achieve that end, "a dialogue between equals," is notably similar to that proposed by Oliver and Shaver and also by Kohlberg; and it seems that, even if their aims are not synonymously defined, they are at least in harmony with Freire. Oliver and Shaver advocate dialogue on issues of public controversy, with generous use of analogous cases to clarify value positions.

---

[22] Maurice P. Hunt and Lawrence E Metcalf. *Teaching High School Social Studies*. New York: Harper & Row, Publishers, 1968; Donald Oliver and James P. Shaver. *Teaching Public Issues in the High School*. Boston. Houghton Mifflin Company, 1966; and Lawrence Kohlberg. *Stages in the Development of Moral Thought and Action*. New York. Holt, Rinehart and Winston, Inc., 1969.

Kohlberg, in his work on moral development, has used the dialogic method to help youngsters raise their levels of moral-judgment making.[23]

Kohlberg's work constitutes a contribution of the highest potential to the survival curriculum. It fulfills most of the criteria posited by Shaftel and Scriven, and also by the U.S. Office of Education study *An Examination of Objectives, Needs, and Priorities in International Education in the U.S. Secondary and Elementary Schools.*[24]

Kohlberg's research base is multinational: it assumes no cognitive-affective split; it relates levels of moral judgment to levels of analysis and asserts that abstract justice as the final criterion for judgment is the highest moral level. Persons making judgments on the basis of abstract justice have also developed abstract reasoning ability; and, even though Kohlberg concludes that persons who make all or most of their decisions at such levels are usually not tolerated by the rest of society (he cites as examples, Jesus, Gandhi, and King), his work should be a source of optimism, for it suggests that capacities for abstract reasoning and intellectually sound analysis can be developed to much higher levels than have been heretofore assumed.

It is only by developing these capacities to the fullest in all human beings that we can hope to move toward a society that is truly democratic and just. Democratic revolutions and various periods of enlightenment notwithstanding, the fundamental egalitarian revolution has yet to take place. Yet now, for the first time in history, we are at least beginning to see what the operational-behavioral components of that revolution are. Education for humanization should embrace as a goal the eradication of the basic hierarchic organization of almost all 'human' society. Racism, sexism, favoritism to specialists, all forms of elitism must be subject to thorough critical analysis and moral evaluation. Should not, for example, James Becker's assertion in Chap. 6 that there appears to be a 'moral' advantage to power be subject to critical examination in our classrooms? These subjects should be among the main themes of the educational conversation and the foci of the educational revolution as they are of the social revolutions sought by youth, women, minorities, and all the other oppressed. In a sense each of these movements seeks to achieve the goal implicit in a statement by a 19th-century feminist:

> We deny the right of any portion of the species to decide for another portion, or any individual for another individual, what is and what is not their "proper sphere" The proper sphere for all human beings is the largest and highest which they are able to attain.[25]

In terms of the programs recommended here, the goal is self-definition. Blacks do not wish to have their roles, much less their persons, defined by a white racist

---

[23] For an account of a project conducted among boys in reform school, see "Toward Moral Maturity." *Time*, June 28, 1971, p. 48.

[24] This study was completed by the Foreign Policy Association in 1969. See Chap. 6 of this book.

[25] Harriet Mill, quoted in *Life*, August, 1971.

society. Nor do women wish to be imprisoned in a definition of femininity emerging from male sexism. And the young will no longer tolerate subservience to age imposed by those who have lived long enough to acquire the power of imposition. Institutions which perpetuate such forms of elitism do violence to the persons oppressed by them and are as guilty of institutional violence as are nations which govern by totalitarianism or states which impose de facto segregation. Recent studies and other data cited in this Yearbook leave little doubt that the school is *among* such institutions. Schools should be inquiring into these problems, helping to formulate solutions and working to enact solutions.

5.10 Professional Responsibilities

Professional organizations have a great responsibility for initiating the revolution. This is true, not only because they have access to a significant communications network within a given profession, but especially because they bear a primary responsibility for the development of the kind of dysfunctional specialization described by Illich and for the entrenchment of the elitism which is both an obstacle to dialogue among equals and an impediment to self-definition. Professional organizations in general follow an order of service which must be reversed. They now give service first to the professionals, next to the profession, and last to the clients. This is one of the main reasons that students have remained until now on the bottom perch of the educational hierarchy.

As the hierarchal structure of education must be disassembled and reconstructed into a circular community of equals, so too must the professional organizations reorder their service priorities. They must open themselves to invite and be enriched by others. Professional apartheid impedes the educational conversation and reinforces the disparate and fragmentary nature of learning within the present school structure. Students, parents—in fact, anyone interested—should be invited, at least for periods of time, into the ranks of the professional organizations. Professional as well as national exchange programs should be undertaken. Educators can learn much from scientists, lawyers, artists, and the like, and we have much to offer other professions. Constructive multidisciplinary programs to serve the needs of peace and survival require conversations *among* professionals and *between* professionals and nonprofessionals.

Schools, too, should be opening their doors. As many educators advocate more off-site, experiential learning opportunities, we should also advocate that non-educators participate in school programs, not just as the important resources they may be but also as co-learners with students, parents, and teachers. There should be more opportunity for ongoing education in which the learning experience is shared by students and parents and by teachers and students. We must be striving toward "learning communities" in both senses of those words. Schools should be both communities *for* learning and the centers of communities which *are* learning.

The structures of these learning communities should be truly democratic, striving toward the realization of a set of universal human values and attempting to equip all human beings to participate fully in the global community of mankind. All people should have an opportunity to educate themselves to their ultimate capacities. All should have available the knowledge and techniques of mathematics, the sciences, and the learnings of human experience. They should be helped to express themselves in various languages and art forms. They should be enabled to become significant parts of the political processes that affect them, from the selection of curricula (which is, indeed, the result of a political process) to the reorganization of international institutions.

Just as the world should be brought into the schools, the schools, through the students—those they are designed to serve—should be brought into the world. Why not, for example, organize more work and travel programs, offering students experience in actively contributing to community change and cultural exchange? Let more of them work in development projects and service organizations, go abroad to teach other students their languages and life styles, returning to their schools to share their learnings and insights with others in their communities. By actually practicing survival skills as part of the process of their education, they may help to further refine those skills and to bring new, constructive perceptions to the central issues for education, survival, peace, and justice.

Readers of this book could help initiate the conversations sorely needed, to transform schools from custodial institutions segregating the young from the rest of society to centers for personal, social, and global development; to keep our cities from further polarizing into violence; to reintegrate communities and minorities into the total life of the nation; to heal the wounds of generational conflict, and to reach beyond our nation to the other peoples of the earth—particularly those who suffer deprivation of a fair share of the values of well-being and justice—to structure a world community. To do this we must have help from and interaction with colleagues in all parts of the world, an opportunity now provided through membership in the World Council for Curriculum and Instruction. Let us begin the conversation in each of our communities. Let us endeavor to forge a chain of concentric conversations similar to the concentric communities Elizabeth Mann Borghese recommends for a world political structure.[26]

Let us converse about the themes of survival, peace, and personhood in all realms of human experience—in the world political structure, in the network of human societies, and in every human person. Let the conversations of the 1970s prepare the way for the real survival revolutions of the 1980s and, we hope, an emerging worldwide, peaceful, and just society in the 1990s. Let us use these

[26] See Elizabeth M. Borghese "The World Communiites." Unpublished paper (1971).

conversations to develop in ourselves the skills of survival and the capacity for building the community of man. Such conversations may kindle the courage to hope, which, as Shaftel asserts, is the essential component of our programs:

> Erich Fromm in his book *The Revolution of Hope* says that hope is a decisive element in any attempt to bring about social change in the direction of greater aliveness, awareness, and reason.... The real problem is whether we, especially teachers,... have the courage to be truly hopeful.... We must project a survival curriculum in the schools. By a survival curriculum I mean not just physical survival, but survival for living in a humane world community.[27]

[27] Shaftel, *op cit.*, p. 405.

Chapter 6
Conclusions from "The Knowledge Industry"

Retrospective Reflection on "The Knowledge Industry" (1978)

This essay, though quite widely circulated among the international network of peace educators that in the 1970s had been brought into collaboration in the Peace Education Commission of the International Peace Research Association, was never formally published. And while it is now available in its entirety in the Canaday Special Collections at the University of Toledo Library, it is known by only a few in the field. An extract is included here because the piece further illuminated the critique of formal education that informed "Education for Survival." As noted in the introductory Retrospective Reflection to that selection, it foreshadowed much of the normative and conceptual bases and pedagogical preferences of later work.

This piece was written five years later than "Education for Survival" and six years before "Comprehensive Peace Education." Taken together, the three provide a forecast of the principled foundations of the developmental work that followed thirteen years (1963–1976) of 'introducing' world order studies through the Schools Program of the Institute for World Order. One of the reasons for moving on from that post was my failure to convince the men on the staff of the inadequacies of formal education as then constituted to achieve the purposes of world order education. I had come to hold a firm belief in the need for a radical change in the organization and delivery of education, especially in teacher preparation. Without significant change in educational practice, education could not serve as an instrument for the changes necessary for the 'transformation' of the international system, the primary goal that then informed the work of the Institute.

The analysis offered in "The Knowledge Industry" was undertaken in response to a request from a UN agency concerned with development policy, asking for an outline of how universities might serve the process of advancing the economies of

B.A. Reardon and D.T. Snauwaert, *Betty A. Reardon: A Pioneer in Education for Peace and Human Rights*, SpringerBriefs on Pioneers in Science and Practice 26,
DOI 10.1007/978-3-319-08967-6_6

poor countries. In the 1970s that process still meant pretty much increasing the GDP of the former European colonies (that came to be called "The Global South") mainly through the application of the assumptions that had propelled the development of the industrial North. Little was considered in the realms of human development and fulfillment that I had taken to be the traditional concerns of higher education. What I came to see as I reflected on the processes and actors within universities determining what knowledge was pursued for what purposes, by what methods and shared with what audiences was a system that was antithetical to preparation for the participatory, inclusive, democratic forms of economic and social development, preserving of cultural integrity that I believed to be essential to achieving a truly equitable global economy. What Freire saw in formal public education I perceived to be structurally embedded in universities, a system in service to the prevailing power elites. I set about to specifically describe the components and functions of this 'knowledge' system, so that it might be reformed to meet the needs of human as well as economic development. (It was decades later that the UN embraced the concept of human development.)

Needless to say, the paper was not greeted with enthusiasm by the requesting development agency. But it did prove useful to some of my colleagues struggling within universities to devise and practice forms of education suited to prepare learners for the social and political tasks being undertaken toward global change. While, we fully recognized and wrestled with the institutional constraints which faced us, we continued to work within our respective institutions, trying often with only little success, even when peace related programs became institutionalized, to affect some of the essential changes. The idea that there is need to work both within and outside existing institutions for authentically transformative change, has been since the 70s integral to the strategies for change that framed my work, both in proposals and, when possible, in practice. The selection from the essay reproduced below deals with such strategic proposals and illustrates my contention that if we educators diagnose problems, we have a responsibility to envision and design prescriptive educational responses to those problems.

It was from this sense of responsibility that I worked within a methodology that encouraged the design and consideration of institutional alternatives to replace the violent oppressive systems and structures that perpetuated war, poverty, social and political injustice and the destruction of the environment; and to follow the exercises in institutional design with planning and assessing potential strategies to achieve them. Such methods are the basis of much of the curricula developed during these years archived in the Canaday Center for Special Collections at the University of Toledo Library.

Within the years from 1980 to 1985, my reflections on what appeared to be the unchanging nature of the fundamental hierarchical authoritarianism of the global order would take me deeper into consideration and speculation on patriarchy as the underlying, continuing core of this power order.

Betty A. Reardon
March, 2014

6.1 Introduction

This essay is a "speculative sketch" of current systems and processes for the acquisition of and access to stores of human knowledge.[1] It attempts to identify the component parts of the processes and systems; to analyze them in terms of the degree to which popular participation in decision making effects their outcomes, and to assess their impact on ideologies of development. The purpose of the analysis is to initiate reflection and discussion on ways in which the components might be integrated into a strategy of change, a strategy intended to achieve s global social order based upon the value of justice, designed for the achievement of peace and the pursuit of human fulfillment, in short the antithesis of the present world order.

I wish to emphasize the speculative nature of the essay. While I will attempt to outline a responsible and honest analysis, the paper is not meant to be 'scholarly'. Scholarship, as I will attempt to demonstrate, like most components of the systems and processes of contemporary education is characterized by the same authoritarian elitism which is the core of the established social order. It is a significant example of the anti-participatory institutions, and practices that must be overcome to achieve a truly just social order. Further, scholarship as it is currently practiced values precedent above inventiveness, and tends to stifle speculation, the most fruitful mental process through which human beings might seek creative solutions to contemporary global problems, primary among which are social oppression and economic deprivation, the hallmarks of authoritarianism and injustice...

6.2 Conclusions and Recommendations

6.2.1 Effects upon Development Ideology

When communications and educational processes are viewed within the knowledge industry framework, they can be seen as the purveyors of an ideology of hierarchy and efficient mass production which espouses the goal of conspicuous consumption as the aim of the development process. This is an ideology which accepts gross disparities in consumption in order to permit one particular segment of society, namely the middle class, to consume at the conspicuous level as demonstration of the productive capacity and power (and in some cases the 'virtue') of the society. While the disparities in socialist societies are much more narrow than those in capitalist societies, when the whole human family is viewed as a unit, the major disparities between the industrialized nations and the so called

[1] This text has not previously been published.

"developing countries" is made painfully apparent, and the degree to which even socialist 'prosperity' depends on Third World poverty can be discerned.

At the global level even Communist countries can accept a bit of "trickle down" theory. But as neither socialist nor capitalist industrial nations have been moved to "share the wealth" through any type of transfer, from unconditional grants to offering truly just prices for primary commodities, the underlying inequities and elitism of the industrial ideology has suffered little erosion from either political or economic 'democracy'. The ideology of development transmitted through the knowledge industry is one which conditions the poor to tolerate their deprivation and encourages the comfortable to defend their privileges. So long as the knowledge industry maintains both the unchallenged control of information and education and the value system which accepts inequity as the result of innate inequalities, the disparities and injustices will prevail.

So long as managers function by the criteria of efficiency above justice, and view ethical criteria as a luxury suitable only in a super abundant society, inequity will not be viewed as a primary problem and inequality will be rationalized by new and even more thoroughly validated scientific evidence to support the superiority of the privileged and to defend their right to consume more as a reward for the greater social responsibility they must bear. These are the norms which are explicitly taught in the industrial societies and which are being exported to those developing nations who are pursuing industrialization, and in the process, loosing many of their traditional values, values which in many cases are far more humane than those of the technologically advanced societies. Indeed, the valuing of technological progress over cultural integrity has led to conflict both personal and political and has transferred to developing peoples a sense of inadequacy so frequently found in the oppressed. Clearly, this ideology is not one to be tolerated by those who pursue participatory structures as the manifestation of the principle of the equal human value of all persons, and who seek to purvey an ideology of equitable and truly democratic development.

Equally clear is the urgent need for a fundamental value change among the managerial class and a critical consciousness of their limitations among the populace at large, a need which can be fulfilled only through experiences in active, participatory learning for both groups. What the managers need most to learn is ethical responsibility and moral decision making and the importance of ethical criteria to that form of development concerned with the whole range of human needs, especially the fulfillment of humane cultural values. The people are most in need of learning to acquire and exercise power in their own best interest, This, too, in its own way, is moral education. In both cases it could result in the application of ethical standards to public policy making, that which is most needed for the formation of an ideology of humane development. The need calls for a renewed emphasis on and a significant role for philosophy in both education and public policy making. Most especially it demands ever increasing popular participation in the creation and transmission of knowledge.

6.2.2 Working Within the System

Although this general review of the knowledge industry and its role in maintaining the elitist structures of the managerial industrial society discloses the extent of authoritarianism and the limits on present possibilities for participatory development, it also reveals some significant points of entry for the initiation of processes of structural change. Additionally it indicates the urgent need for such change if the managerial ethic is to be replaced in time by a participatory one. Some fundamental changes in world views and values are a basic requirement for the achievement of this replacement. Clearly, such changes cannot come about without education, and the temptation to abandon not only schooling but all formal education as a significant route to structural change must be resisted.

While the analysis supports the position that instruction alone cannot make a significant contribution to change, it also reveals the degree to which the present system is kept in place by the modes of production and transmission of information and education. Any serious efforts or plans for change must, therefore, include these functions. And in the absence of viable alternative institutions through which to overcome the power of the knowledge industry as presently constituted, ways must be found to effect some change within the existing institutions.

There are both tactical and ethical reasons for those of us who are committed to the struggle for higher levels of participation in all human institutions to continue to work within the existing system. Tactically, there seem to be few ways of obtaining resources outside the established institutions, and it is certainly clear that the capacity to communicate with large numbers through alternative channels is extremely limited. Ethically, it seems that we have two serious responsibilities to fulfill if we denounce the present structures. First we should try to envision and articulate alternative structures and offer strategies for achieving the desired structural transformation. Second, we have a human as well as professional responsibility to those who are subject to the present structures, who have no possibility of 'dropping out'. These responsibilities cannot be fully met unless some forces for change continue to view the established structures as their primary arena for action.

It needs to be emphasized, however, that change of the dimensions necessary to achieve a participatory society cannot be achieved if we count only on efforts within the institutions, even if they affect the entire knowledge industry. Such efforts within the structures must be coordinated with and of collaborative origin with the various extra institutional and alternative movements which make up the broader movement for global social change. Indeed many individuals working within the knowledge industry can also play significant roles in other strands of the movement.

At the moment, one of the most significant arenas; for the pursuit of change is development, and it is evident that the current norms and practices of the managerial industrial society run counter to a form of development, which is participatory and humane. Therefore, the recommendations made here focus on the possibilities of working for change in the development ideology communicated by the knowledge industry by working to maximize the possibilities for change within the present structures.

6.2.3 Entry Points for Change

Within each sector of the framework outlined in this essay there is one component, actor or stage in the process most likely to come to support of the need for value change and therefore a potential entry point for the change process. These tend to be those whose authentic function has been most distorted by the managerial value system. Among them are scholarship, creation, instructors, and media and methods.

It must be recognized that the power exercised by scholarship has a legitimate base in its authentic function. An authentic scholar inwardly aware of and outwardly acknowledging her own value system, engaging in objective study and balanced dialogue in examination of the speculations of the philosophers and the findings of researchers could be the most effective liberating force for the transformation of the production of knowledge. The scholar could make demands upon researchers for objective data, which could in turn provide researchers with wider parameters in their search to disclose reality. Scholars could also insist upon the consideration of moral and ethical questions, and could actively involve philosophers in the process whereby scholarship determines the content and method of education. Most significantly they could serve as role models for all who study with them, especially those who are preparing for the teaching profession. More than any others they can affect the whole system.

Creative functions, most especially the arts, have the possibility to recast both the substance and the transmission of knowledge to the broad public. Those who produce the content for the public media like those who develop the curricula for public schools, have a very great influence over the world view and the ideological perspective of the majority of the populace of the industrialized countries. The emergence of socially conscious advertising agencies, public relation firms and artist cooperatives holds promise of a significant contribution to social change. The promise could be fulfilled if those among the creators who espouse alternative values to those of the managers can receive support and reinforcement from those among the public who respond to the alternative visions and realities they attempt to design and communicate.

Instructors more than any other component of education and information systems affect the way the public processes, or thinks about the information made available to them. The cognitive styles and human values they communicate through their regular contact with students deliver important messages about the reality of the social system as well as the possibility and desirability of changing it. The values and world views which influence their behaviors and interactions with students far more than subject matter or methodology imprints upon the majority of those enrolled in schools a value stance and a perspective on human and social relations. Instructors committed to an alternative, humane ideology of development, could radically change the transmission process. Such instructors are likely to be authentic teachers and thereby exercise even stronger influence. If the medium is the message, teachers as a transmission medium could deliver a strong message to countervail that of the industrial managerial system.

Authentic teachers can often be discerned by the media and methods they employ. Media and methods, which demand authentic participation and engage students in active learning, could be very effective means of eroding the role of students as objects and passive receivers. Methods which engage all students in critical analysis leading to action for change could affect significant change in educational institutions and, thereby, in education, helping it to become an instrument of positive social change.

6.2.4 Approaches to Change

The possibility for development of skills of analysis offered at the entry point of educational methods constitute the most crucial element in a general approach to change in the managerial macro system, the knowledge industry which upholds it and the educational institutions which replicate it. Large scale social change for the normative purposes advocated here require changes in values, world views and assumptions, and institutions. These types of changes depend upon the capacity to analyze social reality so as to diagnose the impediments to preferred social values. Most of all, they call for a deeply held commitment to the values of equity and justice.

These specific values would probably be given a higher priority in the scale of social values which guide development planning, if both managers and populace learned to identify and value themselves and others not by what they have and how much they consume, but by what they are culturally and individually, learning also to value what cultural and individual commonalities and differences can contribute to a more rich and diverse ideology of development. The educational task is to teach the principle of the equal value of all persons within the context of cultural diversity and integrity; a context which recognizes that there is a wide variety of modes of meeting human needs, and respects the right of persons and peoples to choose the modes most meaningful and satisfying to them.

The modern industrial mode is only one way of meeting economic needs. Human beings have the creative capacity to devise many others; others less personally dehumanizing, socially alienating and ecologically destructive than the managerial industrial mode. Recognizing this creative capacity while developing critical capacities in the general populace is essential to a change in the world view which continues to replicate hierarchy and assumes that industrialization is an inevitable step in a narrowly construed concept of human progress as the development of mechanisms to provide ever expanding possibilities for consumption.

Education toward a humanly constructive change in this world view should encourage the critical examination of this assumption and ethical reflection on the responsibility of social systems for meeting a whole range of human needs beyond the satisfaction of physical needs.

An education so directed could produce an alternative ideology of development based on the assumption that just as there is diversity in modes of meeting needs there is universality in the range of human needs of all people. All have spiritual, social and aesthetic needs which development should strive to fulfill. These "higher needs" are not the exclusive experience of the economic and intellectual elites. While the physical necessities for survival are the prime requisite to experience and pursue the satisfaction of these needs, their satisfaction is not sufficient means for true fulfillment for any person. A world view and value system which is based upon this assumption about human needs could be developed by an educational system designed to contribute to human fulfillment rather than to replicate the industrial system.

In striving to affect such changes in values and world views we must recognize how deeply rooted are the assumptions and values of the present system in the world views and behaviors of all of us who have been conditioned by it. Much of the educational struggle must take place within even those who most ardently advocate these changes. Few, if any, of us have escaped some infection by the elitist ethic, be it the belief in intelligence differential, or the higher value of abstract thought over plastic skill or blatant sexism or the rationalization of other forms of oppression. Educators who hope to contribute to these changes need to be aware of these elements of infection within themselves. Without such consciousness changes in educational institutions will be little more than cosmetic. And such institutional changes are essential—however, they must be inspired not only by empirical analysis but also by inner reflection on our own values and world views.

Institutional approaches to change might be worked upon as the outward manifestation of the desired changes in values and world views. Like all other institutions in the managerial industrial society, a trend toward smaller, more community based units would better serve the purposes of those to be served by the institution and provide more relevant models for development based on lower resource consumption. Smaller units would also increase possibilities for participation, not only in educational institutions, but in most components of information systems.

Successful education to smaller units calls for the changes taking place within the context of the general system and the emphasis on interrelationships among the components suggested by the knowledge industry framework offered here. Constructive changes of this kind will be most effective if undertaken simultaneously with similar changes in other parts of the knowledge industry framework. Failure to understand the impact of the general system was in large part the reason for lack of success of earlier reforms of similar nature. Indeed, simultaneity is a major aspect of the approaches advocated here, not only institutionally, but also in terms of values and world views. The re-establishment of the link between science and philosophy is a good example of the principle of simultaneity in which changes of the same substantive nature are pursued at the same time in all possible areas of the knowledge industry and the information and education systems which it controls.

The re-establishment of this link could result from two types of efforts. First and most significantly the previously noted introduction of ethical criteria into all public decision making would help to make ethical concerns a part of most social relations and interactions. Secondly, specifically within the educational area, philosophy equally with critical analysis should become part of the general education of all citizens. As philosophers should become more fully involved in knowledge production in the area of policy making, if knowledge is to be more relevant to the concerns of a more democratic social order, citizens should become more capable of philosophic reflection, if broader citizen participation is to result in significant qualitative change in that order.

Equally important to the changes advocated here, are the principle of equal human value of all persons and the imperative of the ethical responsibility of all human persons. The lack of ethical responsibility manifest by the elites in the managerial industrial society was made possible by the acceptance of ethics as something apart from pragmatic politics and economics and the companion notion that ethical responsibility seldom resides in the economic or political actor acquiring and executing power. We came tantalizingly close to affirming the principle of ethical responsibility for our own actions in the formulation of the Nuremberg principles. Tragically these principles ran counter to the growth and consumption ethics of the managerial industrial society which grew to mammoth inhuman proportions in the decades since World War II. The tragedy resulting is that we live in a system where it is not only unusual for individuals to accept ethical responsibility, but even worse it is damned difficult to exercise it. Even those who want to do so find the route so convoluted that most, like those disillusioned teachers, just drop out of the system. Conditions which by most 'civilized' standards as defined by any culture, constitute crimes, grow ever more criminal in a system where culpability is easily avoided because ethical responsibility has never been established. Corporate structures in economics and politics obscure responsibility and impede the development of ethical standards sorely needed to transcend the human distortions of the managerial industrial society.

The infusion of ethical considerations into all efforts for change, in values, world views and institutions is the primary condition for bringing about the fundamental change toward a preferred ideology of development, an ideology which espouses the aim of human fulfillment over economic growth. This infusion can most immediately be initiated within the channels of the existing educational system. It will not be done easily, but it offers the best possibility presently open to us. Or so it seems to me within the framework of these speculations.

Chapter 7
Disarmament and Peace Education

Retrospective Reflection on "Disarmament and Peace Education" (1978)

As selections for this collection were being made in the winter of 2014, the issue of disarmament was reintroduced into the peace discourse by some who did not fear breaking the taboo of speaking the unspeakable, of actually speaking truth to power in the conference rooms of the United Nations. When the International Peace Bureau and some other NGO's called for the essential necessity of reducing military expenditures to the achievement of the "Sustainability Goals" being proposed to carry forward the unfinished agenda of the Millennium Development Goals (2000–2015), they unsettled the "gentlemen's agreement" of the member states to sideline the issue as most continued to increase military expenditures and build greater arsenals. So I find the re-reading of this article to be timely and sad. The sadness comes from the foiled hopes that the late 70s the early 80s exhibited for disarmament, reflected in the UN Special Sessions on the issue, held in 1978 and 1982, the latter being the occasion of the most massive peace demonstration in the history of New York, demanding an end to the nuclear arms race, as the Second Special Session on Disarmament was about to convene. The event was a high point in the anti-nuclear movement that had some effect on education, but even the many educators who through the early 80s advocated teaching about the dangers of nuclear weapons did not address the possibilities for peace integral to general and complete disarmament (the demilitarization of the international system) envisioned by many in the years immediately following World War II as a means "to bring an end to war."

Between those two sessions with the encouragement and assistance of an international network of peace educators, UNESCO had convened at its Paris headquarters, "The World Congress on Disarmament Education" as called for in the Final Document of the 1978 Special Session. The 1980 UNESCO Congress

B.A. Reardon and D.T. Snauwaert, *Betty A. Reardon: A Pioneer in Education for Peace and Human Rights*, SpringerBriefs on Pioneers in Science and Practice 26,
DOI 10.1007/978-3-319-08967-6_7

produced a document (http://www.un.org/disarmament/education/docs/uneco.pdf), *which like the issues raised in this article, still has relevance to peace education, yet like most aspects of disarmament remains outside the major themes addressed by the field. While there was, especially in the United States, a reluctance to address any truly political aspects of peace, the structural aspects of system change and critical study of sovereignty were 'alien' to the thinking of the majority of secondary school peace educators. Granted, the field was still viewed with suspicion by much of the public as well as governing authorities, and there was evidence that the topic was a red flag to the member states. (Note that in this piece published by an arm of the inter-state system of which it was so critical that 'State' is capitalized, as is the custom with the name of the deity.) In the wake of the Congress and its final document (which in fact raised little of challenge to the system) some member states withdrew from the organization, most notably and most damaging, the United States and the United Kingdom. UNESCO itself retreated from pursuit of this area of peace education, so only a few voices continued to try to bring it into the peace knowledge discourse. Since mine has been one of them, I can but view the attempts to gain serious considerations of arguments such as those put forward in this selection as professional failures. Were it not for the fact that a few NGOs continued to put forward proposals and offer strong support for weakly pursued state efforts at "arms control," I might have lost hope that others would succeed. Developments, such as the Secretary General's report on Non Proliferation Education in which there is fleeting but definite recognition of the long-range goal of general and complete disarmament, also served to "keep hope alive." As do the efforts of civil society and the non-nuclear nations to strive toward nuclear abolition. This piece is included here, as it is one of my essays on the topic that illustrate the significance of the concepts of disarmament and alternative security systems to all the phases of my work.*

I see here, as well, elements of the arguments about control put forth in "The Knowledge Industry" that also influenced the evolution of my thinking about patriarchy that gained some attention with the publication of "Sexism and the War System."

Betty A. Reardon
February, 2014

Among the crucial controversies of peace education, generally acknowledged but seldom discussed, are the issues of whether its methods should be primarily cognitive or affective and whether its purposes should be intellectual or political.[1] To my mind there is no question about how these issues should be resolved. The methods should be both cognitive and affective and the purposes both intellectual and political. Given these premises peace-education programs and curricula should

[1] This chapter was initially published as: Betty A. Reardon, 1978: ''Disarmament and Peace Education'', in: *Prospects: Quarterly Review of Education*, 8,4: 395–408. The permission to republish this text was granted by Ms. Alice Eisenpreis, Springer Publishers, Heidelberg, Germany in March 2014.

include the most central substantive concerns of peace, disarmament as an alternative to the arms race and the present State system which breed war and violence. However, issues regarding the nation-State system and the techniques it uses to maintain the ultimate power position in the world political system have little or no place in current peace education as it is practiced in schools and universities. Until these issues become universal components of the content of peace education, the field cannot be true to its' own purposes.

The purpose of peace education is to provide learning which can be applied to the problem of reforming and/or restructuring present human society so as to make it more just and less violent. The subjects which should constitute the bases of such learning are those manifestations of violence and injustice which dehumanize and threaten the very survival of contemporary world society. Clearly the most significant among these manifestations are the war system and the global economic structures which divide most of the human species into categories of poverty or affluence. When the two are carefully examined, it becomes apparent that an insidious, symbiotic relation-ship exists between them; that they are indeed one system maintained by armed force or the threat thereof, that force residing primarily in the hands of the most powerful nation-States.

The neo-colonial world economy, a system in which the industrial nations provide a high standard of living for most but not all of their populations as a consequence of having virtually free access to the resources and the raw materials of the so-called developing nations, is buttressed by military superiority in the form of highly sophisticated weapons systems and large-scale industries for the production of both nuclear and 'conventional' weapons. The technological 'progress' which has brought the developed countries to post-industrial affluence has also provided these nations with weapons technology which make the destruction of human society not only possible but, according to some, highly probable (cf. the 1976 report by the Stockholm Institute for Peace Research).[2] Although most peace research acknowledges these relationships, they are not yet studied in peace education.[3] The reasons hark back to the ambiguity about the methods and content of peace education and raise the questions: Why should peace education place equal emphasis on cognitive and affective modes of learning, and how can disarmament be a significant vehicle for such learnings?

7.1 Emotions or Politics?

During the early years of the present period of peace education, some practitioners favored a primarily affective approach, assuming that if certain feelings were

---

[2] Extracts from this article appeared in a newsletter of the World Education Association in December 1976.

[3] Betty A. Reardon, 1975: "A Social Education for Human Survival: A Synthesis of Practices In International Education and Peace Studies", in: *Social Studies Review*, 15, 1.

touched, people would be moved to behave differently, thus lessening violence and war. So the early 1960s saw efforts to make students and the public contemplate the horrors of nuclear war. From the mid-1960s onward, the Viet Nam war caused many who formerly identified themselves as 'peace educators' in the United States of America to scurry off into the less 'political' field of global education, which places emphasis on 'interdependence' without considering political structures. Many who stuck with peace concentrated on the atrocities of an illegal war, giving little attention to the whole field of weapons development or to the larger issue of the war system itself. Since that time there has been a surge of efforts to educate about the Third World. These programs focus on the inhuman conditions of dire poverty in which the vast majority of the peoples of the 'developing countries' are forced to live, but offer little structural analysis of the world economy. Indeed, many of these efforts were and are very effective in arousing horror, fear, sympathy and shame. But as often as not, they also release the feeling which more than any other stands in the way of serious endeavors to overcome war and poverty-impotence, the feeling of powerlessness so widespread in the face of the arms race and the rapidly declining capacity of the world to feed its growing population. This feeling of impotence may well be the strongest bulwark of the status quo.

Horror, fear, sympathy and shame are genuine and legitimate human emotions which should be confronted in any responsible program of peace education. They should, however, be acknowledged within the framework of efforts to analyze the system and structures responsible for the conditions giving rise to them. Such analysis should not only include the systemic and structural as well as the ethical causes of these conditions, but even more importantly should consider alternative systems and structures, encouraging students to conceptualize their own preferred alternatives. This is not to advocate avoidance of the present realities, but rather to insist on approaching them from the perspective of alternative solutions, to make it possible to deal with the painful feelings of fear and shame, by coming to understand that the situation is not inevitable or hope-less of change. The conditions resulted from particular political choices, and they can be altered, improved by new choices, perhaps even transformed by new structures or alternative systems. By coming to understand that the problems may be approached from alternative perspectives with varying solutions, impotence may be eroded by hope. Students need to be aware of and to feel the suffering and dangers of the present system, but they need also to hope for a better future and to be motivated to act. Action-oriented education is political education and some peace educators, particularly among the Europeans, have long argued that peace education is and should be political education.

Peace education as political education is not a view very widely held in the United States. There seem to be two main lines of reasoning for this situation. First, the popularly held notion that violence and war are largely due to aggressive attitudes and lack of understanding of other peoples has tended to place great stress, especially in the lower grades, on the attitudinal and cultural, pretty much avoiding the political and structural. The idea that peace education at the elementary level should attempt to cultivate attitudes which accord human dignity to all, and provide familiarity with some of the variety of human cultures as a means to create respect for other ways of life *is* a sound one and should be supported. Indeed such attitudes are essential to motivate people to want to relieve human suffering, but these attitudes alone will not prepare them to do it.

It should also be noted that even at a tender age children have the right to have their questions answered truthfully and as fully as they can comprehend. When they ask about war and 'the Bomb', they deserve a truthful answer, not some simplistic reply about people simply not understanding each other, or even worse, that it is all too complex for them to understand. If they understood enough about reality to ask the question, then they surely can comprehend a direct and truthful answer. It is sheer folly to think that avoiding these questions with young children is shielding them from the 'awful truth'. If they are exposed to the media, they know about the realities. Not only do they know, they worry. 'The Bomb' is one of the main sources of anxiety among children. This is substantiated not only by personal experience with the questions and fears of young children, but also by research.[4]

It is the responsibility of educators as well as parents to deal with these very real and legitimate fears and anxieties. The job of peace education is not to create abhorrence of war through encouraging fear of it; but rather to cope with fear by approaching war as it is, a complex, dangerous but ultimately solvable problem. Although the adult public has been fairly successful at employing the 'denial mechanism to close out the specter of nuclear annihilation, the monster manages to rear its head with sufficient frequency not to be completely denied. Whether it is the indiscretion or careful political calculation of one of our 'leaders» letting us or 'the enemy' know by way of assurance or threat that we have this capacity or the cold, dry fact of the mathematical possibilities of a nuclear exchange released by a peace research institute,[5] we all know that we can as easily as not be blown out of existence.

What only a few of us know, however, is that there are alternatives, and whether we survive or not is in most respects more of a matter of human choice than of statistics. We all have as much right to know this as we have to be aware of the threat of nuclear annihilation. It should be taught to us not just by our 'leaders, but deliberately and systematically by our schools. Small children need to learn that human society is the handiwork of human beings, and that when we use both our reason and our foresight we can generally make the world better. We can overcome even the most severe social and political problems. War in all its forms, from border skirmishes to the Dr. Strangelove ultimate attack is not a natural disaster to be endured like typhoons and earthquakes. It is the result of human actions, and it can be avoided, indeed eliminated, by human action. Such action, however, is not only unlikely, it is impossible so long as the driving force of the

---

[4] "Children of War", *Journal of World Education, 1971.*

[5] The Swedish Peace Research Institute released a report in September 1976 stating that the rapid escalation of the arms race makes the occurrence of nuclear war very possible.

war system, the nation-State monopoly on the legal application of force continues. The best way to bring that issue into question is through the study of disarmament, in all its political and emotional ramifications. This can be done in an intellectually responsible way in any and all learning environments, and it should be done, and very soon, at no later stage in formal education than the secondary level. Just as the issue should not be deliberately excluded from the elementary level, it should be very deliberately included at the secondary level. No university peace studies program should be without full and careful analysis of the arms race and the war system.

Advocating the inclusion of the arms race and the war system, particularly in terms of the power monopoly of the nation-State, as a required part of the content of citizenship education, almost inevitably provokes a second line of reasoning against peace education as political education. Such content, it is argued, would cause a 'backlash' from the authorities which could thwart the acceptance of peace studies. It is pretty well recognized that to evaluate the desirability of the unlimited power of the nation-State or to question the concept of national sovereignty is 'off limits' in the schools.

Curriculum innovators know much better than to jab at the most sensitive spots of the entrenched course of study and the values and—interests which underlie it. This is virtually a law of survival in the public schools, which in the area of social education still have some pretensions to a value-free curriculum, even while some districts have tolerated the introduction of 'values education'. The latter, it must be admitted, has in some cases caused a furor similar to what might be expected if the issues of arms and the sovereignty of the nation-State were to be raised in our classrooms. Those of us who advocate that curriculum should deal with such questions as who should disarm, when, under what circumstances, should be sensitive to the perceptions of many of our fellow citizens, that including disarmament in the curriculum is tantamount to advocating an end to sovereignty, just as sex education is sometimes seen as advocating promiscuity. Unreasonable as that may seem to many who believe that education should help people to cope effectively with the realities of life, it is a very real and, indeed, very understandable fear. For in both cases there is implied that the established and familiar patterns of life, institutions and behaviors that seem almost part of the natural order, are subject to change and we ourselves will have to change. Most people find the notion frightening.

This situation need not mean that the introduction of the topic of disarmament into the schools has to cause public controversy and risk the future of peace education. What it does demonstrate is that there is a crucial relationship between the community, the parents, the school boards, the central offices and the like, and the schools. The schools are not just an instrument of the community to be controlled and stifled by it or to be ignored to enjoy 'academic freedom'. They are part of the community with equal participatory rights and commonweal responsibilities. All who are part of the community should participate in the decisions about the needs to be met by these schools and all should have the advantage of the education which comes from making decisions about education. This is to say that the very question of whether or not the issue should be discussed in the schools should be a subject of public discussion and the vehicle for wider public education about the most crucial issue of our century, the nature of the political institutions which can best assure human survival, peace and justice. All educators, parents and students should be debating the questions of whether the war system and the human species can continue to coexist and what the schools should be doing about the question.

7.1.1 Public Values

The foregoing implies that in essence all education is political and that preparation for politics is a major task of education. Education serves public interests and should be guided by public values. It should also equip people to analyze values, not only their own, but perhaps more importantly those of the society in which they live. For if education, as has long been presumed, is supposed to contribute to a better life, then those educated should be able to make reasonable decisions about what is better. The techniques for learning about and analyzing values and public issues are intellectual techniques, and developing their mastery should be an essential task of education, if it is to fulfill its responsibilities to prepare for politics. The failure to provide full analytic education for all students is a political failure of democracy, because it effectively denies those who miss it full rights of participation in policy-making. Further, it debases both the pragmatic and the ethical quality of politics by limiting not only the numbers but also the capacities of those who do participate. Thus education in general and peace education in particular should be both intellectual and political. In fact it cannot adequately fulfil the one responsibility without attending to the other. Therefore, the most crucial current political issue and problem, the consequences of an international system of heavily armed States, should be a central topic of education for citizenship.

There are two main approaches to citizenship education. One which has been the most widespread, and still seems to prevail in areas where a high value is placed on tradition, is the 'producing good citizens' approach. Here there is a great emphasis placed on the cognitive mastery of governmental process and affective stress on building loyalty to the traditional values of representative democracy. It does not usually encourage the critical analysis of the processes nor does it require clarification of the values. It is the approach which buttressed the educational contribution to national unity and the 'melting pot' theory, and which was at the root of much of the dismay over the 'lack of patriotism' of the Viet Nam dissenters. The other approach, which has gained currency, with the recent emphasis of social education on methods of inquiry and problem-solving, is the 'critical responsibility' approach. This approach puts more emphasis on structural analysis and values analysis while including instruction in such things as constitutional process and the values of the political system. Although the two approaches are not necessarily dichotomous, and in actual practice most citizenship education is a mix with the emphasis stemming from somewhat different assumptions, it is important to point out the different assumptions. The 'good citizens' approach appears to assume that if the government, particularly that of the nation-State in the modern world, is to carry out its functions, it must have a strongly supportive citizenry which, when the 'national interest' is at stake will not question nor harass those in charge of the State. On the other hand, the 'critical responsibility' approach assumes that if the government is to function well, it must serve its citizens and put their interests above its own. In order to assure an adequate assessment of those interests and the efficacy of the processes and policies designed to meet them, people must observe and evaluate the government and its policies with a constructive critical eye. If the national interest is to be defended, it must be constantly reviewed to assure that it is, indeed, the sum of the best interests of the nation's citizens. Since peace education is basically about change, the latter approach is more compatible with its purposes.

7.2 Global Interdependence

The acceptance of the concept of 'global interdependence' as a fact of life has led many to conclude that individual national interest can no longer be construed as independent of the global interest and some to advocate that citizenship education should be education for 'world citizenship'. However, even among the latter there is often hesitancy to advocate that such education should address the value conflicts and structural dilemmas in the concept of a world polity which is the basis of the notion of world citizenship. Yet can they responsibly advocate world citizenship without confronting the issues raised by the contradictions between sovereignty and interdependence, and between the notion of a single polity and its components armed against each other? Even those who espouse the idea of world government have been somewhat reluctant to face the contradictions and dilemmas of creating such a structure, particularly those issues relating to questions of peacekeeping and security, i.e. the contra-dictions between the freedom of States as we know them and the existence of one heavily armed superstate. All this is by way of saying that the major issues of interdependence and whether it can become a peaceful and just state of affairs are structural issues, most of which revolve around questions of security and force, raising such questions as who shall have the responsibility to maintain the former and who shall have the authority to apply the latter? If citizens are to have anything to do with answering these questions they must have two vital bits of equipment, a responsible critical capacity and an adequate set of facts about arms and security, i.e. the comparative advantages and disadvantages of the war system as opposed to a disarmed world.

I submit that most present education, even peace education, does not equip people to know anything about disarmament nor about proposals for its achievement. I further submit that, at the very least, peace education has the responsibility to rectify this glaring error in citizenship education. None should get through formal education without some comprehension of the fact that a disarmed world is a practical alternative to the war system, that a great deal of scholarly and practical political thought has gone into designing structures and strategies for constructing such a world (although none of them may be adequate to the task, at least the task does not defy the human imagination), that there are foreseeable costs and benefits to such a world, and most important, how those costs and benefits compare to the foreseeable consequences of the continuation of the war system. All this can be studied without necessarily coming, as so many fear, to the conclusion that the nation-State should be abolished, any more than Luther came to the conclusion that the Christian Church should be abolished. Painful, costly and traumatic as that critical questioning of the most powerful institution of medieval Europe was, there are few Christians who would deny that it was not in the end a good thing not only for Western society, but for the Church itself. Can calling into question the nation-State's monopoly on ultimate force and violence be any more frightening or earth-shaking than calling into question a monopoly on the way to eternal salvation? After all, here we are only discussing human and time-bound institutions. It is, in fact, quite possible that the nation-State could emerge from such a critical analysis a stronger and healthier if drastically revised institution.

If education should not avoid the issue, how can *it* be raised? If we look at the present topics which comprise peace education, it can be seen that the arms/security issue is a natural part of the inquiry into just about every one of them. Only a few examples will suffice to demonstrate the case. As noted, poverty and underdevelopment are widely studied topics in peace studies and global education. The crucial component in this study is the distribution and use of resources. Can the study be adequately conducted without examining the facts of arms expenditures and the cost benefits of those expenditures, or noting that some economists claim that poverty can never be overcome so long as so great a percentage of the world's resources goes into military expenditures?[6]

Another popular topic is conflict and conflict resolution. How can either of these subjects be explored if the differences between the intent and consequences of both armed and non-violent conflict are not examined? Yet there are many courses in conflict which do not even cover the concept of non-violence!

Human rights is another issue which, though not yet widely enough taught, may become more familiar if the UNESCO recommendation gains currency. The phenomenon of the growth of military regimes collaterally with the increase in conventional arms trade and political repression, cannot be ignored if we expect to achieve any understanding of current trends, opportunities and obstacles *in* the field of human rights. Would it not be interesting to have students make

---

[6] Ruth Leger Sivard, *World Military and Social Expenditures, 1976*, published by WMSE Publications. This report estimates that close to $300,000 million per year is spent on arms and the military.

comparative maps of the 'geography of torture' and the geography of arms trade and military assistance?

Most programs in citizenship education as well as some in peace studies and global education devote some attention to problems of the environment. The effects of nuclear testing and the current debate over the use and sale of nuclear technology is perhaps the most crucial of current environmental issues. Can any aspect of this issue be properly analyzed or debated without taking into account the military aspects of the question?

In short, I contend that the questions of arms and security and the competency and legitimacy of the presently constituted nation-State system to maintain a monopoly on them are at the core of all peace education, and should, as well, comprise a major aspect of citizenship education. The questions are pragmatic, political ones, which are also ethical and intellectual in the best problem-solving sense of the word. They are also profoundly affective, for they deal with the most powerful and deeply rooted human emotions, fear of death, in this case the death of us all, and love, love of life and of our fellow beings.

Education should equip people to deal with their feelings and to think critically about reality. Peace education should help people to feel more for other people, and to envision ways to change reality, the reality of the presently violent and unjust world. A key to the opening of such educational processes is the subject of disarmament. It is the single concept which embodies the idea of an end to violence and which opens the broader inquiry into the really thorny problems of achieving a better future, by creating world institutions which are equally adequate to the twin tasks of maintaining security and promoting justice.

Part III
Generations of Reardon's Professional Formation and Practice as Reflected in Selected Essays: Second Generation—The Formation 1985–2000

Chapter 8
The Fundamental Purposes of a Pedagogy of Peace

Retrospective Reflection on "The Fundamental Purposes of a Pedagogy of Peace," Chapter 5 of *Comprehensive Peace Education* (1988)

Comprehensive Peace Education, *the collection of essays from which this essay is selected, being among the first general theoretical works in the field, was received as a useful contribution to a field still seeking to define itself several decades into its current phase. The term comprehensive peace education was coined in attempt to bring some cohesion to the multiple and varied forms of curriculum and instruction practiced as peace education. I sought to find not only common social purposes, but to identify the foundational concepts that lead educators to see their respective materials and practices as peace education in the 1980s. I found that all were informed by a compatible set of social values, but few were cast in the broader holism or clear conceptual frameworks that I perceived as essential to educating toward citizens' capacities to conceive and work toward the achievement of a transformed world order. That educational goal, I believed, required systematic, holistic and multi-disciplinary thinking. The book was comprised of primarily previously published attempts to argue for the holistic and essentially normative approach to the field, an approach that I asserted to be consistent with the values that characterized the affective goals of the field as they were developed during the first two decades of my experience in the developmental process.*

During the first stages of the post-World War II development of peace education, a variety of topics and practices emerged, all seeking to educate toward bringing an end to war and subsequently to overcoming what were to become the various other forms of violence conceptualized by peace researchers. While all peace educators were not linked into networks of their peers, a significant number had sufficient contacts to exchange, not only their own experiences, but also those

B.A. Reardon and D.T. Snauwaert, *Betty A. Reardon: A Pioneer in Education for Peace and Human Rights*, SpringerBriefs on Pioneers in Science and Practice 26,
DOI 10.1007/978-3-319-08967-6_8

of others in their respective countries and regions. My own work intersected with several international networks, the chief one being the Peace Education Commission of the International Peace Research Association, which for a period of time was the main source of international exchange on the theoretical and methodological development of peace education. Europeans in the network were particularly productive in the development of theory, largely based on the problematic of peace as defined by European peace researchers.

With Prof. Ted Herman at COPRED meeting, mid 1980s. *Source* personal photo collection of the author

In spite of this flourishing "on the margins" of institutional education, peace education had yet to take on any common conceptual or pedagogical definition, rather clinging to the notion of "let a thousand flowers bloom," largely I now believe, due—in spite of some significant common values—to a reluctance to accept the premises of others' delineations of the peace problematic and its underlying causes. So, when I took up the development of a peace education graduate degree program, although there were already dozens of undergraduate peace studies programs, there were but only a few courses in peace education per se. The substance I worked with came from the various international peace education sources with which I had familiarity, some of the peace research which informed it, and the focus problems of the American peace movement as known by prospective students. In my case the main body of foundational research came from world order research and the work I did among NGOs at the United Nations. An outline of that degree program is archived in the Ward M. Canaday Center for Special Collections, University of Toledo Library.

I also called a bit upon a wide variety of school curricula being independently developed by individual classroom teachers. In later years, I regretted not giving more attention to some of these curricula the product of an international survey sponsored by the Institute for World Order. Selections from the survey conducted with the assistance of team of TC students were published in a compendium of those most transferrable to other classrooms in Educating for Global Responsibility: Teacher Designed Curricula for Peace Education, K-12, *a companion volume to* Comprehensive Peace Education. *While the collection demonstrated that peace education was being integrated into all grade levels and most curricular subjects, no common definitions, conceptual parameters or common educational purposes emerged from the survey, nor were there general frameworks that might form the basis of what I believed to be the requisite holism. Yet it was clear that most practices were productive and fell within the substance and purposes of what was traditionally considered to be civic or citizenship education; hence the subtitle of the book,* Educating for Global Responsibility.

For my own professional purposes of developing a peace education degree concentration to be offered as one of the choices of focus in masters and doctoral programs in international education at Teachers College Columbia University, I embarked upon an effort to outline proposals for the fundamental substance, purposes and conceptual parameters of the field. Specifically stating, that these efforts were not to be the 'definitive' work in the emerging field, but rather an attempt to open discussions that might bring some of the conceptual clarity so essential to fulfilling any possibility of institutionalizing the field, I undertook in this essay—that began as a seminar lecture other versions of which were given at other universities—to suggest some guidelines for that purpose. Reprinted in several publications, it became widely known as "The 7 R's."

As I believe that establishing interrelationships in holistic perspectives is important to understanding problems and designing responses. It has proven useful in teaching to use devices such as putting forth a set of interrelated concepts staring with the same letter, not only to facilitate remembering the concepts, but for perceiving their interrelationships. It is a device I have used on various occasions in the evolution of my work in the field. Here it is found in what has come to be known as "The 7 R's". These R's represent capacities that I would now certainly further refine, as I have in an unpublished 2013 piece.

Though the tone and form of "The 7 R's" is distinctly different from that of "The Knowledge Industry", that analysis was the basis from which I speculated on the forms of learning and the citizen capacities to be developed to address the problematic as defined in that earlier piece. As the conclusions of The Knowledge Industry *attempted to propose ways in which the academy might be changed to restore the socially and humanly constructive educational purposes many educators believe should be fundamental to its mission, this essay was written as a reflection on the question of what education might do to prepare citizens to be actively and effectively committed to the public pursuit of peace within the structures and values of the society that infuse the institutions in which they are educated.*

While Comprehensive Peace Education *was not the definition and 'cannon' that some sought, it clearly resonated with many peace educators who were themselves seeking some potential framework for "putting it all together," within which to establish interrelationships and commonalities among the various practices so that taken together they could become the basis for a substantively sound and responsibly purposeful field of citizen education. Indeed, some of us claimed—given the conditions of the world order and our respective national situations—peace education was the most relevant and potentially constructive of all possible approaches to that field. Although the established order did not agree, and the field, while continuing to mature and deepen, remained on the institutional margins—even in the universities in which it was being devised—the conceptual challenge had been launched. As the piece proved useful to others, it also was a significant landmark in my own peace learning, the way in which I engaged in continued teaching and on-going development of the field and, most important, my own understanding of what purposes it should serve and how to become more effective in achieving them.*

Betty A. Reardon
March, 2014

8.1 Introduction

Peace education, like most educational fields, aspires to excellence.[1] If excellence, as the *Oxford English Dictionary* indicates, is the "possession of... good qualities in an eminent or unusual degree," the good qualities needed, l would argue, are those that would come closest to the current concept of "positive human potential." Efforts to fulfill this human potential for authentic excellence would be a major animating force of the peace paradigm basic to the transformational approach. And although contemporary education seems very much preoccupied with excellence in the sense of preparation and capacity to compete, it seems to have little concern with qualities; it is so much obsessed (as is the competitive mode) with quantity and measurement that it is an impediment to transformation rather than a means to it.

Education should be devoted to the development of the ability to learn and should concern itself with deepening and extending the capacities that are comprehended by the notion of the positive human potential. Positive peace and positive human potential are inextricably linked—both are developmental and organic. Many peace educators and activists would define peacemaking as conceiving, gestating, and nurturing those conditions in which all can develop their good qualities, their capacity to be fully human. Education today is not really living up to its potential. My own experience and my own activities have been, it seems to me now, more often focused on instrumental than on fundamental purposes. Much of my work-indeed the dissertation on which this volume is based-emphasized conceptualizing and designing curricula for particular learning objectives derived from earlier work (Reardon 1981, 1982) that now appear to me to be quite limited.

Many of us continue to engage in an educative process that is much more a matter of the teacher's transmitting information or interpretations to students than a process of mutual exchange. We set our tasks too much in terms of achieving 'objectives'—not only the much-maligned "behavioral objectives," but all the narrow learning goals from which we develop our curricula. When we measure our professional success, we assess our achievements by quantifying them. There is certainly a role for quantification, as there is a role for specific objectives, even

[1] This chapter was first published as: Reardon, Betty A. *Comprehensive Peace Education: Educating for Global Responsibility*. New York: Teachers College Press, 1988. According to Francesca King, Rights & Permissions Department, Teachers College Press, New York, the Rights returned to the author.

behavioral objectives, in a comprehensive program for peace education. But we have placed so much emphasis on these aspects, that we have held back the possibility for developing a broader range of human capacities. For example, we put a great deal of emphasis on developing the skills of analysis, a very important set of skills. But when it becomes the dominant mode for our teaching and learning, analysis alone tends to reduce knowledge into small, isolated components. It fragments our learning and our thinking, and thereby our lives. Goals and objectives, without a larger value framework, do the same.

Goals are desired states that we work to achieve. *Objectives* are intervening points along the way, partial achievements. Because neither *goal* nor *objective is* broad enough, and neither seems to encompass the aspects of process and complexity that are so important to the field, I use the term *purpose* to describe the intentional ends of peace education. Purpose seems to connote continued pursuit of a value or good. The concept of purpose provides the larger value framework and pushes us to less instrumental thinking.

Peace educators might well review the preamble to the charter of the United Nations Educational, Social, and Cultural Organization (UNESCO), which states that "since wars begin in the minds of men, it is in the minds of men that the foundations of peace must be constructed." Putting aside a temptation to make a feminist comment on the wording, I must agree that wars begin in the minds of men-indeed, in *all human* minds-and that it is in all our minds that the foundations for peace must be constructed. If we are to be peacemakers, then we must learn to be peace thinkers. We must pursue that change in our thinking that Einstein exhorted us to seek, if we take seriously the need to change our way of thinking, then we have to look toward the reintroduction of qualities and capacities into the educational pursuit. As Douglas Sloan has suggested, in the introduction to the special issue of the *Teachers College Record on* peace education, "A change in our way of thinking would, if nothing else, recognize and re-orient itself, in method and substance, around the *reality of qualities….* The qualitative enhancement of life and of culture would become more important than their quantitative manipulation and control."[2] He argues that pursuit of quality should be at the very center of education. I would add that developing our capacities for peacemaking should also be at the very center of education, for practical as well as moral reasons. Given the complexity and dynamism of only part of what is meant here by reflection. We need to encourage a type of reflectiveness that permits us to look beyond our ordinary understandings of reality, to move into something approaching a meditative or contemplative process through which we deepen our understanding of personal, social, and global realities. Such a process would enable us to see things more clearly at various levels, and teach us to value silence as the occasion or 'space' for reflection. It is in these reflective spaces of silence that we can most readily discover our connectedness to others and to the living Earth.

[2] Sloan, Douglas. "Toward an Education for a Living World". *Teachers College Record*, 84, no. 1 (1982): 11.

Teachers will need to learn to tolerate silence in their classrooms. We will all need to learn to become more comfortable with periods of silence in our interactions as we work together in decision making and peacemaking processes.

We need, too, to develop a capacity for another form of silence, reflective listening. This is a capacity comprised of various skills like those of concentrated attention and interpretation, which is especially needed by the most articulate among us-statesmen, teachers, and students alike. The high rewards accorded skills of verbal expression often impede the development of listening skills. Lack of these skills is, I believe, a major obstacle in many of our efforts toward peace, especially in our negotiating processes. Many of the techniques developed for business negotiation and successful group dynamics are quite relevant to peace and disarmament negotiation. They need, however, to be transposed from the win-lose to the win-win context, and beyond that to the context of deeper understanding of and interconnectedness with others.

Reflective listening skills would assure far more effective communication and would certainly enhance learning. They include the forms of affirmative, non-judgmental listening that accord equal respect to all parties to a communication or a learning experience. They also call for full engagement to 'read' all signals for the full meaning; to 'interpret,' or place the meaning in context; and to be critical, in the sense of looking for points of both agreement and disagreement, but to do so in a manner that maintains fundamental respect for the human dignity of all, no matter how deep the disagreements are. Peacemaking can be in many ways as conflictual as war making. The adversarial modes of discourse now used in academic discussions and political debates should be replaced with transformative ones. Paramount among these modes is respectful, reflective listening. Reflection is a requirement for responsible action, both individual and social.

Responsibility is the most essential active peacemaking capacity, one that requires as preparation rational, meditative, and interpretative reflection. Active responsibility is responsibility *for* and responsibility *to*. Responsibility *for* involves acknowledging and assuming the cost of our own complicity in the violence and injustice of the war system and the values that uphold it, acknowledging that we as individuals and as a society have accepted and gone along with the systems of violence and exploitation, exploitation by the northern industrial nations of the southern, the so-called underdeveloped, poorer nations, whose poverty in large part results from our having enjoyed their resources, having access to them at less than just prices as we purchase commodities in international trade.

Responsibility *to* is a responsibility to those with whom we are inextricably interconnected in the global web of life, a responsibility for acting to change these conditions. Responsibility to the others in this world system who have been deprived of a fair share of the world's benefits calls us to critically evaluate that system and create alternatives to it. This responsibility to take action is one that involves risk.

So *risk taking*, too, is a peacemaking capacity. The capacity to take risks is the capacity. to face the consequences of change, the capacity to willingly involve oneself in the process of change, changing systems and structures, changing-our-own circumstances within systems, structures, and relationships, and ultimately even changing the ways in which we live our lives and the ways in which we relate to others. The capacity to risk how we live and indeed how we perceive ourselves, and, in some cases, our very identities, is one of the most essential challenges to peace education. Without the capacity to risk, will we have the courage to live in new public and private realities, or will we be able to involve ourselves in creating them? For we will need to confront and resolve the conflicts that these changing realities are bound to produce, as well as the conflicts that will continue to be produced by the inequities of the present system. We must be able to work through such conflicts and reconcile the conflicting parties, all of whom are members of the human family and part of the unity of the living Earth.

Reconciliation is often recognized as a significant peacemaking capacity, yet we have not adequately addressed ourselves to developing the specific modes, behaviors, and attitudes that foster reconciliation, nor have we pursued the development of this capacity as an educational goal. We need to develop the capacity to reconcile not only the politically conflicting parties in the world but also many of the other elements now in conflictual, destructive relationship to each other—those fragmented relationships that characterize personal as well as international systems and processes.

Most especially, we will have to do some reconciling even of the parts of ourselves that we find in conflict, of the very ways in which we think. Our fragmented and adversarial patterns of thinking may well lie at the very heart of our problems of violence and injustice.[3] The self-healing will be as important as the healing of the society. Certainly holism and integrity cannot characterize either persons or societies developed from the reductionist thought that still dominates both our educational and our policy-making processes.

The metaphor of the "broken world" is one that pervades all aspects of the current human experience, from the planet ravished by "progress and development" and threatened with destruction by conflict and war, to personal relations and individual senses of personhood. All of life is in bits and pieces; the human family is broken and bleeding. Healing the wounds and reconciling the estranged and alienated are fundamental to the process of transition to the transformed society necessary to peace. That transformation must take place in our structures and our relationships but most important, in the way in which we view the world and our part in our paradigm. Yet even the emergence of a holistic paradigm will not do away with the need for the capacity to reconcile. For as long as conflict and change are part of the human experience, reconciliation will be necessary to the continuation of the experience. And without the capacity to reconcile, we cannot expect to recover from the trauma of the paradigm shift essential to the change from a war system to a peace system.

Recovery– the transcending of that trauma of the excessive change and conflict of a system change, returning to health and wholeness requires strength and a form of courage that we have not yet acknowledged as the essence of heroism. But recovery also refers to reclamation, uncovering or rediscovering, regaining that

---

[3] Sloan, Douglas. *Insight, Imagination, and the Emancipation of the Modern Mind.* Westport, CT Greenwood, 1984.

which has been lost. The regaining of much of what has been repressed and forgotten of human capacities may be essential to the transcending of the pain and shock of paradigm shift. It may indeed be the most hopeful aspect of our search to develop the capacity to recover. As indicated earlier, there is much to be recovered from our past, much that we know about how to build positive human relations and create peace. There is also much that is repressed in our images of the future. Feminist scholarship is bringing to our attention a whole realm of human experience and modes of imaging that can contribute to peacemaking.[4] Surely we have much to learn from uncovering other parts of the human experience that have been devalued or repressed in the present paradigm.

We also need to build a new reality, to reconstruct the fragments of our broken world, to bring together the positive elements that we can uncover, create, and imagine in a new paradigm of integrity and wholeness, to reconstruct a healthy, wholesome human society on the planet, to answer the call for new notions of power and courage, to put into action constructive uses of imagination that we have long neglected in our education.

The capacity for *reconstruction,* more than any other of the Rs, involves the uses of imagination for peacemaking. The development of imaginative capacities is one of the most commonly cited purposes of peace education. It is the main purpose of several of the curricula in the K-12 curriculum guide[5] and has featured in much of the theoretical literature. In terms of the capacity for reconstruction, it seems to me that there are three distinct manifestations of the imagination, which range from the deepest level of insight to the practical level of design skills.

The deepest of the three is *envisioning*, which enables us to experience insight into the full range of possibilities for realizing human potential through the expression of the most fundamental human values.

Imaging, as distinct from envisioning, is more readily integrated into conversation, particularly in the sphere of the exploration of values. Imaging is the visualization of the conditions that would prevail if those values were realized. Where visions seem to require the arts, poetry, and philosophy for expression, images can be described in the narrative of discourse.

Modeling, the most practical of the three, the closest to the sphere of skills, involves the design of social and political structures, of economic and political processes and patterns of human relationships that manifest the actual realization of the values in our lived experience. We often use models as "blueprints for preferred futures." The capacity for modeling has been significant in the reform and reconstructionist approaches to peace education. Imaging links these approaches to the transformative, which struggles with the releasing of our visionary capacities, our talents for the prophetic.

---

[4] Boulding, Elise. *The Underside of History: A View of Women Through Time*. Boulder, CO: Westview Press, 1976.

[5] Reardon, Betty A. *Educating for Global Responsibility: Teacher-Designed Curricula for Peace Education*, K-12. New York: Teachers College Press, 1988.

The prophetic capacity leads us to the seventh and the most comprehensive-and, I think, the most meaningful-of all the fundamental peacemaking capacities, *reverence.* (This concept is adapted from Douglas Sloan's contribution to a discussion at the Peace Education Seminar at Teachers College, Columbia University, in September 1986.) But reverence should not be ascribed only to the prophets of the great social visions nor limited to religious education. It is a universal capacity, one that our scientific paradigm has denigrated, and democracy has misinterpreted, but from which authentic joy in life can most readily spring. I use the term *reverence to* mean not only respect for truth and goodness but also the deepest appreciation of the fullness and infinite possibilities of life, possibilities that, it appears, we have experienced only in limited fashion in those centuries since we first became conscious of ourselves as human beings. Reverence is the source of wonder, which is the parent of authentic learning. Reverence is the source of our capacity to hope and the ground from which human compassion springs, the primary manifestation of the sense of connectedness and understanding of interrelationship that is at the center of the three comprehensive value goals of peace education, stewardship, relationship, and citizenship. Reverence provides the wholeness and integration of the other six capacities.

Developing educational programs to nurture these capacities is a major challenge to peace education. It calls upon us to venture into new, sometimes frightening, territory. It calls us to restructure our own professional realities. It challenges us to practice our profession in ways that we have done only in bits and pieces in the past. What Douglas Sloan has referred to as the "recovery of wholeness" will enable us to put those bits and pieces together and to imagine and create the missing pieces so that we can pursue the authentic purposes of education, the enrichment of the human experience, and strive more effectively toward the superordinate goal of peace education, assuring the continuation of the human experience by transcending the true cause of violence, alienation from life.[6]

8.2 Teaching Toward the Development of Peacemaking Capacities

Although the classroom pursuit of the seven fundamental capacities will indeed require significant changes in educational practice, it is apparent, especially from the results of the World Policy Institute survey, that many classroom teachers are already actively engaged in teaching that reflects these purposes. The resulting curriculum guide contains units and teaching suggestions that are readily adaptable to the recommendations that follow.[7] Indeed, these recommendations are largely inspired by those curricula and other current practices in peace education.

[6] Sloan, Douglas. *Toward a Recovery of Wholeness*. New York: Teachers College Press, 1983.

[7] Reardon, *Educating for Global Responsibility: Teacher-Designed Curricula for Peace Education, K-12*.

Teaching for the development of reflective capacities will require a renewed emphasis on the kind of approaches advocated by Hunt and Metcalf [8] and by some of the discipline-based analyses of the "new social studies" approach of the sixties. In these practices, reflective thinking was an essential component of the modes of inquiry and problem solving that were widely advocated for teaching the skills essential to citizenship in a democratic society, However, new dimensions will also need to be explored. As noted earlier, the creative potential of silence has largely been overlooked. The need of all, even the youngest learners, for private time and silent spaces in which to engage in reflection has to be recognized. The meditation techniques currently being introduced into some peace education programs have great potential for the fulfillment of this need. The silence of affirmative listening and the silence of contemplative meditation both provide conditions in which reflective capacities can be developed, and both are conditions that should be encouraged in peace education classrooms.

Teaching responsibility is also teaching for empowerment. Responsibility can best be learned by taking responsibility. Students need to have the opportunity to make real choices, not simply to form opinions regarding issues-a subject of study but not of real decision making. They need opportunities to make choices that will lead to action directly related to the issues. Opportunities for individual actions and group actions to be pursued within the general community and the larger society need to be integrated into peace education curricula. Students who engage in social and political action at every age have an invaluable experience of reality that teaches the difficulties of and the possibilities for social change. They are given a sound basis on which to make judgments about social reality as well as to assess the effectiveness of their own actions. It is important that teachers communicate to students that even the most carefully chosen actions do not necessarily lead to the desired ends, that taking action is part of the ongoing process of learning to be effective change agents, of learning to refine action and to direct it more effectively toward the desired purposes. Education for empowerment, responsibility, and action is also a form of process learning. It is closely related to the cycle of reflection and action, or praxis process, integral to Paulo Freire's method of consciousness-raising for political empowerment and liberation.[9]

Another element in teaching for responsibility is equally important: helping students to appreciate the responsibility of having and creating knowledge. This responsibility has been most discussed in the realm of the sciences, particularly as related to weapons development. However, students need to be aware that all knowledge, the derivation of knowledge and the transmission of knowledge, carries responsibilities, and that responsible learners are those who retain that sense of responsibility as they incorporate the knowledge into their own paradigms and behaviors.

---

[8] Hunt, M. and Metcalf, Lawrence. *Teaching High School Social Studies*. New York: Harper & Row, 1955.

[9] Freire, Paulo. *Pedagogy of the Oppressed*. New York: Herder and Herder, 1970.

The exercise of responsibility is the exercise of values reflected upon and values pursued in personal, social, and political interactions. Authentic valuing produces action and involves risks. Students can be helped to learn that risk taking is integral to commitment to values, that if we must pursue changes in order to realize our values, then risk is inevitable. Indeed, in the Freirean context, and in the experience of those who have applied it to their own liberation, risk taking is a profoundly significant part of the empowerment process. The taking of risks empowers the risk takers to take further risks and to develop the capacity to deal with the consequences of actions. It should lead to more reflection on the changed conditions, so that further action can be taken, and to an understanding that at each level new risks are likely to arise.

Risk takers are confident people, and education has not been very effective at building confidence in learners. We tend instead to undermine confidence and to teach students to avoid risk by reinforcing the social norms that encourage conformity, and we limit as we assess the potential of particular learners, by grade levels or by learning style, in quantifiable terms. We undermine confidence by using competitive grading systems and standardized curricula and teaching practices. We do not create in our classrooms a favorable climate for risk taking and confidence building. Creativity and individuality, though given much lip service, are not given much chance for development, except among those who exhibit the specific talents that the prevailing paradigm values so highly. Those whose talents lie in different areas are, too often, discouraged from exploring their talents. The competitive nature of our classrooms impedes the development of individual talents and aborts the potential for complementarity that is so important to positive peace. Rather than measuring students against each other in assessing their learning and their learning capacities, schools must help students to develop complementarities, ways in which their special talents can be integrated into communal capacities for striving toward the realization of common goals and shared values. If we are going to encourage the values of diversity and universal dignity, then variations in learning styles and approaches to problem resolution must be handled very differently in our classrooms. These variations must be looked upon as examples of the wonderful array of human potential and possibilities. Complementarity is, in essence, the core of much of what is practiced in cooperative learning.[10] Much relevant work is being done in this field. Cooperative learning is certainly necessary for the development of the positive attitude toward otherness that is so important to transformational education.

Consciously nurturing positive attitudes toward otherness and human differences is fundamental to developing the capacity of reconciliation. Reconciliation, in fact, might well be pursued by having the classroom be a place for the celebration of otherness and diversity, much as is the practice in peace-related, multicultural education. Instruction needs to communicate the notion that reconciling differences does not mean eliminating them. Rather, it means accommodating to differences in a constructive and positive, and a cooperative rather than a

[10] Johnson, R. and Johnson, D. (editors). *Structuring Cooperative Learning: Lesson Plans for Teachers*. Minneapolis: Interaction Books, 1984.

destructive, negative, and conflictual manner. That differences represent an exciting challenge to the integrative needs of our society, to the search for integrity and wholeness, is a concept that can be intentionally taught. Differences should be presented as the pool of possibilities for other ways of knowing and other ways of being that may help us to transform the realities of the war system. Most especially, the capacity for reconciliation must be included in education for conflict resolution. It should, perhaps, be considered both as a culminating phase and the context of conflict resolution. Not just the settlement of disputes, but the true reconciliation of the disputing parties might well be the purpose of transformative conflict resolution processes. The notion of reconciliation and the capacity to reconcile can be integrated into much of what we now teach in world studies, in comparative systems, in the analysis of conflicting ideologies, and the problems of sexism, racism, and colonialism and world community building. Reconciliation is the manifestation of wholeness, relatedness, and integrity. Teaching for the recognition of interconnection is teaching toward reconciliation.

Recovery, both as healing and as discovery, as a concept and as a capacity, might well become a major theme in our teaching of history. The notion of recovery as healing might be illustrated as we emphasize authentic moments of reconciliation in history or instances in which destructive situations and relationships were overcome or transformed by human actions. Recovery as the discovery of human capacities practiced in our past or by those of other cultures and other places in the world can open for students a significant possibility to be hopeful and constructively idealistic. If an ideal can be found actually to have existed in our own past or in the history of other cultures, then we can be hopeful of the possibility of achieving it in our own space and time.

Recovery also calls for us to open up more possibilities for imagination and spontaneity and for a sense of adventure. If we enable students to have experiences in which they look for specific capacities and conditions in their own environments, their classrooms, schools, families, communities, and within the problems with which they actually are faced, as well as within the history they are studying, they can also become aware of their own capacities for recovery. By practical application of exercises in imaging and modeling, they can become aware of their capacities not only to mend the broken world but to rebuild and transform it.

Mending and rebuilding are essential components of the capacity for reconstruction. In some ways, the capacity for reconstruction pulls together the other five capacities, for reconstruction requires reflection on what in the reality needs to be mended and what needs to be newly created, as well as evaluation to determine what needs to be discarded. It requires the responsibility to formulate the proposals and take the actions necessary to make the changes. It requires the risk of trying the new, the often untried. It requires reconciling elements that have been working against each other into a common endeavor. And it requires recovering all the skills, all the knowledge of social planning and of creating social structures that humans have used in the past to bring about new social orders. Such capacities can be exercised and learned by giving students opportunities to engage in actual social planning; planning the structure of their own relationships in the classroom;

planning the sequence and method of their own curriculum, to whatever extent it is practical; and, where possible, working with outside groups that are actively involved in planning for social change. Schools that now use their own communities as learning laboratories have shown that we already have many opportunities to teach toward the development of these and other capacities.

Finally, teaching toward reverence can be done only in an atmosphere of reverence. The classroom must be a place in which mutual human respect is the norm, in which children and learners of all ages are valued and experience is valued. Respect for the unique gifts of each individual, complemented by reverence for the common humanity we all share, and joyous wonder as the stance toward life and the Earth that sustain it, are attitudes to be manifested by teachers, nurtured in learners, and struggled for in the consciousness *of* society.

8.3 Transformational Approaches to Learning

The various pedagogical purposes just discussed are largely brought together in the capacity for reconstruction, for it is in reconstruction that we engage in the actual transformational process. As noted earlier, world order studies has developed reconstructive teaching practices appropriate to comprehensive peace education. The world order method of inquiry, although it lacks some of the important transformational components, lends itself well to the development of essential peacemaking skills and can be integrated into a process learning approach, if placed within the context of a holistically oriented pedagogy. For this or any other comprehensive mode of inquiry to be truly transformational, however, it must, as we have seen, start from a base of superordinate purposes and fundamental capacities, rather than from the present skills orientation. As an example of how such educational methods rooted in the development of specific skills might accommodate a capacity-development approach, I want to suggest a process that is, like world order inquiry, essentially reconstructive, but that, because it is more cyclical than sequential and is not confined to rational analysis, may have somewhat greater potential to be transformational. I propose this process as a means to integrate my former emphasis on skills into my emerging concern with the notion of capacity development, and I offer it here as a contribution to the ongoing exploration of appropriate and effective approaches to peace education.

The educational process that currently preoccupies me is one of phases or cycles of learning experiences, composed of activities that exercise various skills (skills that I now see as components of the more general peacemaking capacities). Each cycle begins and ends with confronting reality and moves through phases, which merge one into the other, of capturing visions, formulating images, articulating preferences, constructing models, assessing possibilities, planning policies, taking action, reflecting on and evaluating change, and, again, confronting reality.

Confronting reality is essentially the kind of process that world order methodology designates as diagnosing problems and that Freire describes as the development of critical consciousness. The skills of this phase are primarily critical skills, the kinds of interpretative and analytic operations that Brookfield, in his discussion of how learners deal with the media (1986), has referred to as 'deconstructing' and 'decoding.' A transformational process learning approach to this phase would also emphasize that the reality, and therefore the diagnosis and the interpretation, are constantly changing and are so complex that we must continually reassess the adequacy of our knowledge as we confront problems.

Because most of the present reality, viewed and assessed from the perspective of the values of peace and justice, is antithetical to human purposes and human possibilities, the imperative of change toward a preferred reality produces the next phase. The need for direction and hope brings forth the attempt to envision a transformed world. Fundamental values are identified and articulated—values of even deeper significance than the five world order values, values of the order of the affirmation of life and universal human dignity, and the three core values of stewardship, citizenship, and relationship. These are values in which the feminine capacity of sensitivity converges with the masculine values of rationality to provide a more holistic framework for formulating images of a preferred reality. This phase is one through which capacities for envisioning and speculating can be developed by the practice of the skills of meditation and reflection and by the creative and constructive uses of silence. From these visions, in which insights into fundamental and holistic value alternatives can be derived, images can be formed.

The process of formulating images develops imaginative capacities by the intentional conceptualization of alternative realities. It exercises both conceptual skills and valuational skills. As the envisioning process brings insights into an awareness of fundamental values, imaging enables us to identify and define them in descriptive terms. Defining values is necessary to articulating and determining preferences and to the formulation of policy alternatives and options for action.

In a complex and conflictual world, different value systems strenuously compete with each other. Even as more commonality of values is identified among human groups and as we seek to reconcile our values and transcend alienation, the range is still broad enough that if values are to be a unifying force in social transformation, value preferences will have to be articulated and negotiated. In the discourse that will be required to reach consensus about communal values for a transformed world society, peacemakers, if they are to communicate and defend their value preferences, will need to be skilled at reasoning and advocacy as well as at description. The articulation and selection of value preferences is the learning activity that can best be served by-and will also be most effective in developing-the capacity for conversation in which images, and preferences are described, exchanged, and advocated.

Once the common preferences and values have been agreed upon, the structural and normative changes required for transformation can be conceptualized. Constructing models will require even more refined skills of specifying, analyzing, and clarifying values. It will also require the development of skills for understanding the relationships between structures and functions in the social order, as ecologists seek to understand these aspects of the natural order. Modeling will also contribute to the development of the invention and design skills that are needed for devising procedural means to achieve human purposes. Once there is a proposed alternative structure for global society that embodies the preferred common values, or, as it is described in world order literature, a "model of a transformed international system," policy planning to bring about the new system can be undertaken. Social and political action can be pursued in the light of the vision, guided by the model.

In order to move from the present reality to the preferred reality described in the model, learners require experience with planning policies. Policy planning requires skills in choosing appropriate actions for implementing values and in integrating various action plans into a general approach to realize the intention embodied in the model. When such policy plans initiate action for change, the capacity for risk and for reconstruction are also developed. Policy planning depends upon the assessment of possibilities for change. Such assessment requires the skills of analyzing and identifying resources, as well as assessing the conflicting and common interests of the parties who need to consent to the process. This type of analysis shifts into an authentically transformational mode when learners engage in activities that allow them to develop their capacity for reconciliation, as they do when they seek to reduce conflict and enhance cooperation in using resources and pursuing of interests. Policy planning in a transformational mode brings into play the essential need to accord primacy to the interests of the entire human species as a whole and to consider as the fundamental unit of analysis the entire world system.

Assessing possibilities for change requires constant confrontation with reality and continual review of the complex and changing nature of the problems. It also provides an occasion for reminding learners of the interrelationship among different problems and the importance of basing problem-solving skills on this interrelationship. In other words, peace education should help students to confront reality, not so much problem by problem-but as a set of interrelated problems presented within the context of a 'problematique.' The interrelationship might be articulated in the curriculum as "problem clusters", clusters of issues, concerns, and conflicts that surround the major value issues, which are so interdependent in their causes and manifestations that their resolution cannot be sought in isolation. The notion of problem clusters also carries with it the notion of cycles and changes, as well as complexity. While inextricably interrelated, the problems also have their own respective dynamics and causes, and they may evolve at different rates and in different places. The cluster relationship can help students to see problems in a multidimensional, dynamic context. It can also help learners, as well as teachers, to appreciate the need to design learning experience that will extend and deepen their fundamental peacemaking capacities as they recognize that the resolution of complex, volatile issues calls for more than one set of problem-solving skills. Such an approach will help students to learn to understand change as a constant of life, to celebrate it as the means of widening human possibilities, and to direct it toward a more humane social order.

Although the phases outlined here are in need of testing and development, each of them is already manifest in some of the classrooms and other learning settings where education for peace is pursued. I know that practical methods for implementing process learning for transformation can be designed, because many of them already exist. Yet the task of elaborating specific methods and designing the necessary comprehensive curricular programs remains a major challenge to peace education.

Chapter 9
Toward a Paradigm of Peace

Retrospective Reflection on "Toward a Paradigm of Peace" (1989)

This essay is to the second phase of my peace learning what "Transformations to Peace and Survival" is to the first phase, a conceptual summary of the main concerns and essential concepts animating both my teaching and my writing during this period.

Based on a presentation on a theme assigned to me for a conference organized by Linda Forcey of The State University of New York at Binghamton, editor of the volume in which it appeared, it evidences the influences of the period's collegial conversations and co-teaching with Douglas Sloan. Sloan's cogent critique of academic reductionism and advocacy of the return to holism in teaching and problem solving reinforced the intuitions of my first phase of learning, which I brought to our exchanges. The critique shared, as well, by some peace researchers challenging political realism as the main framework for addressing issues of the international system resonated with arguments being advanced by those who were developing the critical pedagogy approach peace education, which was to become the dominant mode of the field in the first decade of the 21st century. This pedagogy formed a complement to the critique of political realism, and is certainly consistent with arguments made in "The Knowledge Industry." This essentially normative critique of "banking education" and the realist school of international relations have also been challenged in the work of Dale Snauwaert, editor of this collection. At the time this piece was written, normative holism (that which Snauwaert identifies as cosmopolitanism)—though still underdeveloped in pedagogical practice—was coming to be perceived as an appropriate framework for peace education.

While the piece calls upon feminist insights, there is little integration of some of the fundamental arguments about patriarchy made a few years earlier in Sexism and the War System, *but rather seems to set the roots of the realist war paradigm*

B.A. Reardon and D.T. Snauwaert, *Betty A. Reardon: A Pioneer in Education for Peace and Human Rights*, SpringerBriefs on Pioneers in Science and Practice 26,
DOI 10.1007/978-3-319-08967-6_9

more in primal fear. While I still could entertain notions of the actual causal significance of the emotions and mindsets that have predisposed us as a species to violence and war (The Seville Statement not withstanding), were I to make these arguments today, I would give far more attention to patriarchy as seminal to the formation of the dominant realist-reductionist paradigm.

While I continued to see the significance of the structural, I now saw, as well, the need to integrate the ecological into our pedagogical conceptualizations. The concept of living systems as possible peace paradigms appealed to some peace educators concerned with the links between environment and peace—especially concerns about the atmospheric effects of nuclear weapons testing—is likely what gave rise to the advocacy of ecological thinking, becoming central to other aspects of my work during this time. Abuse of the natural environment as an issue for study in peace education became a focus of discussion and research among peace educators. I called upon those discussions in forming the notion of "organic peace" *that features in this essay, a concept I began to substitute for "positive peace" to suggest that it was a developmental and evolutionary process not a fixed state. I complemented this notion with that of "foundational peace" in lieu of "negative peace" here referenced as the structural–institutional requirements of peace set out by Warren Wagar in another chapter of the Forcey volume. Asserting that subtraction of violence from the international security system was indeed essential to peace, but that it also involved the addition of stronger institutions for keeping the peace that would provide the foundations for the evolutionary changes of an ongoing process of organic peace.*

The concept of "ecological thinking" was later to emerge as the core of ideas and assertions developed through the Project on Ecological and Cooperative Education, a collaborative endeavor of Soviet and American peace educators brokered by Eva Nordstrom, a Norwegian educator-activist. The project produced Learning Peace: the Promise of Ecological and Cooperative Education, *a selection from which is included in this collection.*

Betty A. Reardon
March, 2014

9.1 Preface

There may be no more significant responsibility and challenge to peace studies than the engagement of learners in the search for a new paradigm of peace to replace the present paradigm of war, which delimits all thinking and determines our culture.[1] That search is the great intellectual adventure of our time. This chapter is intended as an initial inquiry into that search.

[1] This text was first published as: Reardon, Betty A. "Toward a Paradigm of Peace." In *Peace: Meanings, Politics, Strategies*, edited by Linda Rennie Farcey. New York: Praeger, 1989. The permission to republish this text was granted by Ms. Tracy Ayres, International Sales Support Coordinator, ABC-CLIO, St. Barbara, CA, on 17 March 2014.

Three convictions are central to the assertions and arguments to be made. First, there is the fundamental feminist conviction that there is no essential separation between the personal and the political. Nor is there a legitimate basis to separate means from ends. Second, there is the conviction that processes and methods are equally as important as, sometimes more important than, goals. The educational implications of the second conviction produce the third conviction that learning modes must be organically, systematically, intentionally, and ethically related to instructional goals. Both peace studies and peace education will be used in this discussion of paradigm change. The former is used to focus on the substance or subject matter of the field; the latter on the learning and the educational methods.

9.2 Taming the Lion Within

The perspectives and parameters of my arguments, set forth by the title Linda Forcey has assigned to this chapter, are totally congenial to these convictions. As she points out in her introduction, paradigms are perhaps the most important conceptual tools we have and they not only constrain and influence the way we think but also the way we behave, the way we organize our societies, and conduct virtually all human affairs. As a feminist peace educator, I argue that the present paradigm is at once the source and the product of a war system that, for generations, has been transferred from our minds into our experience and from our experience back into our minds. We engage in war and violence because we think violently in images and metaphors of war. If we are to experience an authentic, fulsome peace, we must think peace. If we are to think peace, we need a paradigm of peace. We need not only a vision of peace but also the concepts, the language, the images, and the metaphors that will comprise a functioning and equally vigorous paradigm *of* peace, so that from it we can construct paradigms *for* peace, those explicit conceptual and political models around which we can organize a peaceful society in which we can conduct human affairs in a more humane manner. Searching for and speculating on such language, images, and metaphors is the stuff of which peace studies should be made. These concepts should be about transcending the war paradigm to enable us to think in terms of a peace system. Peace, then, of necessity, must be conceived in dynamic, active, challenging terms. It must provide for us all of that which we have sought in and through war. It must become the means by which human beings strive for the highest achievements, their most transcendent goals.

'Toward,' the word with which Forcey began the title, is most important for the purposes of this chapter, for it is a word which connotes process and action as well as thought. It is the notion 'toward' which helps to inform these reflections with the sense of dynamism that is so essential to bringing forth a vigorous peace paradigm that can instill vibrant peace images, images of new forms of power and accommodation that contrast sharply with the present concepts of peace and how it might be achieved.

The shapes and tones of such images are vividly expressed in a story by a naval chaplain, and fellow peace educator, about a Biblical zoo in Israel, in which the various animals mentioned in the Bible were arranged in tableaux, or Biblical images. The most problematic image was the lion lying down with the lamb. The zookeeper was working on this particular tableau during the time when Henry Kissinger was pursuing shuttle diplomacy for peace in the Middle East. "If anyone could give me the secret of how this might be done," thought the zoo-keeper, "it will be Henry Kissinger." Sure enough, the very day after he had the good fortune to encounter Dr. Kissinger, the lion and lamb were lying down together. The next day, they were lying down together, and the next day and the next. One frequenter of the zoo was determined to discover the secret, and when pressed, the zookeeper did confess that the way to accomplish this was to put in a new lamb every morning. The zoo-keeper had considered a number of alternative structural arrangements to make this possible, but in the end, because the tableau depended on the behavior both of the lion and the lamb he took a pragmatic political solution. The sacrificial lamb is very much a part of our politics and our paradigm, an image and symbol of peace through propitiation. It is suggested that the only way the lion and lamb image could be realized without continuing to incur a very high cost on the part of the lambs, would be a profound personal change and major paradigm shift, mainly on the part of the lion. In some respects, that is what we must be about in our attempts to construct a peace paradigm. We are about taming the lion in all of us.

Among the changes that have to be made for the achievement of such a shift, the most significant ones are within ourselves. The way which we move toward these inner changes, the way in which we envision and struggle for peace and try to construct that new paradigm, is the most essential means through which we will be enabled to make the larger structural changes required for a peace system. Thus the journey is really more personally meaningful to us than the destination. What we are about, on a day-to-day basis, is actually how we change paradigms. We must change ourselves and our immediate realities and relationships if we are to change our social structures and our patterns of thought. We've known this for a long time. Shakespeare told us that the fault is not "in our stars, but in ourselves." St. Augustine reflecting on his own journey wrote, "I have sought thee outside and thou were within." His was a long and tortuous route to a new paradigm. A few decades ago, the Cunard Line tried to convince us that in traveling to Europe "getting there was half the fun." However, there are very few passenger ships that cross the Atlantic these days. We prefer to take the rapid route, by plane, to get to our destination incurring jet lag and any other negative consequences. Paradigm changing is not only a difficult inner struggle, but also a time-consuming journey, so we had better be ready for a long voyage on turbulent waters.

Long voyages on turbulent waters require patience, steadiness, and strong stomachs. The journey toward a new peace paradigm is not likely to be undertaken by the faint of heart. Those who still fear sea monsters, and tremble at the possibility of sailing over the edge of the present paradigm, will certainly not board the good ship "Peace Studies" on its exploratory ventures. We know full well that few came to wave us off and wish us well in those early years when we first hoisted anchor with but a few courses, and only two programs; when we still purported to know our destination. Indeed, the queen did not pawn her jewelry, nor did foundations offer portions of their coffers to finance the earlier voyages to peacemaking knowledge. Yet, as the statistics indicate, the fleet has grown and we have the feeling that more are now following our route as we traverse the familiar waters of academe in search of a truly new world. If we are to entice even more educators and students into this search for new horizons of thought, the exploration of the terra incognita of a peace paradigm, we will need the equivalents of the maps of the Indies, the products of the imaginations of early global explorers who captured the minds of seamen and monarchs. For those we would have join us on the journey, we need to evoke images of what the new world might be like, and in which directions we should sail to reach it. World order scholars would say we need models of peace systems and transition strategies for the change from a war system to a peace system. We need an image which may well be as Utopian as the lamb lying with the lion, but we also need specific and particular approaches to the learnings, political movements, and personal behaviors which will take us toward our vision.

Personal and political changes are very much interrelated and both will be the product of learning processes. It is for this reason that peace studies is central to the task, not only of paradigm change, but also in the achievement of structural and systems change in the global order. Peace studies must take on the task of nurturing new modes of thought. We cannot achieve a change unless we can think it. And we cannot rally others to support the changes if we cannot communicate our visions of change to them. Thus we need not only images and maps but also effective and appropriate language. If both the lion and the lamb are to undergo the personal changes that would make a new relationship possible, first they must be able to communicate the changes to each other.

Reflect for a moment on the language we tend to use most, on the shades of violence and combat which color so much of our discourse. Such language even creeps into the literature and discussions of peace studies and the peace movement. We speak of "fighting for peace" and "ammunition for peace makers." Feminist peace research is no exception. I received an interview questionnaire which included the following questions, "What has sustained you so long on the frontlines of the feminist battle?" We need only to monitor ourselves and others for less than a day to see how such language pervades so many of our exchanges, and includes not only the substance of the subject at hand, but also the standards of the war system which we salute constantly in our choice of words and metaphors. Our language and our metaphors reveal just how we think more clearly than our arguments and proposals.

Our thinking, thus, is frighteningly combative and antagonistic, a fact which has been at the core of much feminist criticism of our culture and scholarship. If we do wish to journey toward the peace paradigm, would it not at least be worth the attempt to change our language as a step toward changing our thinking? Many have conceded the significance of language as the reinforcement of racism and sexism. Can we not admit the same of militarism and the war system? Would it not be more productive to try consciously to substitute alternatives for combative and militaristic terms? We might at least become more aware of the concepts that influence our thinking.

For example, could we use ‘struggle’ instead of ‘fight’? ‘Struggle’ does not necessarily require an enemy or adversary, or even an opponent, as does ‘fight.’ It connotes vigorous effort to transcend an obstacle, resolve a problem, or bring forth a desired end, none of which calls for harm of others. Indeed, we need to think more in terms of avoidance of harm as a primary criterion for behaviors and policies. To do so is hardly a full commitment to nonviolence, but it can help us become aware of how violence evolves and how it might be limited, if not eliminated. In lieu of ‘ammunition,’ we can substitute ‘nourishment’ or ‘food’ or ‘fuel,’ something that can convey a source of energy for struggle without carrying along the concept of injury and death. I prefer to think of my involvement in the women’s movement as tilling the fields of feminism, attempting to cultivate more humane attitudes and social structures. Can we not think in terms of tools and tasks instead of weapons and battles, nourishment and cultivation in lieu of artillery and victory? As we change our words, we will also begin to change our images, and our metaphors may be transformed as we move from the language of war and death toward one of peace and life. If we speak differently, we can become more intentional about changing how we think and teach.

Using images of cultivation in lieu of those of battle to connote energy concentrated toward the fulfillment of a purpose comes very close to common images of peace often articulated in drawings by children, or the pastoral paintings and poetry of some of the great artists of all cultures and languages. Serious peace people, educators, researchers, and activists, especially the “hard heads” among us, have often cited this type of imagery as evidence of our inability to think in as complex and concrete terms about peace, as about war. This assessment is questionable, although the fundamental assertion of this volume is that our education does not prepare us in any systematic way to think about peace. It is precisely for this reason that these types of images are so significant, for they do demonstrate our capacity to image peace. The thinking which rejects the pastoral as a practical or useful image of peace is the same kind of thinking which permits us, in a manifestation of the war system, to abuse the environment, which is even more threatening to life on this planet than nuclear weapons and war. That is the same kind of thinking which has, in fact, produced weapons of mass destruction and reinforced the war system. This argument, too, has been a major assertion of feminist critiques of peace research and peace education.[2]

9.3 Peace as a Dynamic, Organic Process

There are several assumptions and assertions that point to peace as a dynamic, organized process. These assertions pertain to notions of peace, concepts of what peace education is and should do, and concerns about the way the present paradigm impedes the purposes of peace education, and is a virtually insurmountable

[2] Brock-Utne, Birgit. *A Feminist Perspective on Peace Education.* New York: Praeger, 1986.

barrier to peace. So long as this paradigm prevails there will be no authentic peace. We may cease to experience as much organized hostility and armed conflict as we presently do but at best, any peace we experience will be truly negative, for it will be nothing more than the kind of peace which oppresses not only women, as Christine Sylvester points out, but any who are vulnerable, less powerful or 'lamblike.' Such is indeed the case in areas of the world where there is no serious armed conflict, but structural violence is most evident. We might cite Brazil or Korea as examples of such peace.

There are perhaps as many reasonable and useful definitions of peace as there are approaches to peace studies. My own definitions have become more open, wider in scope-an organic concept of peace. As Warren Wagar asserts, "peace is it." If we define peace in its fullest, most varied sense, it reflects pastoral images. If we need to think of peace in structural or political terms, then we may say that peace results from social and economic structures, and public policies which sustain and enhance life; hence, the notion of avoiding harm and injury as primary policy making criteria. Admittedly, these are feminine notions, and to some degree 'feminist.' While such notions are, of course, repressed by patriarchy, they are in no way exclusively female. We need only look to some of the great religious and ethical traditions which were articulated to the world by such male prophets as Gautama Buddha, Jesus Christ, and Mohandas Gandhi to see that these notions are in fact, human universals, only now beginning to be seen as new sources of actual as well as spiritual power, power in the positive life enhancing sense of the capacity to realize values and achieve goals. This is in essence the energy source which 'inspires' (i.e., breathes life into nonviolence as social action and political mode, demonstrating quite clearly that authentic or 'organic' peace is an active, dynamic state).

Organic peace is a source of energy for development, the breath of life which impels action. It does not exclude conflict, as is well argued by Dean Pruitt, but it governs and guides it to become a source of growth and change rather than harm and destruction. Organic peace is, above all else complex, as are life processes in general. It is not so easily modeled in static structural terms. While clearly we need the new structures, institutions, and systems emphasized by Warran Wagar, the structural is but one, quite limited dimension of organic peace, which comprises all those social processes and personal behaviors which facilitate change, growth, and fulfillment. Should we achieve peace by the twenty-first century, it will not be the same peace that prevails in the twenty-second century, else it will not be peace. As Tacitus instructed us, peace does not bloom in a desert. Deserts have limited forms of life, fewer varieties of flora and fauna than other natural environments, the richest being the rain forest which, literally, "is crawling with life." The most complex environments are the richest in diversity and are full of life. Yet we have confronted these natural phenomena as we have the questions of human social order. We reduce everything to its simplest, most manageable form. We seek to control and manage life rather than to live it. We have, in fact, not developed that far emotionally from our forebears who cowered in caves in fear of natural phenomena and other life forms. While the sophistication of our means of subjection has become greater with the evolution of modern science, human attempts to subdue, control, and simplify as a means to security may be as old as the species. It is no coincidence that in the process of seeking security through control, we have destroyed many life forms and are to the point of cutting off the very air we breathe through the destruction of the rain forest.

Critics of the present paradigm, such as Douglas Sloan and Jeremy Rifkin, attribute much of the reductionist character of contemporary thought to the initial intellectual separation of philosophy from the sciences.[3] Other critics, particularly of the sciences, see the drive for control of nature as patriarchal, and a primary cause of the evolution of a dehumanized technology which produces nuclear weapons and isolates genetic material.[4] However, this drive would seem to be far more deeply rooted in our history and our psyches than in Cartesian science or even patriarchy. It may be as much a cause as a consequence of patriarchy, other forms of repression, militarism and war itself.

The linear thinking which has been the dominant mode of thinking not only in the sciences but also in all of academe, is the most serious impediment to us who seek peace through education. Clearly, within the present paradigm, the primacy of a negative peace notion could be replaced with that of a positive one, much less one of organic peace. So long as this and the present forms of empiricism are our dominant intellectual values, we will not be effective learners about, or partners with, the complexity that is life. While some physicists and biologists are revealing startling notions about apparent randomness reflects a beautifully choreographed pattern of interrelationships and repetitions from the smallest to the largest bits of creation,[5] and proposing through the Gaia hypothesis that the Earth itself is living system, such concepts are by and large subjected to the rational, positivist version of the Galilean syndrome. If it is not revealed in our present scientific scriptures, nor pontificated by the highest authority, it is not true. This circumstance reflects the notion of fixed and limited truth, which cries for the kind of questioning advocated here, in order to open the windows of the frequently stifling ivory towers of academe to the air of new possibilities. The inquiry of peace studies should be based on queries mutually derived by instructor and student, each posing problems calling for various alternative responses, rather than predefined questions by the instructor, calling for predetermined answers from students.

9.4 Peace Education as Life Enhancement

What more comprehensive definition of peace education could we offer than learning to learn about, and functioning in and with complexity, so as to enhance the richness and diversity of life? Such a definition would apply to, and provide

---

[3] See Sloan, Douglas. *Insight, Imagination, and the Emancipation of the Modern Mind*. Westport, CT Greenwood, 1984; Rifkin, Jeremy. *Declaration of a Heretic*. Boston: Routledge & Kegan Paul, 1985.

[4] See Easlea, Brian. *Fathering the Unthinkable: Masculinity, Scientists and the Nuclear Arms Race*. London: Pluto Press, 1983.

[5] See Gleick, James. *Chaos: Making a New Science*. New York: Viking, 1987.

deeper purpose for cross-cultural education, conflict studies, world order modeling, human rights education, environmental studies, and most of the themes and subjects which comprise the broad and varied field of peace studies. Profound changes in present educational systems and methods are essential if we are to move toward a new paradigm. For starters, it would help us to comprehend more fully the significance of pastoral images of peace. We should see them as pictures of life in process, of cultivation, of intentional enhancement of life, and, hopefully, of diversity. The reductionist thinking which permits us to dismiss the importance of the loss of some species because they are, but rare insects for which we have no apparent use, is the same mode of thought that prevents us from seeing descriptions of peace in the drawings of children, whose imaginations have not yet been imprisoned by "fixed, demonstrable truth." With such a start, we might open and develop our capacities for imaging, which Elise Boulding sees as necessary to inspire us with viable concepts of peace. Imaging is a skill which can and should be developed through peace education.[6] To develop skill, however, is but a means of directing and giving communicable form to a fundamental capacity of the human imagination. These imaging capacities must be freed by a liberating form of education based on authentic inquiry, rather than the probe for predetermined answers. Only through such open authentic inquiry as described by Forcey, with students and teachers exploring the terra incognita of peace together, can education make a significant contribution to the formulation of a new paradigm.

Thus, a primary method of peace education should be authentic inquiry. Such a method would be derived from the posing of queries, which would perform three functions: Reveal apparent obstacles to peace, open avenues for exploring the causes of and alternative approaches to transcending the obstacles, and assess the alternatives according to criteria which would result in the most life-enhancing choice. The exploration would be conducted to maximize the possibilities for reflection, creativity, and full participation of all engaged in the study. It would reward rather than impede speculation, the most open form of inquiry, and the most encouraging form of creativity. It would preclude the premature narrowing of the broad creative process of speculation into the limitations of too few scientifically testable hypotheses. It would provide space for, and honor the need for, reticence and silence as a sometimes necessary environment for reflection-that deeper inner questioning that is essential to personal change and evolution on which the political and social changes of a new paradigm will depend. Without such reflection, learning cannot be fully integrated into the thinking and world views that condition our personal interpretations and assessments, from which we make the choices that lead us to action. An emphasis on integration reflects the notion of education and learning as part of the seeking of a wholeness that is the authentic meaning of integrity, and the essence of what has been most trampled upon by the reductionist nature of the present paradigm. Peace education, if not all

[6] See Reardon, Betty A. *Comprehensive Peace Education*. New York: Teachers College Press, 1988.

education, should be intentionally designed to contribute to the search for integrity by individual learners and the whole society.

Integration of diversity in a mutually enhancing relationship is a fundamental process for maintaining life and for achieving peace. Our present emphasis on analysis has encouraged separation at the cost of integration. The reluctance to see things holistically also may well contribute to the current alienation of individuals and to the disintegration of society. Rather than try to heal and reintegrate it, we have attempted to simplify it to better manage and control the conditions of separation and alienation, conditions largely responsible for the high degree of personal and social insecurity from which we suffer. This insecurity has, in fact, alienated us from life. We shun and fear difference, diversity, and complexity because we have not learned to live with them, and in the process we have shunned life itself. Peace requires the embracing of life in all its problematic fullness.

9.5 Metaphors of Birth and Life

We need also to devise a life-affirming metaphor to replace the death- prone, war metaphor of destructive struggle that so conditions our language, our thought, and our learning. Since we want a set of images for positive struggle, the most likely new metaphor of life would be one centered on the origins, development, and maturation of living things-one based on conception, labor, birth, and parenting.

Were we to think in terms as all-encompassing as conception, gestation, labor, birth, nurturing, parenting, education, and caring, we would have a whole new way of thinking about the human experience and social organization. We might think of the desired paradigm shift as one which moves us from a warring society to a parenting or caring society, in which all adults parent the young and care for the vulnerable. Care of the vulnerable, like avoidance of harm, is characteristic of both good parenting and a peaceful society. Our thinking would tend to focus on the long-range health and welfare of living beings, and on the enhancement of life. We might begin to organize intentionally planned learning toward development of the capacity to care, thus embracing one of the most fundamental purposes of peace education- an overarching concept for a comprehensive education for justice and peace, and for humane and fulfilling human relationships.

The concept and value of care as a core notion of peace education illuminates the inextricable interweaving of the personal and the political. As a primary learning goal, care brings into focus the essential significance of diversity and complexity. It makes it possible to sustain the struggle for integrity in the apparent chaos in which the emerging patterns and intricate order of actual relationships give us a glimpse of the multiple possibilities for a transformed reality and a paradigm of peace. In such a paradigm, peace and life would be perceived as the products of a diverse, dynamic, continuous set of processes of change in a magnitude of aesthetic quality we have only begun to grasp. If we can learn to become creative participants rather than destructive controllers of these life processes, we may yet reach a truly new world.

9.6 Learning: Merger of Personal and Political, Means and Ends

Learning is primarily personal, inward, and interactive. We learn as we use our paradigms (our world views, assumptions, and values) to assess and integrate our experiences. We learn in relationship to experience, to systems, and to persons. Mostly, we learn from and with each other. Authentic learning is a complex and sometimes chaotic process. Our notion of cognitive dissonance as a primary instigator of learning, is evidence to support the argument of authentic learning as far more varied than the linear processes on which most present instruction is based. Learning, like life, is an inter-relational and holistic process. Thus, methodology cannot be separated from purpose. If we seek truly new and transformed realities, we need to construct courses and learning experiences on genuine holistic inquiry and speculation. Social and political processes, if they are to be viable and effective, must also be holistic and integrative, recognizing that society, comprised of persons and politics is an aggregate of personal choices. If politics are to be altered to change the society, then people must also change. Personal change, if it is to be sustained over time, and not subject to repeated manipulation of outside forces, must be autonomously and intentionally embraced and integrated into the self. Just as a value consensus within a society is a necessary prerequisite to viable political and structural change, only change in people can change the culture which 'cultivates' the values of the society.

With Prof. Willard Jacobson at Teachers College Library 1986. *Source* Personal photo collection of the author

Clearly, peace studies must begin to pursue holism as the framework, process as the primary method, and peace in its widest sense as the goal, if it is to energize the intellectual transformation necessary to a paradigm of peace. The lion can lie down with the lamb in a nurturing rather than devouring relationship, only if each is able to transform its reality by transforming itself. These transformations are what peace studies should be about.

Chapter 10
Learning Our Way to a Human Future

Retrospective Reflection on "Learning Our Way to a Human Future" (1994)

The Project on Ecological and Cooperative Education (PEACE), which produced this essay, was pivotal in the evolution of my approach to peace education, inspiring conceptual developments that impelled me more than ever toward a professional consciousness of the significance of process, a wider perspective and a new conceptualization for the diagnosis of the peace problematic. And, most especially, because of the participants in the project and the relationships we developed.

Conceptually the notion of anthropomorphism lead me to identify ecological thinking as an alternative and complement to the structural thinking that had been for long so paramount in the lenses through which I perceived the central problematic of peace, violence. This concept, introduced to the project by Soviet science educator, Sergei Polozov, more than any other idea, illuminated the bias of the human perspective on the environment as patriarchalism, another concept entering my work at this time, the masculine bias in most social, political and academic thinking. I became even more convinced that central to all problems of peace were our ways of thinking; and, therefore, the primary task of peace education was to bring about changes in modes of thought more conducive to constructively addressing the goals of global transformation. That transformation had to be addressed within the widest frame of the whole living system of Planet Earth. This belief was articulated in advocating "ecological thinking" as explicated in this piece, a perspective wider even than the holism I had learned from Douglas Sloan.

B.A. Reardon and D.T. Snauwaert, *Betty A. Reardon: A Pioneer in Education for Peace and Human Rights*, SpringerBriefs on Pioneers in Science and Practice 26,
DOI 10.1007/978-3-319-08967-6_10

At IIPE 1989 at Teachers College with in *first row* Eva and Odd Nordland (Norway), Willard Jacobson (*second row*, second from *right*), and Soviet authors of essays in Learning Peace. Foreground, Sr. Kathleen Kanet, Network for Peace through Dialogue

PEACE in which Willard Jacobson and I were the American participants, as initiated by the Norwegian peace educator, Eva Nordstrom, was a fulfillment of a possibility that Willard pursued through most the years we had been working together on the development of peace education at Teachers College, Columbia University to undertake cooperation in peace education with Soviet colleagues. In the midst of the Cold War and its nuclear arms race, this may have been "the impossible dream," but we continued to pursue it, and it turned out not to be so quixotic after all. One of the few advantages available to us from the university base was the 'legitimacy' it gave us over and above some NGOs, such as Educators for Social Responsibility, who were also making contacts with Soviet educators as part of the movement of "citizen diplomacy." Beginning as the project did shortly before Perestroika, our academic base helped Eva in her invitation to the Soviet Ministry of Education to send representatives to the meeting at which the Project would be conceptualized.

Among those sent by the Ministry was Dr. Valentina Mitina. Neither of us knowing who the representatives from the other "super power" would be, we were both delighted to encounter each other in Oslo. We had met earlier at a UNESCO organized consultation in Turin, Italy, where we were pushed into collaboration at the session somewhat by the mistrust other participants had of both our respective nations, but more by recognizing in each other an educator dedicated to the same ends, educating the young to live rewarding lives in just societies in a peaceful world. Even then we had spoken of the possibility of a cooperative peace education curriculum project, while recognizing the political obstacles that could be posed by our respective governments. Eva's focus on the common environmental problems all nations faced seemed to vault that barrier. PEACE enabled us to work together and to become close personal friends. Her death in 1994 was a great personal loss as well as a blow to the project and the field, as was that of Willard Jacobson a few years later. Both had profound influence on my professional development and both enriched my life and personal development. Willard and I never agreed on approaches to the arms race; and Valentina's political formation was quite different from mine. The difference taught me first hand in my own life the great learning benefits and the possibilities for individual human enrichment offered by diversity.

Some of what PEACE envisioned has become integrated into peace education through environmental educators who perceive the links between abuse of the environment and armed conflict, and by peace educators who believe that ecological violence should be a significant entry in any general typology of violence. In Sexism and the War System *I called attention to the parallels between the crime of rape and the crimes against the integrity of the Earth, noting both as forms of violence clearly related one to the other as evident in the feminine terminology used to describe our planet.*

Again as was the case with some other initiatives that produced the essays in this collection, our visions were never fully realized, falling victim not only to the loss of key participants but also to a complete waste of the transformational opportunities for peace described in this essay. The power structure of the war system continues to push back against those ideas and initiatives that most challenge it. Though it may seem to be financial or institutional problems that impede us, I believe the obstacles actually lie in the system and the thinking that sustains it. Grasping and confronting those impediments continue to be the main challenges of peace education.

Betty A. Reardon
March, 2014

10.1 Introduction

The ideas and arguments set forth in this essay summarize a variety of learning experiences, each of which has contributed to broadening the conceptual framework within which I view peace education, and each of which has moved me from a systemic structural view of the world and education to a process, organic view.[1]

---

[1] This chapter was first published in: Betty A. Reardon and Eva Nordland, eds. *Learning Peace: The Promise of Ecological and Cooperative Education*. Albany, NY: State University of New York Press, 1994. Permission to republish this text was granted by Ms. Carla Shute of the State University of New York Press (SUNY) on 12 March 2014.

Many of us now consider our work in terms of pre- and post-*ecological consciousness.*

For me my work with the Project on Ecological and Cooperative Education (PEACE) was, and for the moment continues to be, an experience of the awakening of ecological consciousness. Certainly I had factored the global environment into the diagnosis of problems threatening human survival when considering the content to be addressed by peace education. However, although even in the earliest stages of my work in the field I applied a global perspective and a systematic analysis of world society, the anthropocentrism pointed out by Sergei Polozov was, I believe, for many years an unrecognized barrier to the prescriptive tasks I advocated as an element of peace education. I have long believed that the prime requisite of being an effective peace educator is to be, as well, an intentional learner.

Workshop in Ramallah, Palestine, organized by the Israeli-Palestine Center for Research and Information, with (on Betty's *right*) Louise Diamond, co-facilitator, 1998. *Source* Personal photo collection of the author

My years of work in developing theoretical bases for peace education and in the design and execution of a graduate program in the field have reinforced this belief. My deepening acquaintance with ecological thinking has been an exceptionally rich learning experience.

It has helped me in achieving a paradigm shift that when applied to a global perspective can best be described as a shift from a "spaceship Earth" view of the world as a mechanical (if unified, closed-system) structure controlled by human society, to a *Gaia* view of Earth as a living organism with human society as a living subsystem within the whole, responsible but certainly not in control. That, it seems to me, is a learning to be further pursued and disseminated.

10.2 The New Moment: The Educational Challenges and Opportunities

To those of us who have been involved in peace education for several decades, the last years of the twentieth century have been the most surprising, frequently the most hopeful, sometimes depressing, and unfailingly the most challenging.

Over the years, while some have tried to take a positive stance and educate *for peace*, most have found it necessary to spend much of our efforts to educate *against war* in order to define and describe the actual and potential consequences of weapons and violence, often to the detriment of education about other global issues and problems. Rarely were our students' minds opened to the real and potential possibilities of peace. Consequently we all know a good deal more about what we don't want and how it is affecting the quality of our lives than about what we do want and how our lives can be directed toward achieving it. We in North America watched in surprise and awe as the peoples of Eastern Europe took action to shake off what they did not want; and we reflected, in the same confusion and uncertainty as our European brothers and sisters, on what should replace it, with little or no notion of how to deal with the problems and conflicts of the transition from one system to another.

Many of us believe that neither of the economic or political systems that dominated the twentieth century are truly adequate to a viable, just, and attainable common future, but little has been done to develop authentic alternatives.

The challenge then for all, but most especially for educators, whose main social responsibility is preparing people for the future, is to envision such an alternative and to devise the educational means to learn to achieve it.

10.3 What the New Moment Means for Learning: The Responsibilities of Educators

In virtually every nation of the world, and most certainly in the industrial nations of the North, contemporary educational systems have been organized around two major purposes: keeping the respective system or nation ahead of its competitors, and keeping the managers of the system in power by popular support or repression or a combination thereof. None have fully succeeded. While the early nineties saw the Western "industrial democracies" engaging in an orgy of self-congratulation on the defeat of Communism in the "former socialist states," the truth is that both systems had exhausted their capacities to maintain a limitless arms race, manipulate the destinies of the rest of the world, and at the same time satisfy the authentic needs of their own peoples.

All the industrial states, both capitalist and socialist—even intensely rich Western Europe and Japan—emerged from the period of the cold war with larger portions of their populations in poverty than was to be admitted freely. They also experienced spiritual poverty, with unprecedented levels of alienation, widespread feelings of emptiness and meaninglessness. Among all income groups worldwide, educational systems were in deep crisis.

What was most disturbing about the crisis in education was that it was almost universally misinterpreted as a cause of, rather than as the consequence of, the inadequacies of the general social systems All societies, particularly in the industrialized democracies, failed to acknowledge that the schools were but a reflection of the failure of the entire society to recognize that it was not focusing its learning processes on what people most needed to know and understand, and not taking into account the severe alienation and despair among the most deprived classes who depended upon public schooling.

Once again schools were scapegoated for larger societal shortcomings. Unlike their socialist counterparts, they did not quickly recognize that they, too, were in a new moment the task of calling it to their attention fell largely upon peace educators.

What peace educators saw in the new moment was an opportunity to at last come to terms with the shortcomings of the society, to take a leaf from the Eastern European book and assess needs and possibilities in a new light. Most especially, I would argue, the major need was to come to terms with the damage done to others in the world system and to the most vulnerable m their own societies by the obsessive competition with the other industrial states, particularly those aspects of competition manifest in the cold war. While the decade opened with a new awareness of the fragility and abuse of the natural environment, the degree to which that fragility was exacerbated and the abuses allowed to run rampant through the behaviors of the agents carrying out the economic, ideological, and strategic competitions of the international system was hardly recognized by either the environmental or the peace movements, or even by the budding ecological education movement. Coming to terms with the environmental and human rights abuses of the cold war thus was taken up as a learning task of PEACE.

Learning to understand the nature and consequences of the abuses, to take responsibility for them, and to find alternative possibilities for education, personal behaviors, and public policies became a central concern of the project. The project tries to focus on positive alternatives, not just on what it means to be *against war*, injustice, human rights violations, and environmental deterioration, but what it is to be *for* peace, justice, the realization of human rights, and ecological balance. The task it assumes is to give concrete form to a peaceful, just society that respects human rights and protects the environment, and to educate people to achieve and maintain a global social order of such form.

We seek to move educational inquiry from the questions of what are the dangers of war, injustice, and environmental abuse, and how they can be avoided, to what are the advantages and forms of peace, justice, and ecological balance, how they are inextricably interrelated, and how they can be achieved and maintained—a seemingly simple but profoundly transformative shift of learning focus.

10.4 The Particular Responsibilities of the United States and the Countries of the Former USSR for New Learning

If we conceptualize the human species as a family and this century as a generation, we can begin to understand the human and historic consequences of nearly half a century of superpower competition. The human family has been through a painful and devastating experience not unlike that suffered by families parented by addicts (to alcohol, drugs, gambling, or whatever). The family resources are laid waste by the addiction while the family members suffer from lack of care and mutually enhancing, supportive relationships. The co-addictive parents engage in mutual recrimination while the children and other family members must endure the atmosphere of tension, of potential and actual violence. The parents abuse their power, abjure their responsibility, and seek to impose their own will on each other and all others in the family system without regard to the immediate or the long-range consequences.

Such behavior usually continues unless there is a crisis or an intentional intervention by those affected. In terms used to describe approaches to therapy in addictive families, "an intervention" is an occasion on which those suffering "the fallout" from the addiction gather around the addicted member or members and describe in full and frank detail their own suffering while acknowledging the value and potential of the addicted ones. In essence the message is this: "Look, we are all one family, part of one system, we have received much from you that is positive and nurturing (i e., economic support, defense, etc.), but your addiction is inflicting damage on us we can no longer bear. We may not survive as a family, or group of friends or associates. You have to stop if you want to maintain a relationship with us."

The Soviet and Eastern European crises, the emerging integration of the European Community, the multiple continued regional conflicts such as that which produced the war in the Persian Gulf, and the growing recognition of the environmental crisis—together these offer the opportunity for such an intervention. Some peace educators seized the opportunity. The participants of PEACE were among them.

The intervention message to the former adversaries of the cold war (and perhaps to the newly emerging power constellation first demonstrated by the Gulf War) from such peace educators is this: "Look, you must take mutual and respective responsibility for what you have done to the world You have to reconstruct your relationship to each other and to the rest of the world. You are no longer able to control either your own people or other peoples. You and other great techno-industrial powers must construct a relationship that is based on the values of planetary healthy and an ecologically viable system that attempts to meet human needs equitably and respects human rights universally. You have much learning to do, but you have rich and varied learning resources. You can learn from each other, and from other peoples, particularly the primal peoples who have lived in harmony with the Earth. Above all, much can be learned from Earth itself, particularly about balance, restraint, and renewal. You must acknowledge now that you must be learners from rather than instructors to the world."

10.5 An Emerging Paradigm for Security and Community: Learning for a Transformed World Order

The new moment provides an unprecedented opportunity for the two former superpowers that emerged from World War II to bring to actuality many of the values that informed that particular struggle and that formed the basis of a vision of the world the peoples of the two nations had embraced together as their soldiers embraced each other at the Elbe, a vision they sought to enact in the founding of the United Nations. We now have an opportunity to view the four decades from 1949 to 1989 as an aberrant interruption in the history of humankind on the brink of recognizing and experiencing its fundamental unity. The human liberty of any people cannot be achieved within the context of a debased environment or reduced quality of life for other humans. While we were preoccupied with our competition with each other, we stepped up without reflection our common competition with the Earth, and equally carelessly ignored the consequent impoverishment and oppression of our brothers and sisters in the South.

Thus we are challenged by still another common learning task, a radical restructuring of our relationship not only to the planet, but also to the majority of those who inhabit her, the poor of the Earth. As nations we need to learn our responsibility to world society; as educators we need to prepare our students to carry social responsibility at all levels, from local to global. Social responsibility requires that we recognize ourselves as members of a world community held together by concepts of common security, liberty, and humanity.

The peace movement has indeed been proven correct in its insistence that the arms race, the major dynamic of the cold war, has eroded security, and that true security involves much more than the capacity to defend against or prevent military aggression. Authentic security lies in the welfare and dignity of people, in relationships that reduce conflict and prevent violence, and in a viable environment that can sustain life on this planet. The task of building a world community involves the design and adoption of a security system that gives equal attention to all four elements of authentic, viable human security, environment, justice, dignity, and nonviolence.

The attention of research centers, educational institutions, and all other learning groups must be turned to learning to design and achieve such a global system. In short, we need to learn how to transform the institutions and relationships that comprise a world of violence, inequity, and environmental devastation.

10.6 The Project on Ecological and Cooperative Education: A Response to the Challenge of Learning to Transform

PEACE emerged out of the common recognition of a small group of Norwegian, Russian (later also Ukrainian), and American educators of the urgent need for this kind of learning. The essays in this book, our first reflections on the task, are one step toward developing appropriate common learning processes centered on the transformational tasks as we mutually define them.

We worked together first in Norway to define the problems and approaches; then in New York to share practical workshops in specific educational methods; and later in Moscow to elaborate the plans for this volume. We continue to work together to move the learning process forward by learning from and with each other and, where possible, from and with educators from other parts of the world. While we seek to define common approaches and concepts, we also recognize and try to fulfill the unique and special responsibilities of our respective societies.

10.7 The Task and the Goal for the North American Educational Community

If American peace educators designate a healthy environment, economic equity, human rights, and nonviolent conflict resolution as the major needs for a transformed world order, then we must accept some very challenging goals for the American educational community. These challenges arise in large part from the role the United States has played m the creation of problems of environmental degradation, global poverty, human rights abuses, and armed conflict.

Our schools should study the nature of the resource exploitation and the flow of primary resources from South to North that gave rise to American affluence at the cost of increased poverty for many in the developing countries, a consequence of terms of trade negotiated to the advantage of "Northern industrialized" over "Southern developing" nations.

A curriculum on the consequences of the cold war should certainly include a global review of the history and condition of human rights concepts and abuses, including consideration of American support for policies that resulted in such abuses as apartheid and the military repression of liberation movements. And study of the history of armed conflict in the twentieth century must offer the facts on the technological achievements of the American defense industry that fueled the cycles of the arms race, as well as American interventions in other nations. Such interventions were often viewed as serious threats to world peace by allies as well as adversaries.

10.8 An Ecological Framework

It has become very clear that the substance of our first phase should be derived from issues and concerns about the environment. In the eighties, with the rise in tensions between the two nations, public concern centered on the threats to world peace, human survival, and global security posed by nuclear weapons. At the beginning of the nineties, with the decrease in cold war tensions and the greater openness to nuclear arms control, it came to focus on "ecological security" and the threats to human survival posed by the degradation of the biosphere.

As the peace researchers of the late sixties and seventies extended the *problematique* of violence beyond armed conflict and war to include the problems of the structural violence of poverty and oppression, broadening the concerns for peace studies and peace research, so violence against the Earth now has taken a significant place in the field of peace knowledge, with the planet seen as inextricably interwoven with peace among and within nations.

The field of conflict resolution is applied to environmental disputes at all levels, from international to local. Environmental issues give rise to actual and potential international conflicts "environmental security" is a major issue before the United Nations. The environmental damage caused by the Persian Gulf war is significant evidence of the ecological costs of those hostilities and of all war. The environment is a "hot topic" for peace educators, and ecology is a theme linked with many other issues of global concern.

For PEACE, however, ecology has meaning beyond the study of environmental problems, and beyond the broad study of organisms in their environments. By "ecological education" we mean, of course, those two areas, but even more. For this project the ecological approach emphasizes relationships and interlinkages. It is a way of thinking that is grounded in *holism*, in the consideration of an issue, a topic, or a problem in the broadest possible context—where possible, within the largest system of which the topic at issue is a part. In most cases this means bringing a planetary perspective to bear on the themes of study.

There are a number a characteristics of an ecological approach that serve to illuminate much of the value base of the project. Perhaps the most central concept of the approach is balance, or *harmony within a whole.* Among the fundamental ecological concepts, this one also reflects the aspirations we as educators have for the world system of nations and for human-Earth relations. We see the desirable goal as the achievement of a mutually enhancing balance of relationships and functions within the whole system concerned. This idea relates to political, economic, and learning processes that maintain living systems. Thus we can see several important value-reflecting balances in an ecological approach, among them, fragility and resilience, vulnerability and sustainability, anticipation and avoidance, extraction and replenishment, and even conflict and security. Exploring ways of maintaining these balances within social and economic as well as ecological systems reveals some of our hopes for what ecological learning can contribute to the achievement of a just, peaceful global social order.

10.9 The Meaning and Promise of Cooperative Learning

Balance as a characteristic of ecological thinking also connotes *inter-dependence.* While it has appeared to the human observer that there are elements of competition in natural systems, this seeming competition is in essence a component of the succession and sustainability of the entire system. It is the form that interdependence takes, and it is kept in balance for the health of the system.

Components of natural systems do not encounter each other's existence as threatening the survival of the system. Predators prey upon other life forms, but the intent is their own survival, not the weakening and destruction of the life form represented by the prey. Indeed, in some cultures the reflective predator, the human who hunts for food, offers prayers of thanksgiving to the prey and observes the hunt as an act to sustain not only human life but the great chain of life itself. Far from being an act of competition, so observed, the hunt is a reflection of interspecies cooperation. Yet we humans have brought the hunt, and other modes through which we have come to seek to sustain *only our own survival,* to the ultimate stages of competition, modern warfare, in which humans can wipe out entire groups of our own species, even the species itself, in the name of their own survival.

That competition and aggression are intractable attributes of human nature was long upheld by popular wisdom and even by scientific treatises. However, in recent years we have come to learn that it was more likely the attributes of cooperation and association that enabled the human species to survive and culture to evolve.[2] Unfortunately, more of the former assumptions than the latter notions still characterize educational practice, especially in those industrial nations in which the market determines production.

In these nations a high value is placed on competition, and preparation for success in competition is seen as a major task of education and socialization.

---

[2] Howell, Signe and Roy, Wilbs (editors). *Societies at Peace: Anthropological Perspectives.* London: Rutledge, 1989.

Individual and group competition pervades the Western and, to some degree, other educational systems, from sliding-scale grading to often potentially dangerous physical contact sports. Some have interpreted these educational practices as being as much preparation for warfare as preparation for the marketplace. Even in some socialist societies there has been the element of preparing to compete against other systems. Creativity and cooperation, two human capacities essential to the survival and development of the species, have traditionally been given little role in the educational systems of most industrialized countries.

Over the past decade this condition has been not only the subject of criticism by educational reformers, but the theme of a growing movement in educational practice, *cooperative learning*. This practice has thus far been used more in the elementary grades than in secondary and higher education, but among some peace educators, at the more advanced levels, some aspects of cooperative learning are now being adapted to broaden and intensify the learning of high school and university students.

Cooperation is a basic component of all sustainable social systems, even those of authoritarian dictatorships, for without the cooperation or the acquiescence of the majority of a population such systems could not maintain themselves.

In essence, any system is a set of interrelated parts operating together to perform a function or achieve a purpose. Even if that purpose is the repression of some of the parts, those parts, just like the others, must work together, 'cooperate,' else the function cannot be performed or the purpose achieved.

Refusal to cooperate is a major form of passive resistance that has weakened and sometimes crippled systems as effectively as have rebellions. All systems can tolerate some dysfunctional parts for some time, but none can sustain themselves when dysfunctionality extends over long periods of time or involves multiple components.

Indeed, we can say that the world political system found the competition between the United States and the former Soviet Union to be dysfunctional and weakening. The two powers, themselves part of that system, suffered in some ways equally seriously. Both paid a high price in long-range economic well-being, social integration, and cultural development.

Each had viewed the other as being so threatening that they interpreted the threat as one to the entire system, and behaved accordingly, to the point where they brought the entire system to the possibility of collapse. Predation without reflection, or thanksgiving without the authentic purposes of balance or survival, destroys interdependence, often decimating essential parts of a system. The hunting of North American buffalo for 'sport' contributed to the devastation of the native American population, whose way of life depended upon that animal; similarly the predatory interventions of the two superpowers in the internal affairs of other nations, when each feared that the rival power was making some gains in the area, weakened and in some cases virtually destroyed the possibilities of freedom in the prey countries while eroding that precious political commodity in their own countries. Predatory intervention endangers the entire system, destroying it or transforming it into another system. The competition between the United States and the USSR brought the world to such a point.

The potential for freedom and democracy that emerged at the end of World War II was transposed into worldwide militarization and repression. We of PEACE believe that the new moment, the possibilities offered by the end of the cold war between the two superpowers, is one of potential positive transformation, a *climax condition* that can move the world to a new political system that is less predatory, less competitive, more peaceful, and more just. We believe this to be possible primarily because of the human capacity to cooperate. Our project is an experiment in such cooperation; we educators are ourselves engaging in cooperative learning.

Cooperative learning as an intentional teaching mode gained wider attention and new adherents in the United States in the late 1980s. Developed out of a theory that acknowledges the significance of personal interaction in learning and emphasizes the variety in learning styles to be found among any group of learners, it advocates setting common learning or problem-solving tasks to be addressed cooperatively by groups of students working together.

It is argued that most of the common learning goals pursued in schools can be achieved by cooperative methods, and further that the learning experience is more rewarding to the participants, whose individual strengths can be applied to the task while their weaknesses can be substituted for by the capacities of others. It is a mode that uses human diversity and complementarity in a mutually advantageous way. It also provides experience that teaches appreciation of diversity and community building in the most practical way, by involving the learners in setting and striving for a common goal approached from diverse perspectives within a context of multiple possibilities.

In this new moment in which we must learn, as nations and as a species, to work together as one system, cooperative learning is probably the most effective educational method. Our greatest need is for all peoples to learn to function together as a single social system whose purpose is to create circumstances that, as Willard Jacobson (Chap. 4) observes, allow "all to be the best they can be"—at the inequitable expense of none. That groups, individuals, even ideologies and whole and varied societies can cooperate, functioning together toward a common end, has been demonstrated within nations by the formation of coalitions around some common national goal. Similarly, it has been demonstrated internationally with alliances and in some regional arrangements. It must now be manifest at the global level. The two major issues that urgently call for such integration of goals and collaboration in efforts to achieve them are saving the natural environment and the abolition of war.

Both of these goals require full, integral, global cooperation, and neither is possible within the present structures, institutions, and policies that comprise the world's sociopolitical system, the international system. Indeed, this system of nation-states is premised upon the sovereign right of each state to do as it wills in its own interest without restraint or consideration of others or the whole system, and most are prepared to do so. This system has been called "the war system." Each nation can at will take up arms against others. Even the United Nations Charter, which was drafted to prevent war, cannot restrain member states from taking up arms against others if they deem it necessary for their "defense." And even though the United Nations peacekeeping forces were awarded the Nobel Peace Prize in 1988, all states are still basically responsible for their own "national security."

Neither can any agent or institution in the system legally restrain others from polluting Earth's atmosphere, destroying her forests, dumping wastes into her waters, or over-cultivating her topsoil. Such actions are physical assaults, forms of aggression against the life and health of the planet. All states are still basically irresponsible toward Earth's "ecological security" and the human species' "environmental security".

Indeed, nations still think and behave in terms that give primacy to "national security" over all other human concerns. Such a view of security has become dysfunctional and dangerous. Its heavy emphasis on the military not only results in the tragic social consequences of military expenditures (see Chap. 1), it results in many other system-damaging consequences that come from the competitive view nations or alliances of nations have taken of each other. Such a view, like the concept of national security itself, is based on a fundamental fallacy: that nations are separate, autonomous entities, systems unto themselves. While the common public discourse now incorporates the concept of interdependence, and the global economy is built upon that concept (though not on an equitable and mutual form of interdependence, as Eva Nordland points out in Chap. 1), respect for interdependence has not been the primary characteristic of international relations. Nations still conduct foreign policy as though they were independent and as though other nations are more likely to harm than help them, for such is how they perceive the "real world." This situation has profound implications for education. As implied in the previous remarks on the dominance of the competitive mode in our schools, education has reinforced the 'realist' view both in the content of what is taught about world politics and in the way it is taught. The deep entrenchment of these notions in the way we think now represents one of the great challenges to education. This challenge, we believe, can best be met through ecological and cooperative education, organizing and presenting content in a holistic, integrated, and interrelated form, following an instructional process in which learners work together to seek understanding and work to build both individual and communal knowledge. Such content and process emphasize both the uniqueness of the components of the content and the capacities of the individuals in the process, in ways that orchestrate these differences for the benefit of the whole and the mutual enhancement of all.

PEACE is attempting to engage in such learning itself as it advocates and facilitates ecological and cooperative education in the schools of our respective countries.

10.10 Toward Global Cooperation and Social Responsibility: Learning for Responsible Citizenship in a Pluralistic World

Just as *ecology* and *cooperation* are the two key concepts that characterize the pedagogy we believe most likely to facilitate learning toward a human future, *pluralism* and *responsibility* are key concepts that characterize the type of global society that we believe would assure a human future. Just as functional collaboration and diversity of life forms are essential to the life-assuring balance of living systems, so too pluralism and responsibility are essential to a just, peaceful, and viable social system. Social systems, to maintain viability and vigor, must nurture human variety of all kinds. In ethnically homogeneous societies, this variety may be said to be adequate if various individual capacities and talents and other forms of human diversity and viewpoints are nurtured. In ethnically (and, we might also argue, ideologically) mixed societies, the varieties of cultures and modes of thought must also be intentionally cultivated. Such conditions are essential to our notion of democracy that derives from the belief that the broader and more varied the human resource base, the more successful a society is likely to be. Above all, a successful democracy encourages full and responsible participation of all citizens.

10.11 Our Vision of a Democratic World Society: The Observation of Comprehensive, Universal Human Rights

A world society in which universal ethnic, cultural, and political pluralism and active social responsibility are seen as central to the success of the society, in our terms, would be authentically democratic. Most significantly, it would be ecological, in this sense it would be understood that the true health, welfare, and sustainability of all the component parts would be fully interdependent, and neither the whole nor any single component or multiple components would take primacy at the expense of others. For should such occur, it would be recognized that the system would no longer be the same. While there may be times when some parts may need primary attention, such temporary attention would signify that the component in need has interests superseding those of other parts. So, too, we recognize that system changes intentionally made for the good of the whole will likely be necessary from time to time.

Indeed, we argue here that such is the case for the present system—that it must be so drastically altered as to constitute a transformation to an essentially different system. The members of PEACE are themselves participating in a process of struggle to articulate a vision of a transformed global society. We hold that this process of diverse entities struggling toward a common vision is an important aspect of an ecological and cooperative approach to peace education. Throughout the world, instructors and learners together should be collaborating in multiple processes of envisioning a transformed world order that is truly democratic, participatory in its origins and its functioning.

As we engage in such a process, we also embark upon the redefinition of many fundamental social and political concepts. Many have lost their authentic meanings in the stagnation of the ideological orthodoxies that have defined and divided the world into competitive interests struggling for dominance in a conflictual system. Thus, what we mean here by "democratic" is not adequately defined by the standard definitions previously applied by the East or the West Differences in ideology have produced contrasting notions of democracy characterized by such standards as full employment (as opposed to universal suffrage), or economic and social (as opposed to civil and political) rights. These differences have certainly fragmented and destructively prioritized the realization of *universal human rights* (meaning comprehensive as well as applicable to all). For us, a democratic society is one that strives to fulfill both sets of rights for all the people, economic and social as well as political and *all* the categories of *rights* the world has defined and continues to define since the Universal Declaration of Human Rights was set forth in 1948. Democracy should mean more than voting and representation. It even means more than the assurance of the wherewithal (learned or provided) to meet basic needs. It should mean, above all, broad, meaningful participation in all public decisions, cultural, economic, and social as well as civil and political. Further, authentic participatory democracy can only exist in a global system where it can no longer be limited "in the interest of national security."

A shift from an international system of win-lose competition and destructive conflict to one of genuine cooperation and collaboration would make the present exclusionary, fragmented notion of national security obsolete. Just to seriously work toward such a system would increase democratic participation and certainly would require more participatory education. The ecological and cooperative notions of security noted earlier can best be put into operation in a fully participatory form of democracy, one that, properly structured, could work at all levels of social organization, even the global. For example, the proposal for a "third house," as an addition to the United Nations Security Council and General Assembly, for the world's peoples or nongovernmental organizations, demonstrates such possibilities.[3] The notion of authentically participatory democracy calls for a redefinition of power as well as an education for empowerment.

10.12 From Domination to Mutuality: Power as Synergy, a Cooperative Learning Task

Power in the present system has come to mean primarily military might, the capacity to arouse fear and to achieve "the national interest." Power, then, has operated as the means to persuade or force others to acquiesce in the policies of the powerful. Clearly, as demonstrated by the Persian Gulf War and its devastating aftermath, this system of deterrence can neither maintain the peace nor provide global security. At other levels of social organization, in communities and within

[3] Boulding, Elise. *Building a Global Civic Culture*. New York: Teachers College Press, 1988; Diamond, Irene. ''Ecofeminism.'' Paper presented at the biannual general conference of the International Peace Research Association, July, 1990; Eisler, Riane. *The Chalice and the Blade*. New York: Harper & Row, 1987; Ferguson, Marilyn. *The Aquarian Conspiracy*. Los Angeles: Tardier, 1987; Gorbachev, Mikhail. *Perestroika*. New York: Harper & Row, 1988; Gromyko, Anatoly and Martin, Hellerman (editors). *Breakthrough*. New York: Walker, 1988.

nations, power used in such a way is perceived as a lack of civility, lawlessness or criminality. Only recently have some begun to recognize the lawlessness and barbarity of the international system itself. From the ecological, holistic perspectives taken here, the lawlessness in the larger system, in fact, makes possible much of the barbarous behavior within nations, most especially that of states against their own citizens. Again the Gulf War of 1991 offers an instructive example, nations coalesced to wage war against Iraq with far greater alacrity than they responded to the plight of the refugees resulting from the internal Iraqi strife engendered by the war. It is evident that we still live in a world in which the state *dominates* rather than *serves* its citizens.

The recognition and application of the imperatives of interdependence among nations would do much to bring authentic democracy to the world society. As power is redefined, the respective governments of the world of nations must learn to relate to each other, in the spirit, and within structures and policies, of mutuality, rejecting the drive for dominance in favor of a struggle toward authentic, fully functioning interdependence.

The formulation of and striving toward mutual goals carries a notion of power now advocated widely by feminists as *power with* rather than *power over*. Sharing power, it is argued, can increase the total capacity of the parties involved to achieve their common goal. Such *synergetic capacity* deriving from cooperative efforts has been demonstrated in the positive educational consequences of many experiments in cooperative learning introduced in the recent past into American schools.

Energy from multiple sources brought to cooperative efforts is often greater than energy from one source, and it is more likely to be renewed or enhanced as the parties involved are increased. In that a purpose of cooperation between the two former superpower rivals is to enhance the possibilities for international cooperation in general, it is hoped that others will soon be brought into the new approach to power as shared capacity, in positive constructive efforts more conducive to authentic security and democracy than the waging of war that has involved many nations.

Developing multilateral, cooperative, international efforts is a learning task, the foundation for which needs to be laid in the schools of the nations involved. Cooperative learning as a standard practice in formal educational systems around the world could be a significant factor in enhancing cooperation in the international system. It would be a significant acknowledgment of the need to enhance interdependence at all levels—to not only teach *about* interdependence but to teach *for* interdependence. Authentic interdependence requires renewed and renewable energy—not only the industrial energy we need to fuel economic production and maintain the world economy, but also, and especially, the human energy to learn and to achieve goals, to carry out equitable, ecologically designed, and environmentally healthy international policies.

Ecofeminists tell us power should be defined as energy.[4] Within the content of ecological and cooperative education, power then is also energy directed toward

---

[4] Diamond, "Ecofeminism."

the implementation of an international process of learning for change. Herein lies the vital task of educators, particularly peace educators committed to learning toward the achievement of nonviolence and the promotion of justice.

Our goal then is the conceptualization of and the struggle to implement an educational system and a pedagogy that can enable us to identify, release, and renew the various sources of energy necessary to transform the present system into the democratic world society we have begun to envision.

The competitive individualism of our present classrooms reifies and reinforces the competitive individualism of the nation-state system. Thus change in the classroom is crucial to change in the world.

10.13 Education for a Healthy Planet, Healthy Society: A Future Worth Hoping for, A Goal Worth Struggling for, A Task Worth Learning

As noted earlier, our concept of a democratic society is, among other things, that of *a secure society*. Security, it has been argued, derives in large part from the expectation of well-being, and well-being is measured in terms of the environment, justice, dignity, and nonviolence.[5] A secure society is a healthy society, physically and psychologically. Health is the realization of well-being. During these years of the environmental crisis we have learned how much the health of the human species depends upon the environment. As the ecological imperative becomes clearer, we are also learning how much the health of the environment depends upon the human species.

Indeed, the relationship between humanity and planet Earth is emerging as the most significant of all global security issues. The most urgent security need of all is that all human beings see themselves as part of the ecosystem, elements of the biosphere, as well as creators of the socio-sphere. Helping learners to grasp that urgency and the nature of that relationship is a paramount task for ecological and cooperative education, one that can only be properly conceived and implemented within a global framework. What the PEACE group is working for is a common educational program as well as a joint vision of an environmentally healthy planet. Energy and attention should be applied to the task of envisioning and struggling for human and environmental well-being. Hope can be kindled in addressing this task. Because security derives so largely from expectations, we can understand now how significant a role hope plays in human well-being. Without hope, there can be no energizing vision of a transformed world, nor is there a source for

[5] Betty A. Reardon and Leslie, Scott. "An Ecofeminist Perspective on Global Security." *International Journal of Humanities and Peace*, 8, no. 3 (1991); Sloan, Douglas. *Toward a Recovery of Wholeness Knowledge, Education, and Human Values*. New York: Teachers College Press, 1984.

renewing the physical and psychic energies that will need regular replenishment in the struggle. For PEACE, then, the inspiration of hope is a significant learning task and goal, inspiring (i.e., 'breathing in') the energies and igniting the possibilities of faith in our capacities to change ourselves, our systems, and our relationships. It represents for us the spiritual dimension of our project.

We recognize that any movement, educational or political, that seeks to transform the human condition so fundamentally as does the change we seek in the Earth-humankind relationship must nurture the human spirit as well as the mind. Perhaps the role of the arts and artists in the changes sweeping the world today more than any other factor instructs us in the spiritual nature of our task. Our classrooms need to become places in which such envisioning is part of the curriculum.

As we help to release the creative imaginations of learners in the imaging of their own preferred futures and the kind of social order that might make such futures possible, we will help to kindle hope and to dissipate the despair that envelops the minds and spirits of so many of the young.

Hope arises from awareness of positive possibilities, from the potential for renewal. So, too, we recognize that ecology itself rests in a view of the world that sees it as the host of possibilities. From such a view derives a spiritual dimension limited neither to philosophy nor to religion, but comprehending all in a spirituality that can encompass the whole of humanity, believers and nonbelievers. Perhaps more than any other element, this spiritual energy will bring us into forms of cooperation that will manifest and apply the unity of humanity and of humanity and Earth.

Certainly for many educators this is what inspires their preference for cooperative learning. It is palpably evident in the sense of community, unity, and possibility that we experience in our efforts as members of PEACE. It is the stuff of friendship, it is the stuff of peace, and it should as well be the stuff of curriculum.

10.14 Learning to Care: The Basis of Responsibility

In small but significant ways, PEACE has been for us, the participants, an exercise in learning to care. Our collaborative efforts have built friendships, and friendships are relationships based on caring. We are willing to risk caring for each other as we risk the struggle toward a still unfocused but mutually and strongly envisioned common future.

Working together has helped us to know each other in dimensions even beyond our professional roles. We see each other whole and human, and out of this comes caring. We see our commonalities and interrelationships, as well as our similarities and differences. We matter to each other as persons and as partners. We seek to find that our differences are usually enhancing and reinforcing diversity. We seek to recognize our own ecology of relationship, to consciously participate in keeping this relationship a viable, productive system. The seeking itself is a form of caring. We are learning something of how caring is learning.

This perhaps is one of the most telling arguments for cooperative education, that it develops the capacity to care. Caring is an active investment in and a kind of twin to hope. Both elements are essential to the abilities to be responsible, to act toward the effectuation of change, to move against injustice, to protest against and intervene in the degradation of the environment. We hope to help learners develop those abilities. We hope to help learners become *responsible,* having the capacity to respond actively and effectively, to live out a commitment to the common future.

This is a goal we embrace in PEACE. This is a goal that will inform the design of content and the methods we use in education for meeting the challenge of the new moment. When we finished our design phase, we cooperated on its application, and we will undoubtedly continue to cooperate on the revisions made ever necessary by the changing world. But we have hope that the care we offer each other will renew the energies we expend in what we know is a long and difficult struggle requiring new learnings as yet unimagined. We hope to continue to learn and imagine together.

10.15 Teaching Toward the Future in the Present

Although our work is inspired by a vision of a transformed global society, a human future of all the Earth's people and a healthy future for our shared planet, we do this work now in the daily context of our present professional positions. It is directed toward small but potentially significant projects that put our values and goals into operation in current learning environments, our communities and our classrooms. It involves efforts to develop respect for cultural differences, build relationships among the young people of our respective countries, and educate teachers in the ways of nature and help them to teach students so that they can see themselves as part of one living Earth.

Our direct and practical steps are to take the form of school 'twinning,' linking particular classrooms through the identification of individual teachers in each of the three countries involved in the initial stages of the project. Middle school, junior high school, and high school students can be in direct contact with each other through correspondence and audio and videotapes, while in their respective classrooms they undertake study and consideration of the same or similar issues under the guidance of teachers seeking to introduce ecological thinking and problem solving within organic and global perspectives.

We hope that such transnational educational projects will become standard classroom practice as collaborative and cooperative ecological education develops and is extended to more and more schools in our respective countries and in the other countries we plan to involve as the project matures and expands. We have begun work to involve more people in East–West exchange, including

Eastern and Western European educators as well as some others from the United States and Canada. Initial investigation into North-South exchanges and networking has also been undertaken to include schools in Asia, Latin America, and Africa.

One important aspect of these practical projects is the intention that they should, as well, involve local communities in the applications of problem solutions. While the problems to be studied are global in scope, their manifestations at the local level will be the immediate concern of the individual school projects. Students will engage with community members of all ages in seeking to resolve local problems of the environment or of human relations. They will directly confront pollution or waste disposal in their own neighborhoods, ethnic conflict or discrimination in their schools and communities.

These are but a very few and limited examples of possibilities for multigenerational, direct action in which ecological thinking and social responsibility will be applied to the actual realities in which the young are living.

Among the problems we seek to address at this stage are various ecological issues, most especially those related to the preservation of natural biosystems in local areas. The study and undertaking of problem resolution on this type of issue will require a form of environmental education that applies ecological thinking to the study and valuing of natural systems and the natural order itself, and learning to understand the Earth through understanding bioregions of various sizes—their unique characteristics, their subsystems, and their relationships to other systems and bioregions. It will require students to learn of the various life forms in their immediate environments, the types and consequences of human intervention in natural processes, and environmental changes resulting from human habitation and organized society.

Such education will also raise questions about the relationship of human society to the natural order, and make it possible for learners to consider these questions within the contexts of their own localities. It will encourage practical action to fulfill social responsibility with regard to achieving and/or maintaining an appropriate and constructive relationship between the local bioregion and the local human society.

Other issues to be addressed will be in the area of mutually enhancing human relations. We plan to stress learning about the alternative ways of expressing human universals demonstrated by diverse cultures, and the learning of respect for human dignity in respect for ethnic identity. The ethnic conflicts that characterize the current rapidly changing global order are a major concern to peace educators, for they express the violation of the very human values and human rights that are at the core of any authentically peaceful order. Our project will address ethnic differences and the study of various cultures as a humanly enriching and necessary characteristic of a world at peace. Ethnic diversity will be taught as a value complementary to biological diversity, necessary to the health of the human family and of planet Earth.

We propose to study, as well, cases of ethnic conflict, and we will attempt to facilitate action programs in which children can in some way offer aid to other children victimized by ethnic conflict. Through such specific cases students will learn the human dimensions of some of the political problems of achieving peace and will come to recognize the meaning of and the need for respect for universal human rights.

The conduct of these pioneering efforts in ecological and cooperative education will require teachers of exceptional commitment with special training in ecological thinking and the pedagogy of cooperation. Thus one of the first major projects of Stage 2 of PEACE is a teacher education program.

Individual schools and school systems are to be involved in a process of teacher education being conducted by members of PEACE. Groups of teachers introduced to ecological and cooperative education are working with project members on the development of specific teaching processes and materials. These will be tried out and revised for publication in a curriculum handbook, which will enable other teachers to attempt similar educational programs.

PEACE also involves a collaborative effort in the common training of teachers/educators, in Russia and in North America, in the use of field techniques. The training occurs in Canada and in Siberia. This common training will provide, at least for those involved, the basis for fully parallel curricular approaches in selected Russian and North American teacher education institutions.

These are some of the specific practical steps to be pursued in our efforts to bring to realization the principles and concepts we have derived during the first stage of our project. We see this as only the beginning of an ongoing, continually widening effort to bring ecological and cooperative education to many parts of the world. We continue to take inspiration and energy from our collaboration and look forward to the contributions and cooperation of other similarly concerned educators wherever they may be.

Part IV
Generations of Reardon's Professional Formation and Practice as Reflected in Selected Essays: Third Generation—Framing for Futures 2001–2014

Chapter 11
Human Rights Learning: Pedagogies and Politics of Peace

Retrospective Reflection on "Human Rights Learning: Pedagogies and Politics of Peace" (2008)

Human rights are a central concern of The UNESCO Chair at the University of Puerto Rico, an active center for Latin American and Spanish language peace education. Communally run by an interdepartmental and interdisciplinary group of scholars associated with the University, the Chair advocates and practices Freirean methodologies in the academy and the community. The historical experience of the island Commonwealth gives them profound insight into colonialism from which to make significant contributions to the development of justice related pedagogies of Peace Education. Chair members participate in The Latin America Council for Peace Research (CLAIP). Having myself, while Chairperson of COPRED, the Consortium on Peace Research, Education and Development (which later evolved into The Peace and Justice Studies Association, North American affiliate of the International Peace Research Association with which CLAIP is also associated) had direct contact with CLAIP in the early 80s, I learned something of how the peace problematic looks from a Latin American perspective. That perspective is deeply infused with issues of human rights, especially as they play out in the politics of the dependency-dominance relationship between the Americas and the politics of striving for authentic democracy within their respective countries. The assertion that peace is realized in the fulfillment of human rights, and thereby integral and fundamental to peace education, long a significant component of my work, fits well with Freirean pedagogy, the preferred Latin American mode of learning and working for justice. Years before

B.A. Reardon and D.T. Snauwaert, *Betty A. Reardon: A Pioneer in Education for Peace and Human Rights*, SpringerBriefs on Pioneers in Science and Practice 26,
DOI 10.1007/978-3-319-08967-6_11

Freire's critical pedagogy was standard fare in European and American schools of education, it was taken up by many in the international network of peace educators. So, when Anita Yudkin, then director of UPR's UNESCO Chair invited me to deliver the 2008 university-community lecture, the Chair's Conferencia Magistral, *it seemed appropriate to focus on human rights learning as critical pedagogy for political change.*

The lecture also reflected my growing preoccupations with the challenge to peace education I see in the moralizing pontificated in the name of social good while ethical reasoning is rejected as irrelevant to public policy (issues further explored in "Meditating on the Barricades" from which Chap. 13 *in this volume is taken). The lecture brought the preoccupation to attention in addressing the adversarial stances being taken at the time among practitioners of various approaches to human rights education as they encountered each other in planning for the next phase of development to follow the UN declared Decade for Human Rights education, each insisting that theirs be the featured approach. But neither addressed the underlying problems of political ethics that produce violations of human right and suppression of discussion and education about them. While I later came to see these debates as reflecting the dysfunctional spirit of acute adversarialism infecting all public discussions, my Freirean instincts led me at the time to speak in favor of human rights learning. The approach seemed to me to hold greater potential toward the political empowerment of learners to actively pursue justice than human rights education that I perceived to be focused more on human rights as subject matter than as keys to practical political learning.*

Later, as articulated in the Klagenfurt lecture (Chap. 12 *in this volume*) *delivered a within few years, I came to see that all approaches had something to contribute to the general field, particularly as addressed by the academy. Yet, I continue to emphasize human rights learning as a vehicle through which politics could be practiced more as social learning and less as a kind of ideological and verbal warfare. Though conducted perhaps without arms, political arguments and campaigns are still waged for victory of one party over another in the language and metaphors of war, which continue to normalize and legitimize the institution of war within a global culture of violence. Above all, my emphasis continues to be on the idea that individual and social learning are the most viable and sustainable approaches to the development of a culture of peace now the most widely embraced social purpose of peace education. I had tried to give that idea specific pedagogical form in* Education for a Culture of Peace in a Gender Perspective *(2001). While not evident in this piece, Volume 27 will demonstrate that I believe gender justice to be the most overarching of human rights issues.*

Betty A. Reardon
April, 2014

11.1 Proposition 1: Human Rights Are Integral and Essential to Peace and Peace Education

As a political framework for the actualization of human dignity, human rights are the ethical core of peace education; not a complement, or a particular component, and certainly not an alternative or an educationally equivalent substitute for peace education.[1] Human rights are integral to peace education, that is, without human rights peace education lacks a primary component of its core and essential substance. Human rights are the essence and the arbiter of peace, the antithesis of violence, touching on multiple and complex aspects of the human experience, illuminating the necessity of holism to the field. The potential of human rights as the means to cultivate transformational thinking lies in viewing all human rights norms and standards as a whole, an integrated ethical system. That system, I propose, holds the promise of a transformed peaceful and just global order...

Human rights learning... refers to a process inspired by an impulse toward social justice that takes place in all settings where people learn for civic purposes. They include—but most certainly are not limited to—schools and universities. Human rights learning (HRL) is the conjoined philosophic twin of critical pedagogy, coming to be the preferred pedagogy of peace education, the two united by a common assumption about the relationship between teaching methodology and social and political learning. An even more significant belief that peace educator advocates of participatory, reflective pedagogies share with advocates of human rights learning is that in itself HRL is political in nature. The efficacy of education for humane and positive social and political purposes is most likely determined by the internalization of values and world views that should complement the acquisition of knowledge and skills relevant to the realization of human rights.

Internalizing values is possible through the acquisition of knowledge and the development of skills if the learning process is mediated through active and reflective involvement of the learner with the substance of study... This is especially so if the process involves the examination and—in most cases—the challenging of the worldviews of the learners and their societies. In distinguishing, as I will here, between human rights education and human rights learning, I intend to argue that such examination and challenge of prevailing social and personal values is still largely missing from standard, formal human rights education, precluding it from being peace education...

Peace education is also of its very nature critical. Not in the sense of criticism as opposition, but in the sense of being probingly analytic and evaluative. Granted

[1] This chapter comprises selections from a paper based on a lecture on "Human Rights Learning: Pedagogies and Politics of Peace," delivered for the UNESCO Chair for Peace Education, Master Conference at the University of Puerto Rico, April 15, 2009. The permission to publish this text was granted by Dr. Anita Yudkin, University of Puerto Rico, on 9 March 2014. Reardon, Betty A. *Human Rights Learning: Pedagogies and Politics of Peace*. San Juan, Puerto Rico: UNESCO Chair for Peace Education, University of Puerto Rico, 2010.

analysis and evaluation may indeed lead learners to oppose some public policies or social, economic or political structures, when they find them to contradict the fundamental values of peace and justice which guide the evaluation; or when the analysis shows failure to achieve just public purposes. For human rights learning, however, such challenge is a core learning goal of critical reflection, with the realization of human rights as social purpose, issues of human rights as substance and observance of principles of human rights in the facilitation of the intended learning, a process mediated within a holistic—and potentially transformative-human rights framework…

With Janet Gerson and Tony Jenkins in the DMZ-Korea, during IIPE 2003. *Source* Personal photo collection of the author

Considering the distinctions I perceive between the largely content-based general practice of human rights education and human rights learning that puts equal emphasis on an engaged pedagogy, provides an arena of discourse on the purposes and processes of social education in general and peace education in particular. We need to enter this arena to grapple with the limits to learning inherent in the information transfer form of education as an obstacle to the ultimate social purpose of peace education, transformation toward a culture of peace through the de-legitimization of violence as a political tool and the development of a social commitment to nonviolent societies, striving to realize universal human dignity in institutions, relationships, and customs. The separations and limits of traditional pedagogies imposed by the fragmentation and reductionism of divided subject matter are characteristic of the "political realism" that still dominates current politics-including issues of human rights and peace. The rationalization and tolerance of various forms of economic and political violence as unavoidable in the face of concerns deemed more significant to order and stability is a given in public discourse. In the names of more urgent public priorities such as national security, human rights fall by the policy wayside. Issues continue to be discussed and decisions made without regard to the essential interrelationships among them. So, too, the ethical and normative dimensions and consequences of public policies are screened out in favor of what is argued to be pragmatism and practicality. Neither do ethical dimensions play much of a role in standard information based education...

11.2 Proposition 2: Human Rights Learning Is a Contemporary Form of Freirean Political Pedagogy

This proposition is... not necessarily new, but I believe it has renewed currency in 2009, the International Year of Human Rights Learning. The basic argument is a call for the fulfillment of the Freirean promise of education as a means to the realization of human rights through that form of human rights learning defined as conscientization-awakening to awareness of the realities of our lives and societies and the interrelationship between these two realms of human experience. It is exactly Freire's focus on the capacity of the inner dynamic of the learning process to illuminate the outer social and political structures that forms the essence of human rights learning as advocated by... the communally based approaches to learning... [that acknowledge] the political nature and purpose of peace education. By political I do not mean the politics of existing political systems, nor the contentions among the categories of political positions ossified into political parties, reifying the dualistic thinking that in the American system plays out in a two-party politics. I mean rather politics in a more profound and basic sense of public deliberation on the aims and purposes of society; the decisions about means to achieve those purposes by sustainably producing and fairly expending the fruits of a peoples' labors, resources and talents. I mean a politics of peace infused with a common commitment to the general public good, a just distribution and equitable enjoyment of benefits and resources; in short a politics of human rights. This is a politics far from the present power contestations of political realism, the win-lose process that obscures and poses obstacles to the learning required to devise and develop a politics of peace. Without an effective politics of peace, peace cannot be achieved. Without an effective political education there can be no politics of peace. I would submit that human rights learning is the most promising vehicle for an effective education for a politics of peace. For it has been devised through such a politics in the places where it has been put into practice as grass roots activism for community change...

11.3 Proposition 3: The Violence and Vulnerabilities of the Global System Frame Ethical Issues for Human Rights Learning and a Politics of Peace

What Freire confronted as oppression of the poor, I would identify as a symptom of a system of social and economic violence, similar to, but not synonymous with what peace research refers to as structural violence. It seems to me that the concept of structural violence is a general abstraction that can obscure the ethical and moral dimension and the individual personal responsibility at play in this category of violence.

Granted, it is accepted that social and economic structures restrict the opportunities for human fulfillment and access to social benefits available to the poor, and the concept of structural violence enables us to discern the institutional and political causes of, and possible alternatives to, these unjust conditions. However, the degree to which personal behaviors and choices conditioned by social values determine the actual processes of deprivation within the structures call for normative reflection that makes ethics and values a significant factor in peace learning and peace politics. Justice and injustice may be mediated through structures but they are not synonymous with nor necessarily determined by structures. Indeed, I would argue that peace and human rights learning and action are not only often inspired by unjust structures, but that they can take place within them. It is this fact that makes peace education possible within our present politics and education systems. It also makes it incumbent upon peace education, especially when it takes the form of human rights learning to pose issues and develop skills for the exercise and application of ethics and morality.

Both ethics and morality may have a place in peace learning and peace politics, but their respective places are distinct and different. They are not synonymous and cannot substitute one for the other. It is not the role of peace education or human rights learning to moralize, that is to teach by moral precept. But they have a responsibility to guide learners in discerning when moralizing is introduced into political discourse as it was so frequently in the last American administration-most lamentably in the case of depicting the war against Iraq as a crusade and the shocking and frightening habit of the then Secretary of Defense of introducing strategic directives with Biblical quotations. In addition to being an egregious violation of the constitutional requirement of separation of church (meaning for legal and political purposes all religions) and state, the habit was a prejudgment on public matters of national security that denied the citizens the right to form and argue for their own positions. Ethical reflection and analysis, on the other hand should be an integral component of peace learning and peace politics. The development of ethical skills can derive from applying global society's agreed principles of justice and equity—such as those that are enshrined in law, pertaining to all no matter what moral system they may live by—to the assessment of political issues and choices. The development and application of ethical principles is a process of engagement similar to my sculpting in clay metaphor. It is a peace education and human rights learning process consistent with Freirean pedagogy…

Accepting Teachers College, Columbia University Distinguished Alumna Award 2004. *Source* Personal photo collection of the author

The differences between ethics and morality most relevant to the transformative learning toward which we are striving are the sources from which they come and the thinking that goes into their application. Ethics, derived by persons wrestling with what might be good and true on as wide a basis as possible derives principles that require deeper reflection on the what as well as the how of the substance of principles and the complexity of their application. Morality, based on precepts set forth by authority—usually but not always religious authority—is more in the area of what is permissible. The range of how is often limited when the authority from which the precepts emanate posits prescriptions, instructing in specific behaviors or imposing specific social norms and policies such as those applying to reproductive rights and sexual practices. There is no area in which the distinctions between the two and the consequences of the application of one or the other is more evident than in the controversies over the human rights of women and children. I would submit the issues involved there are not contending moralities, but contentions between moralities and ethical principles many of the latter having been encoded into the international legal standards of the Conventions on the Elimination of all Forms of Discrimination against Women and the Convention on the Rights of the Child…

A process of public conscientization will of necessity involve ethical reflection. It seems to me that what I know of human rights education in its traditional education form does not assure that the ethical issues of complicity with the systemic violence and social responsibility for the suffering of the vulnerable will be considered. The assumption that substantive knowledge, per se, is the object of education still infuses the mindset in which the privileged are educated. Knowledge is considered to be a commodity to be acquired, a source of power and of "market advantage." The uses to which power is put and the ends served by knowledge are not considered as issues subject to ethical assessment. Power and knowledge are bases of individual, corporate, or familial wealth to be used to the advantage of the possessors, only secondarily—if at all—as resources to be put to the betterment of the human condition or for the fulfillment of social responsibility. Peace education has long advocated the cultivation of the skills and capacities of social responsibility as integral to its purpose. Human rights learning, at its core, is the cultivation of ethical reflection and assessment for the exercise of social responsibility. Both sets of capacities, ethical reflection and social responsibility, are essential to the development of transformative thinking. Both are essential to citizen action to overcome the avoidable harm of structural violence. Comprehension of structural and all other forms of violence is crucial to devising the strategies of a politics of peace.

…I identify violence as the central problematic of peace education. All violence degrades and/or denies human dignity. This is why I assert that the substance of the field should comprise an inquiry into violence as a phenomenon and a system, its multiple and pervasive forms, the interrelationships among the various forms, its sources and purposes, how it functions and potential alternatives for achieving the legally sanctioned, socially accepted, or politically tolerated purposes commonly pursued through violence. I emphasize these structural forms of economic, social and political violence as I believe them to be more significant to our task than, the non-systemic, aberrant violence of crime, interpersonal conflict, vandalism, etc. that I believe are both rooted in and facilitated by the systemic violence of the institutions that uphold the wider culture of violence. [including] gender violence…

I define violence as intentional, avoidable harm—usually committed to achieve a purpose. By designating it as intentional harm, I intend to indicate that using violence especially to achieve economic or political purposes or to maintain social conditions (such as male dominance) is an act of choice, strategic as well as ethical choice. In most situations there are alternative courses of action toward the ends sought.

I also distinguish between violence and necessary, legitimate force. When there are no known non-forceful alternatives, we have recourse to legitimate force—

peacekeeping and police forces for instance-to be used, keeping in mind in its application that harm should be kept to the lowest possible level. I would categorize what is commonly called police brutality as violence. It is harmful force that exceeds what is necessary to achieve the legitimate social ends to which it is being put. So, too we can say that the use of military when all other avenues to defense against armed attack are closed off under the present system—which lacks sufficient institutional alternatives—is legitimate. It is recognized to be so in Article 8 of the Charter of United Nations... There were and are institutional alternatives to respond to and remedy... acts of violence which are crimes, not acts war.

As we can consider police brutality to be violence, so too, there are clear instances of what Okinawa Women Act Against Military Violence (OWAAMV), a Japanese peace organization, have defined as military violence, intentional harm to civilians or avoidable harm inflicted outside combat conditions by military personnel...

My definition of violence derives from the core value of human dignity and respect for the living Earth; and from the concomitant human responsibility to honor them. The values of human dignity and human responsibility are also central to the theories and practices of nonviolence. Nonviolence comprises efforts to pursue goals imbued with an intention to do no harm; and where that may not be possible, to minimize any potential harm—if possible to enlist the consent of those who will suffer some of the harms that sometimes occur in the use of nonviolent strategies. Strikes are a good example here. Those who withhold their labor may have just cause, but all those who suffer the consequence of the strike may not be implicated in the injustice. Such consent was given by large numbers of Black South Africans to the boycotts and sanctions that helped to topple Apartheid in South Africa. These are but two examples of the kinds of human rights issues, the resolution of which involves citizens in consideration of consequences, especially ethical considerations.

Because the values of human dignity and human responsibility from which this concept of violence derives are integral to human rights, human rights issues and human rights learning are excellent lenses through which to seek the requisite clarification about what constitutes violence and how it is implicated in the perpetuation of the vulnerability of the oppressed. Human rights study provides us with tools of definition and diagnosis of what comprises violence, experientially as well as conceptually, and provides opportunities to consider approaches to overcoming vulnerability.

A condition that often produces the impulse to violence is vulnerability. The concept of vulnerability provides another useful analytic tool with which to assess the circumstances that make possible the denial of human dignity to large masses of the human population. Vulnerability,—in particular structural vulnerability—I would define as a chronic disadvantage suffered by person or groups at the lower levels of the prevailing social, economic and political structures, women, the poor, the aged, children and minorities. It is a condition in which the vulnerable are the most likely to suffer harm as a consequence of the prevailing structures and policies, as well as, from the periodic disturbances that shake the structures interrupting their normal operation. Although determined by people's positions in the social and political structures rather than by any personal quality or action on their parts, given the widespread lack of general recognition of the principle of human dignity, the vulnerable themselves are often held responsible for their own disadvantaged circumstances. Too often unaware of their human rights, they seem powerless to make claims on the society for the assurance of those rights. Those at the top, "the rich and the powerful" are least likely to suffer harm from system wide events and developments (other than in natural disasters) and face few limits to the claims they make to the all the benefits of the society. Those at the bottom are most likely to suffer harm, both on a daily basis and in the case of humanly caused or natural disasters. The vulnerable are one of the present system's most exploitable resources, providing minimum cost labor, commodities for the human trafficking markets. In political systems that hold elections, votes are often bought for the price of a meal. As violence is the central problematic of peace education, vulnerability is at the center of the problematic of HRE and HRL.

I think it important to note that the early practice and development of Freirean approaches to human rights learning were among the vulnerable of the world, mainly in the "global south." The intentions of this human rights learning were to enable vulnerable communities to become aware of the structural causes of their vulnerability, to help them to understand that it was not the necessary or inevitable consequence of any legitimate social goal and to inspire them to take action to overcome it. Further, the international standards of human rights were both a recognition that their vulnerability should not be accepted by them or their societies and could serve as tools to overcome it. In order to do so they needed critical skills, not just literacy. In short, these are arguments similar to those Freire made about the relation of standard education practice to the maintenance of existing power structures. So it was appropriate for human rights learning to work with Freire's pedagogy in that these endeavors were directed at reducing the structural harms suffered by the oppressed. These endeavors were instructive examples of learning as politics and learning applied to perfecting ever more effective strategies and political means toward reducing avoidable harms-politics as learning.

Politics as learning is in some significant part, a process of identifying and conceptualizing problems. Indeed, conscientization is in its first stages a process of conceptualization, or 'naming' of the social conditions that impede or enhance human dignity, such as circumstances and indicators of oppression or justice. Concepts are the components from which we construct the holistic frameworks used in peace education, the core ideas of the problems to be addressed and/or goals to be pursued. So, too, they figure in the pedagogies of human rights learning, and provide an instructive mode for the curricular use of the international human rights standards.

Conceptual definitions encapsulate the abstract and philosophic dimensions of human rights imbedded in basic principles of human worth and human dignity. Such are the ethical injunctions articulated in the Universal Declaration of Human Rights (UDHR). The Declaration defines the ethical and normative aspirations that form the principles to guide ethical deliberations about human rights issues and problems. The individual standards of the covenants and conventions are instruments for disclosure of specific, experiential dimensions of denial and enjoyment of particular rights. The standards help us to comprehend and reveal the often unobserved bulwarks or abnegations of human dignity. In their fulfillment they are hallmarks of dignity. In their denial they are indicators of vulnerability in a global system characterized by violence. We can best perceive the multiplicities of violence from a holistic perspective revealing the interrelationships between violence and vulnerability. Our analysis must put us simultaneously in touch with the systemic and the particular. To satisfy this injunction in my teaching practice, I used the metaphor of the zoom lens, mentally shifting from a wide angle view of the entire scope of a subject under discussion, the general, central problematic, to a narrow focus on a very specific detail or datum that relates to or forms part of the central problematic. The term problematic is a formulation that comprehends all aspects and sub-problems that comprise a major problem of peace or human rights, a formulation that facilitates holism as an approach to peace education and human rights learning.[2] Peace education and human rights learning aim to facilitate a learning process in which the skill of making this shift is invoked whenever appropriate to the analysis.

In human rights learning within a holistic approach—applying the framework of the international standards as a whole—the learning process would alternate its focus between the wide angle of the visions of a society universally informed by human rights projected in the UDHR and the specific details of the vision, as outlined by the particular standards of the covenants and conventions, designed to bring about the conditions that comprise the vision. The particular standards, when viewed in the wider perspective of the multiplicities of violations, also help us to see the systemic nature of violence in the present world order, as well as, to recognize and assess specific instances of violence as visible violations of particular rights. So, too, they enable us to see how instances of fulfillment of particular rights manifest the abstract concepts that define the values we espouse, the norms we seek to actualize, the ethics that can guide our actions and policies.

These international legal standards are useful devices for on-going conscientization from awareness of injustice, conceptualized at the systemic level, to recognizing and confronting the specific conditions and incidence of the actual violence in daily, lived experience. Confronting the symptoms requires political action taken—on principle and wherever possible—in one of the nonviolent modes that are integral to a politics of peace, action that can be the basis for learning toward further action toward the realization of the right in question. So, human rights standards need not be consigned to HRE content to be absorbed but not necessarily applied or to legal exotica, confined to the discourse of lawyers and

---

[2] I have dealt in more depth with the concept of the problematic and its function in peace education in Reardon, Betty A. *Education for a Culture of Peace in a Gender Perspective*. Paris: UNESCO, 2001: 128.

diplomats. They can serve citizens and learners, on the ground living in the conditions of human rights violations, as diagnostic tools and instruments for the legal remediation of the injustices that afflict them. Most human rights standards, be they entitlements or protections, designate instances of violence and stand as injunctions to overcome a particular form of vulnerability…

Awakening of publics to all forms of violence and vulnerability, as noted, are goals of peace education and human rights learning. These are goals, which are approached through learning as it is facilitated in programs of education and in the political action that is a medium for so much human rights learning. Among the learning objectives integrally related to this goal is the conscientization of the privileged to their implication in and responsibility for this systemic and structural violence, advocated above as the pedagogy of the privileged. The complement to that goal is the awakening of the vulnerable, not only to awareness of the structural foundations of their oppression but, also and especially, to consciousness of themselves as the subjects of rights they may claim on the basis of universal human dignity, the core principle and foundation of all realms of human rights. Political action to claim human rights is the politics of justice, a potentially transformative politics of learning.

When we assert that human rights are the particular components of economic, social, cultural and political justice, we recognize that just societies are those that are conscious of vulnerabilities, seek to prevent them from becoming the occasions of avoidable harm, and devote resources to care for those who are vulnerable so long as they are in such condition. Much of President Roosevelt's New Deal to overcome the Great Depression of the 1930s… was just such an effort to help the vulnerable through the period of their vulnerability and to provide ways out of it for the long term. I think it is not just an accident of history that the drafters of the UDHR and most of those who drafted the covenants to implement it had experienced the Great Depression as well as World War II. Both disasters, viewed within the philosophical framework of the United Nations and the legal norms it developed, were deemed to be avoidable harms, the overcoming of which the international organization claimed as its fundamental purpose. In so doing, the UN stated to the world that it is possible to overcome the conditions that brought about the two disasters, even to replace the structures in which they unfolded. What I argue here is that the possibility to overcome becomes more probable when publics have experienced human rights learning.

…Human rights standards derive from human experience, from the history of human beings struggling to overcome their vulnerabilities. Lived human experience is the medium of human rights learning, the arena in which social ethics and social conscience are actualized. At its most dynamic human rights learning is infused with the vision of a just world order, an ethical global society, striving to overcome structural vulnerability and the violence that maintains and manifests the power of the structures over the lives of the vulnerable…

Human rights [is] the ethical core of peace education, built upon the value of human dignity. As a set of tools for diagnosing and overcoming vulnerabilities, human rights are also ethical criteria, a code of secular social ethics that is reminiscent of—and doubtless influenced by—the religious ethics and moral codes of the world's great religions... [In] a recent lecture, "Ethics, Economics and Global Justice" (2009)... Rowan Williams, Archbishop of Canterbury addressed contemporary ethics as they pertain to the current global financial crisis. "Ethics is essentially about how we negotiate our own and other people's vulnerabilities... behavior we recognize as unethical is frequently something to do with the misuse of power..." In these observations, the archbishop calls to our attention the power-vulnerability relationship that reflects the relationship between political and civil rights and economic social and cultural rights, a relationship made evident in approaching human rights in the holistic framework essential to thinking our way to a politics of peace, modes of thinking I have referred to as transformative or transformational. [This] is an opportune moment to advance the development of transformative thinking as a significant process in education and political discourse...

11.4 Proposition 5: We Need to Devise a Pedagogy for Hidebound Institutions

Peaceful political processes are learning processes.[3] They are Freirean politics of deliberation—action—reflection—renewed deliberation; action and reflection toward the best possible results, all within a process imbued with respect for and guided by the principles and standards of human rights. Authentic social progress is the product of the learning experienced by institutions and societies, as well as by individuals, each being a facilitator of the learning of the others. Perhaps the greatest lesson to be learned by the institutions that manage our nations and their relationships with each other is to trust and to truly serve their constituencies, to truly attend to them. Good governance as good teaching requires attentive listening to those being served. Attentive listening, a skill cultivated by peace education as the corner stone of critical pedagogy is fundamental to a politics of learning. A politics of learning would be a politics of dialogue, among citizens and between citizens and government. Educating through dialogue, for dialogue has long been a favored practice of the pedagogies of peace education and human rights learning. All citizenship education should include education for dialogue as preparation to mediate institutional learning. Such dialogue should exemplify civility in discourses of difference, made imperative by a commitment to the human dignity of all. This quality of civility would most contribute to the transformative possibilities of political dialogue.

---

[3] Proposition 4 entitled "The International Year of Human Rights Learning (IYHRL) may be a 'teachable moment' to advance critical, transformational thinking" was omitted from this version.

Civility, as a personal and social value, stems from actually experiencing the core value of human dignity, receiving and giving respect. What educators and politicians both need to understand is that it takes the experience of being the subject of rights, complemented by appreciation of the rights of others, to be able to exercise the skills and internalize the value of civility. Skills of civility comprise a behavioral repertoire infused with human rights norms, characterized by habitual use of dialogic and reflective approaches to all discourse, but most especially in addressing controversies that emerge from impulses toward change colliding with resistance. It is for such reasons that I advocate learning through creative/constructive contention as a complement to critical pedagogy.[4]

11.5 Proposition 6: Critical Pedagogy Is the Methodology Most Consistent with the Transformative Goals of Peace Education and Human Rights Learning

… Peace educators who teach so as to cultivate the values of civility and reason and the capacity of reasoning see these values and this capacity as basic to education for reconstructive practice of global citizenship; to preparation for participation in global as well as national politics of change.[5] Peace education's commitment to change toward reducing violence and vulnerability through dialogic critical analysis of political and social structures and relationships distinguish it from standard citizenship education. The political skills of authentic dialogue or civil discourses of difference are not usually cultivated beyond instruction on the general principles and stances of the leading political parties and the skills of the dualistic discourse of debate, a format in which civility has become the casualty of contemporary pit-bull politics. Neither public discourse nor public education has provided a hospitable environment for reasoned and reasonable political discussion or critical learning, particularly as regards reasoned reflection on alternatives to the prevailing order. (One good example among others is the controversy in the United States over health care reform.) I believe that it is in some degree reluctance to risk the consequences of open inquiry and the critical thinking it cultivates that leads some to insist that education and learning are synonymous, opting for education (i.e. transfer of information) as the safer terminology and practice. This reluctance exists among educators as well as politicians. We are not always so eager to open our own behaviors and values to the critical challenges that may lurk in open inquiry.

---

[4] This way of learning is elaborated upon in Reardon, *Education for a Culture of Peace in a Gender Perspective*: 168.

[5] I should like to acknowledge as well John Dewey largely as interpreted by Lawrence Metcalf whose work on reflective teaching has had significant influence on my own concepts and practice of critical pedagogy.

Peace educators who argue for the essential and integral relationship between pedagogy and purpose might summarize the distinction between ordinary civic education and peace education as similar to the distinctions between the generally held notions of the purposes of education in contrast to those of learning as espoused by human rights learning advocates. One very significant distinction is between formative vis-à-vis transformative approaches. The purpose of education is generally held to be formative, guiding formations' inculcating information and skills so as to enable the learners to function in the system as it is. The purpose of learning, as peace education seeks to cultivate it, is transformative, drawing from within learners' capacities to envision and affect change and helping them to develop the capacity to transform the existing system. The determining factor in most formal education is the intent of the educating agent. In learning it is the intent of the learner. The most influential factor in transformative learning is the conscious, reflective experience of the learner. The cultivation of learning strives toward the development of autonomy of thought, the sine qua non of preparation for constructive civic participation in an authentically democratic political system. Learning-centered peace education acknowledges learners as subjects of rights applicable in the learning setting as in all social arenas. Learning directed approaches are consistent with the value of personal autonomy that democratic systems purport to protect, the same value that led to the articulation of First Generation civil and political rights in terms of the individual person.

Fully internalized learning (i.e. learning that is demonstrably integrated into the thinking and behaviors of the learner) is not—as I have asserted above—the inevitable product of education originated outside the learner. It derives from within the learner; a circumstance that requires methods and pedagogies very different from those that characterize information-based instructional education to live in the world as it is. The true art of teaching lies in the capacity of the teacher to draw out the intent of the leaner, to bring it to the consciousness of the individual learner and co-learners in the learning setting, as well as that of the teacher. Effective teaching comprises moments of convergence of intentions, the instructional intention of the teacher with the learning intention of the student. It integrates that convergence into other such convergences to produce common learning for all in the group; to which all contribute and from which all receive elements of their own individual learning. It honors the individual as it cultivates a communal environment. An authentic educator in "leading forth"—the Latin root of the verb to educate—learners helps individuals to form learning communities through dialogues and sharing of intentions and arranging them so as to form common learning purposes. Such a process is what I have taken to be the intention of Freire in his role as educating agent. Such is certainly the essence of what I have come to perceive as human rights learning, and wherein I see human rights learning as pedagogically consistent with peace education.

11.6 Proposition 7: Inquiry Is the Teaching Mode Most Consistent with the Principles and Purposes of Critical Learning

Peace educators seek to devise pedagogies that enable them to draw out learners' intentions, then to discern the point of engagement at which the learner can undertake critical reflection on the subject matter as the basis on which to enter into dialogue with others for shared critique and communal inquiry into responses to the problems being addressed. For example, in human rights learning these responses might relate to how given violations can be overcome or avoided and how to pursue social change to prevent such violations from recurring in the future; or they may analyze forms of violence and/or explore the structural causes of the vulnerability that underlies so many human rights violations. Both human rights learning and the pedagogies of peace education are diagnostic and prescriptive and frequently speculative processes—raising queries into issue of what, why, how and what if—that call for communal discourse preceded by individual reflection on the substance of the issue under study. While the substance—the issue or problem under study—can be introduced by reading and or lecture, acquisition of the relevant information is the medium for learning as I suggested in the sculpting metaphor. The central learning mechanism is a question, a question that engages the learner with the substance, that which is to be changed; describing, assessing, diagnosing and prescribing. The core question or query formulated from the general problematic which is explored through a series of related queries derived from the component sub problems that comprise the problematic.

The inquiry comprises this series of queries and the questions that clarify them. In the construction of an inquiry as a learning process, I distinguish between questions and queries. Questions tend to be narrowly direct and call for answers—usually factual or clarifying. They bring a form of closure to a single aspect of the inquiry. Queries tend to be wider and not specific, calling for a range of possible responses. They open the inquiry to deeper reflection and critical analysis.

A learning process of reflection and dialogue is mediated through the formation and consideration of systematically constructed analytic and valuing queries. Critical thinking derives from confronting such queries and clarifying the questions they may raise. Queries are most effective when formed to produce a variety of responses that facilitate the consideration of multiple, often complex possibilities. A capacity for critical thinking encourages learners to form their own responses to the problems confronted, rather than expecting answers to be included in the curriculum or provided by the instructor. The capacity to devise queries that can produce multiple responses is one that peace educators seek to develop so as to perfect their skills of learning facilitation and extend their capacities for dealing with open critical inquiry.

We also seek to develop our own capacities for risk, perhaps preparing ourselves for the courageous creative politics of peace, but more professionally relevant, to undertake a similar process in our classrooms. When teaching from open ended queries, and deliberately cultivating multiple and varied responses, the teacher relinquishes sole control over the content and direction of discussion, a situation many educators find intimidating. Yet like many risky endeavors, it also can be exhilarating as the learning experience of the teacher is enriched and extended. Sometimes, especially when totally fresh and new possibilities are proposed by students, it can be downright thrilling. I refer to this pedagogical risk taking of fully open inquiry—as opposed to the assurance of a scripted curriculum—as "teaching without a net." As high wire performers and their audiences find working without a net thrilling rather than just entertaining, so too, this form of teaching—requiring even more preparation than transfer type pedagogy—is very professionally and personally rewarding. It is also analogous to the joys of playing and listening to jazz. It is communal creativity without limits; but, like jazz, is not without form and discipline; in the case of teaching the discipline and form are the rigorous standards of evidence and reason, central to responsible critical inquiry.

Critical learning has the potential to capacitate learners to live so as to move the world toward what it might become, toward the holistic vision of a social order based on human dignity that inspired the articulation of human rights in the first place. Human rights as the articulation of the characteristics of a world no longer tortured by violence and vulnerability give form to the vision and serve to deepen the understanding of the injustices of present societies. Inquiring into the means to achieve the vision within a holistic framework of human rights enables the learners to hold in mind two or more possible sets of social conditions, what is and what could be. As the zoom lens perspective provides the broader frameworks of holism, open inquiry cultivates thinking in terms of multiple possibilities, a step away from the limits of prepackaged curricula delivered through instruction and also from the reductionism and dualism of political realism. Most importantly, it helps to inspire hope that these limits can be transcended.

Hope is the energy source for all transformative learning and politics. It comes as we see the possibilities for outward change that lay in the inner reflections openly shared in Freirean dialogue. The process of shared reflection contributes to internalizing human rights values, motivating learners to acquire the knowledge and to develop the mastery of the political skills and social strategies to actualize the values in their own lives and societies, as in the larger world. Human rights learning requires the facilitation of active, participatory, reflective and applied learning. It demands raising the hard questions with open minds, exploring them with civil tongues and confronting them with hopeful hearts. Such reflection and questioning is preparation for the practice of the politics of peace, and the source of adherence to human rights as both goals of and guidelines for peaceful politics.

Peace educators cannot claim to know just how to initiate and implement such a politics as a means to peace or the realization of human rights. Neither peace education pedagogy nor human rights learning, though based on sound, well researched substantive knowledge of various aspects of the problematic have any assured resolutions to offer to the multiple and complex issues involved. Nor do they have readily applicable responses to the questions of how to achieve the reduction and ultimate elimination of violence and vulnerability. We have some guiding principles (human rights), repertoires of problem solving skills, methods for reflective, well-reasoned dialogue, and nonviolent conflict resolution strategies among other peacemaking possibilities. We tend to believe we can devise more and to assert that where the necessary political and pedagogic alternatives do not exist, they can be invented. We have profound faith in the human imagination and capacity to learn. But we do not purport to "have the answers." We tend to see the task as one of perfecting the questions, by formulating cogent queries about the human condition, its origins and possible futures. Perhaps we turn from the transfer model because we see that we have little that can be transferred. We do, however, have means to elicit the critical reflection that is essential to perfecting the questions, to devising the most fruitful queries.

11.7 Concluding Summary Proposition: Holistic Frame-Works and Critical Reflection Are Consistent with and Contribute to Transformation Toward the Actualization of Human Dignity

This International Year for Human Rights Learning is timely in the attention it brings to some of the most urgent political challenges faced by peace educators. It sheds light on the forms of Freirean pedagogy in which our field has been most active in the past few years, calling attention to its ultimate purpose, contributing to bringing about a world in which all can be human.

There may be nothing more human than the impulse to learn, to understand the realities in which we live, to seek the capacity to shape those realities into what we perceive to be conditions conducive to living in dignity. It is just this impulse that I believe leads us to be educators, persons who wish to devote their human talents and energies to clarifying the means to develop the capacities to realize our own humanity and assure the same opportunities for others. It is into this quest that we seek to lead forth the learners entrusted to us.

The history of all that is good in education can be interpreted as the efforts of society to improve and make more effective the ways in which we lead forth to the benefit of the learners and the societies in which they experience their humanity. Throughout most of what we know of human experience these efforts have been made the more difficult by conditions of both unavoidable and imposed ignorance, an oppression resulting from the correlative obstacle of the denial of the humanity of many by the few. The genius and the great contribution of human rights is that it (i.e. human rights taken as a whole) vindicates our rejection of this notion of limits to humanity, to human potential and to the members of the human family who may claim and enjoy their full humanity.

We are becoming aware of ways in which we may—even in the face of these limits imposed and upheld by structures of power—lead forth our own and our students' capacities to shape new realities. Paramount among these ways are holism and critical learning: the holism that enables us to see both the full dimensions of the limits and obstacles to our full humanity, as well as the range of multiple possibilities to overcome them; and the modes of critical learning that can cultivate our capacities to affect transformative change.

It is holism, critical learning and a commitment to transformative change that distinguish critical inquiry based human rights learning from information based human rights education, making human rights learning integral to peace education. The possibilities opened by these three attributes of human rights learning call us to risk undertaking the politically sensitive task of entering into authentic and transparent dialogue with power, so that we may learn together the ways to transformative change. Such a dialogue would be fully sensitive to words such as education and learning and how they affect our thinking and shape our actions and control our politics. Transformative politics would understand that education per se does not necessarily produce socially constructive learning, so that all means available must be used to engage ever wider populations in critical learning.

Above all, we as educators must reclaim and redefine the language of education, from that of an instrument for the communication of limited, selective, standard knowledge, to one for the creation of multiplicities of new knowledge, toward a potentially transformative understanding of the world. As peace educators we can approach this process through the Freirean mode of human rights learning. As Martin Luther King said in his statement denouncing the Vietnam War, we live in a time of "the urgency of now" (1967). There is much at stake and much to be gained by the way we work in what remains of this International Year of Human Rights Learning.

References

Eisenhower, Dwight, D., 1953: "A Chance for Peace", as quoted in Blanche W. Cook (1978) A Divided Legacy: Peace and Political Warfare. New York: Doubleday. Reissued in 1991 as The Declassified Eisenhower. New York: Penguin.

Freire, Paulo, 1970: *The Pedagogy of the Oppressed* (New York: Herder and Herder).

Galtung, Johan, 1996: *Peace by Peaceful Means* (London: Sage).

Hague Appeal for Peace Global Campaign for Peace Education. 1999; at: www.haguepeace.org.

Hans, Asha; Reardon, Betty, (Eds.), 2010: *Human Security: Challenging Patriarchal Violence.* (title tentative) (New Delhi: Routledge).

King, Martin Luther, Jr., 1967: "Beyond Vietnam: A Time to Break the Silence," a speech at the Riverside Church, New York, April 4, 1967; at: www.riversidechurch.org.

Metcalfe, Lawrence; Maurice, Hunt, 1968: *Teaching High School Social Studies*, 2nd Edn. (New York: Harper & Row).

Reardon, Betty, A.,; Eva, Nordland, (Eds.), 1994: *Learning Peace: The Promise of Ecological and Cooperative Education* (Albany: Albany State University of New York Press).

Reardon, Betty, A., 2001: *Education for a Culture of Peace in a Gender Perspective* (Paris: UNESCO Press).
United Nations, 2000: United Nations Millennium Development Goals; at: http://www.undp.org/mdg.
UN Secretary General (A/57/124), 2002: Report on Disarmament and Nonproliferation Education; at: http://www.un.org/disarmament/HomePage/ODAPublications/DisarmamentStudySeries/PDF/SS-30.pdf.
UNESCO, 1994: *Integrated Framework of Action for Education, for Peace, Human Rights and Democracy* (Paris: UNESCO).
UNESCO, 1980: *Final Document of the World Congress on Disarmament Education* (Paris: UNESCO).
UNESCO, 1993: *World Congress on Human Rights* (Paris: UNESCO).
United Nations General Assembly Resolution A/Res/40/184, 1994:*Resolution on the United Nations Decade for Human Rights Education, 1995–2005* (New York: United Nations).
United Nations General Assembly Resolution A/Res/62/171, 2008: *Declaration of the International Year of Human Rights Learning* (New York: United Nations).
Williams, Right Reverend Rowan, 2009: "Ethics, Economy and Global Justice," a speech given in Cardiff, Wales, March 7, 2009; at: http://www.archbishopofcanterbury.org.

Chapter 12
Human Rights and the Renewal of the University

Retrospective Reflection on "Human Rights and the Renewal of the University" (2012)

While human rights as socio-political norms and substantive content have been at the center of the development of my perspectives on and approaches to peace education from the first stages of my thinking about pedagogy and curriculum, my approaches to their role in the pedagogy of peace learning continues to evolve. I might now take a different approach to one of the first curricular materials published under my direction and co-authorship in a series of units published by Random House in 1973 and 1974, "The Struggle for Human Rights." That curriculum reflected the centrality of values analysis, a major concern at the time of the social studies and citizenship education. The leading social educators of the day, Laurence Metcalfe and Maurice Hunt, Donald Oliver and James Shaver, and Earl Johnson, all of whom I worked with and learned from in common efforts to advance what came to be called education for critical thinking, an interim antecedent to peace education's embrace of the critical pedagogy adapted from Freirean popular education.

The 70s also saw the introduction of international human rights law into some American Law Schools and the general topic of law into secondary schools social studies curriculum as advocated by The Constitutional Rights Foundation. Among the leaders of the movement was Professor Frank Newman of the University of California Berkeley who believed in the need for public education in the field. He aided and encouraged my curricular work, and was among those who informed and strengthened my conviction that peace required strong legal institutions for

B.A. Reardon and D.T. Snauwaert, *Betty A. Reardon: A Pioneer in Education for Peace and Human Rights*, SpringerBriefs on Pioneers in Science and Practice 26,
DOI 10.1007/978-3-319-08967-6_12

the adjudication and mediation of international conflict, and that enforceable law should replace armed force in determining the outcomes of the conflicts that led to war. As noted in the biography, my interest and belief in the potential of law as an instrument of peace was first kindled while directing The Schools Program of the Institute for World Order which made much use World Peace through Law *by Grenville Clark and Louis Sohn (Harvard University Press 1958.) The belief in law as an alternative to force was reinforced when I was called upon to prepare a common language version of an essay on international law by Quincy Wright, author of the classic in the field, Swords into Plowshares. I was more than pleased when he made only one minor adjustment in my text as it validated me as a learner, something I valued even more than being an adequate interpreter. It was another example of how the most substantive learning derives from interactions with those from whom we seek to learn, a reinforcement of the predilection for participatory learning first intuited and practiced during my classroom teaching.*

My thinking about human rights was thus initially from the perspective of attributes of citizenship to be protected and fulfilled through law. I also came to see human rights as a practical and heuristic framework for education for organic peace (more widely labeled "positive peace"). Rights provided peace education with practical descriptors of concrete goals that would manifest and serve as measures of the conditions of a just peace; an organic peace, the socio-political circumstances in which society would constantly strive toward the universal fulfillment of all human rights as defined in the international standards and those standards that may come to be established as we recognize and define new forms of injustice. Human rights are what comprise justice of the sort we envision when we speak of peace as the presence of justice. Since authentic justice cannot be achieved by force and in fulfillment of peace principles articulated in the Preamble to the Universal Declaration of Human Rights, I argue still that human rights are integral and essential to peace.

Celebrating 75th birthday in New York with Werner Wintersteiner 2004. *Source* Personal photo collection of the author

Within such a conceptual framework, focusing on the substance of human rights and framing peace education as learning toward their fulfillment, we can begin to envision peaceful institutions as infused with human rights, paramount among those institutions would be ones through which we educate, most especially the university. So, when I was invited Professor by Werner Wintersteiner to come to Klagenfurt University in Austria by the Center for Peace Research and Education to teach an intensive course on human rights as peace education as the first step in envisioning and developing a human rights university, I was delighted. I took up the task with hope that in the waning years of my career I might do something positive toward transcending my on-going critique of the academy initiated in "The Knowledge Industry."

This challenging task also provided me with an opportunity to reflect on the whole field of human rights education that had been developing through recent decades. As with peace education, there were various approaches, differing in

emphasis, methods, and learning audiences. Some human rights educators argued that their own particular approaches were the most effective ways of educating for the common goal of a just world order. I, too, had a strong preference for human rights learning to the point that I advocated it in the Master's lecture at the University of Puerto Rico delivered the year before the lecture at Klagenfurt on which the selection below is based. The Klagenfurt assignment pushed me to revise and refine my position, striving toward a comprehensive view of the field into which all the approaches to the field I was able to identify might be integrated. The major approaches as I perceived them are outlined in this selection in an attempt to acknowledge the particular contributions each could make to an institution seeking to educate for and a society actively endeavoring to achieve an authentically just public order.

Betty A. Reardon
April, 2014

12.1 Human Rights: a Response to the Problematic of Contemporary Universities

The modern university, like so much of society, has taken on the values of the corporate culture and the global market. Knowledge has become a commodity, the currency of success in the market; critical analysis is an exercise in perfecting technique for increasing material value; and wisdom is relegated to history and philosophy, realms that do not enjoy high value in a market-centered academy. The formation of reflective thinkers and responsible members of society would seem to have become the purview of seminaries and religious institutions, as universities prepare students for success in a highly competitive world, governed by a compulsion toward the amassing of wealth and power. Ethical reflection and involvement in the arts are the indulgences of leisure. The purpose of education is read more as perfecting skills of competition than at perfecting the human condition. Practical intelligence is valued while reflective valuing is considered impractical. What, we may ask, might those who still harbor some hope that the human condition could yet become a central concern of the modern academy advocate as a path to realizing that hope? The response, a case for which I set forth here, is human rights.

The state of the university and the social value system it reflects has begun to provoke a world-wide reaction against corporate power and the 'commoditization' of education along with other elements of the social order essential to the realization of our humanity. Some university faculty members have taken courageous stands to resist, in an attempt to preserve the integrity of the academy. There are students protesting on public squares and universities in numbers and vigor not seen since the pivotal year of 1968 in which student 'unrest' exploded in Europe, the United States, Latin America and even some few campuses in Japan. Today

Canadian, Chilean, US-American students among others, inspirited by the call for justice that 'occupy' movements the world over have breathed into the political atmosphere, are demanding change. They are rebelling against a life-long burden of debt as the price of an education less than relevant to the lives they envision. They are essentially demanding the fundamental human right to an education that will equip them to live as fulfilled human beings contributing to a society striving toward the conditions of human fulfillment, a vision that has enlivened centuries of the struggle for the realization of human dignity through the implementation of human rights. That vision, I assert, should inform the mission of the university and all that it comprises in the intentional learning derived from research and teaching in all the fields that constitute human knowledge.

To renew the traditional mission of the university as provider of authentic knowledge and relevant learning in the service of the development of persons and the societies in which they live their lives, there is no better means available to us than human rights. The goals and values of human rights are those most suitable to confront the competitive—frequently corrupt—materialism that has infected society. As the university has not been immune, serving as a carrier of the infection, so too, it can deliver the antidote. The prescription is a university wide infusion of human rights, compounded from the fundamental principles of universal human dignity, ethical responsibility and social justice. These, I argue, are the principles which should infuse the structures and programs of the university, and inform the norms and behaviors of those within it. The faculty members who hope that a human rights university can be developed at Klagenfurt offer an opportunity to test the proposition that a university can be devoted to learning for a more socially healthful human future.

12.2 The University as Learning Community

Above all, a human rights university would be a learning community. The pedagogy of critical, comprehensive peace education, a close relative to human rights learning, cultivates learning communities as environments in which learning is maximized and enriched by education *of* the participants, *for* the participants, and *by* the participants. It is, critical peace education practitioners argue, the atmosphere most conducive to educating for responsible, democratic citizenship, fully consistent with the norms and principles of human rights, most effective for the practice of critical pedagogy, integral to comprehensive peace education and human rights learning.

My conception of the nature and composition of an authentic university learning community derives from ideas advanced by students in a course I offered at Klagenfurt in the spring of 2010 when the idea of a human rights university had first been proposed. Their focused and value-aware reflections deeply influenced what I believe the concept of such an institution entails. The learning process of the course which centered on human rights learning and the possibilities for a human rights university played out in an atmosphere of open inquiry that I felt privileged to be part of. It was an experience that re-enforced my own sense of course convener as participant in a learning community. I am indebted to that community for the origins of much of what follows in this essay.

The university as a learning community comprises all who participate in the planned learning programs and processes and all who make them possible: students, teaching assistants, faculty, administration, office support staff, food services, buildings and grounds crew and custodial-security workers. All play essential roles necessary to establish, maintain, and develop the learning environment of the university. Each is a subject of human rights, endowed with human dignity. All are included in the moral community of the university that determines the quality of human relationships throughout the institution. Moral inclusion is the manifestation of the right to be held within the realm of justice and fair treatment and to have your and your group's interests and perspectives taken into consideration. The full unambiguous moral inclusion of all in the quotidian life of the university, as well as their participation in a human rights-centered institution serves as an indicator of the implementation of and commitment to the values integral to the concept of universal human rights.

As an institution undertakes to become a human rights university, everyone should be involved in all phases of planning and implementation. Reflecting on what the roles of each might be in the human rights learning community of the university would in itself be a community building process. Each person as an individual and the respective groups comprising each component of the community should themselves initiate a reflective inquiry into the possibilities for their particular contributions to the learning environment. Each person individually and each group together should also be invited to assess their current roles and experiences of the moral community of the university. If environmental or institutional change is needed to affect a successful process of development into a human rights university, such assessment could provide a starting point in planning the requisite changes. Such planning would certainly indicate the authenticity of the human rights intentions of those who issue the invitations to participate.

Participants in Teachers College Tokyo, Peace Education Certificate Course 2005. *Source* Personal photo collection of the author

The inclusivity of the community would be sustained by an ethos and ethic of human rights, not necessarily materially evident or visible any more than are the normative principles cited as rationale in the mission statement of a human rights university, but rather felt in the social atmosphere of the learning community. Essentially, an abstract spirit that manifests itself primarily in the attitudes and stances of moral inclusion that would characterize more than any other attribute of a human rights university, a human rights ethos would be the heart—or the soul, i.e., the agent of ethical self-reflection—of the institutional identity. Members of the entire community would recognize themselves personally, as well, as persons who respect human dignity and seek truth.

The ethos of inclusion would be infused throughout the interactions, dialogues, discussions and debates by which the mission is communicated and carried out. It would make it possible to address the most controversial and severe differences as open inquiry into truth to be reasonably and respectfully pursued, knowing that the risk faced would be change in view or position, not denigration of ideas or affronts to personal dignity. Through language, process and stances assumed by the disputants, the ethos would be manifest and moral inclusion would become more deeply ingrained in the mindsets of the participants. Above all, it would help the university to transcend some of the ideological polarization that prevails in the ethos of the current adversarial political culture, a polarization that tramples human rights, represses the seeking of truth and blights the academic soul of the university.

It is not only for the sake of the abstractions of truth-seeking and respecting human dignity that the form of communication I have referred to as "civil disputation" and as "constructive/creative/contention" is nurtured in community.[1] It is also essential to the discourses of difference that evolve from, among other factors, ethnic differences and legitimate political differences, especially the intersection of these two sets of differences that in the larger society often produce tensions and destructive conflicts that obstruct open inquiry. A community imbued with a human rights ethos would seek not only to respect and accommodate differences, but also to use them as learning resources. Different experiences and perspectives enrich learning communities and bring multiple gifts to the communal learning and to the search for responses to social and political problems. Constructively integrating human differences into the learning process prepares the university as a learning community to be a more effective agent of just and equitable societal development…

Wealth and power [have become] the hallmarks of human worth and capability in the corporate culture. Wisdom, integrity and empathy, qualities so evidently required to manage human affairs, are given little social value. The culture so wedded to the scarcity principle of worth in regard to material goods—that is, the less available, the greater the value—does not apply that principle to the human virtues in such short supply and so much needed for the kind of society that human rights standards were formulated to develop and sustain. In terms of the virtues and ethics that I argue to be at the heart of a human rights learning community that is at once educator of and model for the larger society, the current most 'advanced' societies are the least developed. I would argue that they have regressed to an ethically primitive state for which the university must accept some responsibility. Those who advocate for the academy a role of greater social responsibility more relevant to the interest of a just society might well consider agency in societal development, guiding the society to higher stages of moral development, as a learning objective to fulfill that role…

The first step in undertaking the mission might well be the reintegration of ethics into any programs relevant to social concerns in all disciplines. There is no better code of secular ethics than human rights standards, which are in essence specific articulations of principles of social ethics. Human rights standards are sturdy and suitable vehicles to be the carriers of ethics learning. More directly in the common life of the university they could also serve as the basis for codes of academic behavior and guidelines for resolving disputes and conflicts that arise within any dynamic, vital community. Dynamism and vitality are at once the source of action for change inspired by human rights and the product of the

---

[1] Reardon, Betty A. *Education for a Culture of Peace in a Gender Perspective*. Paris: UNESCO, 2001.

creative energies so likely to be unleashed by the action. A human rights university would be a lively community, as it undertakes action to fulfill its societal mission.

12.3 Purpose and Mission of the University Articulated Within the Human Rights Framework

One of the first steps in designing a human rights university is the declaration of its mission statement. In this statement the university would articulate its institutional purposes and the philosophy upon which they are based. The purposes of a human rights university would be infused with the philosophical principle which is the cornerstone of the human rights framework, "the inherent dignity and [...] the equal and inalienable rights of all members of the human family."[2] The means of fulfilling the purposes would be through comprehensive human rights education, integrating the practices of human rights education, human rights learning and human rights training as they are most appropriate to the various spheres of the university. Taken together, viewed and applied in intra- and extra-institutional relationships and interrelationships among all components of comprehensive human rights education, the effort could unfold in the holistic vision of a just society that inspires the philosophic foundations of human rights. The statement, to be consistent with the cornerstone principle, should involve a negotiation process in which all members of the university have a voice. This process would serve as the initiation of community building, providing the social and human foundations for the fulfillment of the commitment to the mission. To prepare the university community for the process of envisioning the mission, the administration could arrange a series of teach-ins involving all personnel in a common learning experience to assure that all are familiar with the basic human rights framework and its core principles, and to introduce a human rights perspective, essential for justice, infused societal development. A human rights perspective views problems in the context of equity and justice, problematizing issues so as to pursue solutions that contribute toward the actual universalization of human rights fulfillment.

---

[2] UN 1948: *The Universal Declaration of Human Rights*; at: http://www.un.org/en/docu-ments/udhr/. Accessed July 16th 2012.

With Dana Minaya, a founder of Samana College Research Center, at the 25th Anniversary of the International Institute on Peace Education observed at United Nations Headquarters in New York in 2007. *Source* Personal photo collection of the author

At the center of the mission should be the reclaiming of the role of the university as the reflective and ethical learning center of the society, wherein the major issues and normative aspects of social and political controversies and crises are fully debated in the spirit of open inquiry that should pervade all learning within the institution. That same spirit should inspire engagement with the larger society for which the university should be the source of relevant knowledge, and to which the university should extend invitations to participate in the normative discussions. In short, one of the main aspects of the mission might be to re-introduce ethics and civility into the public discourse, by the university serving as the facilitator of public discussions conducted with an authentic objectivity and integrity that can contribute to societal development toward the realization of the philosophy embraced in the mission statement.

12.4 Human Rights Education, Human Rights Learning and Human Rights Training: Contrasts and Complementarities

Within the peace knowledge field, activists, researchers and university and school educators have had differences over the significance of each of these sectors to the integrity and effectiveness of the field. Activists have not always fully appreciated the utility of theory produced by research, the modes of analysis taught in universities, nor of the critical thinking which peace education introduces into schools. Similar lack of appreciation of the other realms of the field can be attributed to each of the other two, sometimes insisting on the primary significance of their respective realms. In my view these distinctions and assessments of comparative significance to the fundamental purposes of the field are specious and dysfunctional, presenting an obstacle for the achievements of the whole field, not unlike the reductionist thinking of the corporate paradigm that upholds the system of inequality and a culture of greed, that peace education seeks to overcome. Here I offer a *mea culpa* for having written and spoken of the difference, seeming to imply that pedagogy may have more political valence than substance and thus, I fear, have reinforced some of what I see to be dysfunctional divisions. The point is made here because I want to make it clear in this argument for the transformative possibilities of a human rights university that those possibilities lie primarily in holism in conception, implementation and the assessment of the process of developing such an institution.

Speaking at Hiroshima Day Observation, in background Pete Seeger and Clearwater Singers 2007. *Source* Personal photo collection of the author

Human rights education (HRE) is the overarching term as used by the wider human rights movement and—with the exception of the General Assembly Resolution 173 on the Year of Human Rights Learning, noted in the 2010 lecture at

Klagenfurt—it is the term of preference of the United Nations and its agencies. The topography of the conceptual map of the field is further complicated by the introduction of the term *training*—firmly established with the 2012 UN Declaration on Human Rights Education and Training—as a third element in the whole field of study. The holistic approach to human rights which I believe is most conducive to the meta purposes of a human rights university, functioning as a learning community intended to contribute to societal development, necessitates that all three (and perhaps—in the longer range—conceptualizations yet to come) are constitutive to the structure and process of both the planning and on-going life of the institution. An argument, made in years past for the integration of the multiple approaches to peace education into the general field, applies here.[3] The whole of the terrain of the acquisition and application of human rights knowledge might be conceptualized as *comprehensive human rights education*, a concept consistent with what UN discourse refers to as the *human rights framework,* the whole of the international body of agreements and standards as derived from the foundational normative core of the Universal Declaration of Human Rights.

Within the context of the learning to be facilitated through a human rights university, some conceptual and process differences, as well as the nature of their fundamental complementarity, are noted here as background to describing the learning realms and functions of the *university*. The distinctions that have produced the sharpest differences are those between human rights education (HRE) and human rights learning (HRL), addressed in detail elsewhere[4] and more cursorily in the lecture at Klagenfurt (2010) of which this essay is an extension. The distinctions here will be limited to how these differences are relevant to a human rights university.

Human rights education (HRE) as practiced in universities and in many schools is centered on the substantive content or 'the what, why and how' of the concepts, standards and norms of human rights. Methodologically, it tends to take an analytic and problem solving approach. This approach, teaching interpretation of theory and critical analytic skills, seldom involves direct action (as distinct from the field research and internships required in some university programs). Students studying human rights at the graduate and undergraduate level are often preparing for human rights work in international agencies, non-governmental organizations or in field campaigns. The underlying assumption of some undergraduate programs, like that of secondary school study units, is that knowledge of human rights, particularly the international standards, is a basic and essential component of education for global citizenship that should be included in the education of all, a standard offering in schools and undergraduate university programs (in which comparatively few human rights courses are offered outside graduate schools and

---

[3] Reardon, Betty A. *Comprehensive Peace Education*. New York: Teachers College Press, 1988: 189–192.

[4] Reardon, Betty A. *Human Rights Learning: Pedagogies and Politics of Peace*. San Juan, Puerto Rico: UNESCO Chair for Peace Education, University of Puerto Rico, 2010; at: http://www.paxeducare.org/Documents/iipe2009/BettyReardontalkppt.pdf. Accessed July 16th 2012.

departments of law). This assumption is one I share, as do some, but not all, practitioners of human rights learning. The position I would argue here in terms of standard curriculum planning is that knowledge of human rights declarations and standards are the substance of the cognitive learning objectives and the analytic skills development of comprehensive human rights education. It provides the content base to be studied within the pedagogy of human rights learning. Substantive analytic human rights education is citizenship education directed toward external application of the knowledge and skills in realms of social and political action in the extramural society.

Human rights learning (HRL) is directed toward affective learning objectives, the internalization of values and attitudes, the normative formation of ethical persons disposed toward behaviors and relationships conducive to the realization of human rights. The objective is to lead the learner beyond problem analysis through ethical reflective processes to place high personal and social value on fundamental human dignity and universal moral inclusion. In so doing, it provides—in addition to pursuing another objective held in common with human rights education, the development of critical skills—the formation of habits of behavioral ethics, i.e. acting within a predisposition to universal moral inclusion. These objectives lead many educators to the practice of critical pedagogy that is common to both human rights learning and critical peace education.

Human rights training (HRT), the more recent entry into the field as it is addressed by the United Nations is provided mainly for the purpose of preparing for direct action, with a stronger strategic element than the other two components of comprehensive human rights education. It is most often sought by those seeking to use human rights principles and standards to uphold arguments and pursue political goals to overcome specific injustices or work directly for social change. It provides demonstrations and practice of action skills designed to achieve specific, political, social or economic goals, i.e. ending the denial of a political right, overcoming instances of sexism or racism, gaining fair working conditions, etc. Training is behavioral, strategic and target directed. When necessary, it also provides relevant substantive knowledge of the standards and laws relevant to the action goal.

All three fundamental learning objectives of the human rights fields of study/learning/practice—the interpretive/analytic of human rights education, the critical/ethical of human rights learning, and the strategic/practical of human rights training—are essential to the structures, programs and practices of a human rights university. Each has a particular role to play in offering human rights education to all learning audiences served by a university.

Comprehensive human rights education developed within the holistic human rights framework that informs the mission of the undertaking makes possible educating all segments of the university community in a holistic view of human rights through a pedagogy particularly relevant to each.

12.5 Human Rights Education as the Substance of the Scholarly Components

Content related to human rights norms, standards, treaties, controversies and conflicts surrounding their violation and implementation can be integrated throughout the teaching and research of the academy. All faculty and academic support staff such as teaching assistants could review the substantive focus of their courses and projects in light of the human rights framework and perspective to identify potential human rights topics, issues and concerns. Infusion of questions and readings relevant to human rights could be achieved without restructuring current courses. Reviewing content regularly, especially from the perspective of current human rights issues, would be a useful device for keeping standard course offerings regularly fresh, providing both faculty and students with wider learning opportunities. New courses could be considered if they were needed, or special issues could be addressed through periodic teach-ins cooperatively organized by faculty and students…

Along with human rights *sensitivity*, human rights *criticality* is certainly among the objectives that should be pursued in all human academic programs. Developing the capacity of criticality in the substantive study of the content, history and controversies in human rights is essential to honing the capacities of political efficacy in the pursuit of social, economic and political justice. Sensitivity and criticality are two sides of the agency coin in the realm of civic responsibility that *all* universities should embrace as central to their missions…

12.6 Human Rights Learning: A Process of Ethical and Intellectual Formation, Sharpening the Mind While Strengthening the Heart

Human rights learning…. employ[s] dialogue, but in general is more participatory and interactive than most academic approaches. As a form of critical pedagogy it is inclined to establish learning communities as the learning setting. Such communities pursue communal, as well as individual learning objectives. Individual objectives are set and followed in terms of what they might contribute to communal learning. As interests and capacities vary, each would have some unique talent or experience that might contribute to the sum of communal learning. The process of setting the individual objectives in the communal context helps students to gain awareness of their special capacities and can contribute to a sense of self-worth, empathic sensitivity and appreciation of community, qualities that contribute to ethical and effective political agency. It helps to kindle the sparks of empathic sensitivity into a spirit of solidarity among the learning community. Experience of solidarity is an affective learning that may be brought to larger international realms of solidarity which characterize popular civil society movements on behalf of those deprived of their rights. Another way of affective learning, resulting from more intense communal cooperation, is coming to appreciate human diversity as a resource that can be harnessed to the achievement of communal group goals.

This more intense and common goal-focused process of cooperative learning is one in which the success of the whole cooperative group is counted as the success of each member because it depends on the responsibility of each. The learning gained through planned cooperation produces a sense of the common human predicament, the oneness of the human species and its universal entrapment in the same survival crises. It is essential political learning for planning and carrying out strategies for achieving chosen human rights goals. Cooperative learning and learning communities are a kind of educational rehearsal for social and political action for human rights defense and implementation in the larger society. In some cases cooperative projects and learning within the university may be designed to be brought directly into the outer community. All this is fuel for the engine of societal development.

Human rights learning may or may not be merged with the academic approaches in the traditional disciplines. However, I would argue strongly for the learning approach—i.e. participatory critical reflection on human rights issues and potential avenues to address them—as the preferred pedagogy of courses in education and especially in teacher preparation. The approach is conducive to developing the professional skills and forming the human qualities of a good teacher.

12.7 Human Rights Training: Providing Non-Academic Social Justice Learning Opportunities

Human rights training is another area which should be applied in teacher education. Training in the sense the term is used here refers to imparting, through hands-on demonstration and practice, specific methods and behaviors to provide human rights education skills development for use in non-formal education settings. Skills are crafted for the particular settings in which human rights education and political action are to be pursued by learners/activists being prepared to apply those skills in their respective learning/action settings. These may be classrooms, civil society organizations, worship communities, corporations, political parties—any group who may act together to achieve a common social goal. Human rights training could be offered as a complement to the human rights education offered to the entire university community. It should be designed to serve non-academic personnel and learning audiences outside the university. Such training would raise awareness of the human rights of individual staff members and of categories of the community membership, such as faculty, support staff, grounds and service personnel. More importantly it would provide skills for the defense and pursuit of these rights.

Once so trained, all university personnel would be able to engage in some forms of human rights education, and be of great assistance to the university in bringing appropriate forms of training to concerned citizens beyond the campus… a human rights university could, in renewing the social purposes of its own mission, serve as an unparalleled agent of the social learning that produces societal development.

12.8 Reclaiming the Moral High Ground: Renewing the University to Transform the Society

The corporatization of modern culture has changed universities who have accepted the role of turning out 'the best and the brightest', an elite of high intelligence and low ethical inclinations who preside over the affairs of powerful nations and corporations, whose hegemony coincides with severe survival crises that are, to my mind, more moral than strategic. Even popular journals, such as *The Nation* have commented on the increase in armed violence, the decrease in distributive justice, the debasement of the democratic process and the erosion of fundamental freedoms that these elites have wrought. Many are beginning to recognize what is most lacking. Their maximal education has lacked even minimal ethical formation. "Without qualities like wisdom, judgment, empathy and ethical rigor, extreme intelligence can be extremely destructive."[5]

The mission of a human rights university would be to replace the destructive corporate values and thinking that valorizes technical prowess and economic power with constructive human values and thinking that valorizes human dignity and moral inclusion. This is not a scenario for "mission impossible." It is a learning agenda for saving the soul (spirit) of the university and the body of society. We might say that comprehensive human rights education brings body and soul together.

The point of societal development is the maturation of a social body, inspirited with ethical, reflective integrity. I see that spirit in the Klagenfurt experiment. It is to be hoped that other universities will also be so inspirited and follow in those footsteps on one of the few paths to hope available to us.

[5] Hayes, Christopher. "Why Elites Fail." *The Nation* 294, no. 26 (June 25th 2012): 15.

Chapter 13
Reflective Pedagogy, Cosmopolitanism, and Critical Peace Education for Political Efficacy

Betty A. Reardon and Dale T. Snauwaert

Retrospective Reflection on Reflective Pedagogy, Cosmopolitanism and Critical Peace Education for Political Efficacy (2012)

The most recent of my publications on the context and processes of peace education inspired this selection, an exchange on pedagogy between Dale Snauwaert and I. That publication articulated the political concerns which led to my working on a greater refinement of a pedagogy of reflective inquiry that is the subject of the exchange. The original essay lamented that circumstance described below as "the ideological reductionism" that currently defies reasoned political discourse and the lack of civility in that discourse that violates human dignity, the core and fundamental value of peace and peace education that animates the philosophy of cosmopolitanism.

The concerns that produced the lamentation, indeed, evolve from some of those that informed earlier publications and the work they reflected, yet they are far more infused with deeper worries about the socio-political climate in which civility and integrity were in little evidence, and decisions and policies on war and peace made with little or no reasoned public consideration. Critical thinking as

B.A. Reardon and D.T. Snauwaert, *Betty A. Reardon: A Pioneer in Education for Peace and Human Rights*, SpringerBriefs on Pioneers in Science and Practice 26,
DOI 10.1007/978-3-319-08967-6_13

advocated by peace education is not in evidence in the exercise of the franchise or any other citizen responsibility. The essay also up-dated the critique of the university as put forth in "The Knowledge Industry;" in this case in terms of the academy's failure to rise to the crisis of reason. Nor did I find peace education blameless, sometimes also failing to eschew ideology in favor of authentic critical reflection. I see in today's surveillance policies rationalized by security interests, poverty tolerated as fiscal responsibility, and denunciation and disrespect as the language of political difference; and in some cases the resort to violence as tool of domestic politics to threaten most of what we seek to achieve in peace education as preparation for citizenship. I am more convinced than ever that it is our ways of thinking that stand most in need of transformation; that further developing our capacities for reflective inquiry is one way to approach that transformation. And I am learning that cosmopolitanism provides the philosophic and normative base that may be the practical incarnation of the transformation.

Class photo of Gender, Peace and Security course at the UNESCO Chair in the Philosophy of Peace at Jaume I, Castellon, Spain, 2007. BR front row. *Source* Personal photo collection of the author

Cosmopolitanism brings a perspective to peace education that I have only lately come to see as the normative form of holism for which I was intuitively searching through the years of seeking more conceptual and philosophic clarity on comprehensive peace education. As the selections related to the role of human rights education included in this volume indicate, I had come to be an advocate of Freirean critical pedagogy. But as is evident, too, in those selections, I continued to seek a more widely conceptualized framework. Had the learning come earlier in my career, it would likely have presaged much of my future efforts. This conceptual breakthrough is, like others in my professional formation, the consequence of learning from a respected close colleague; in this case Dale Snauwaert, whose scholarship on cosmopolitanism has so enriched the field. Dale and I have had a fruitful learning relationship since our days as simultaneous visiting professors at Colgate University. I deeply valued his validation of the conceptualization of reflective inquiry and welcomed the opportunity to delve more deeply into the relevant pedagogical processes offered in this exchange in which we sought to model as closely as possible in print, the learning possibilities integral to dialogue. The dialogic element of learning communities engaging in the various forms of reflective inquiry may well be the fuel that propels the transformation of our thinking. Certainly this exchange has considerably pushed forward the continuous changes in our own thinking. Were I to be able to assign but one piece of my writing to students, it would be this dialogue with Dale Snauwaert.[1]

Betty A. Reardon
April, 2014

In a recent publication entitled "Meditating on the Barricades: Concerns, Cautions and Possibilities for Peace Education for Political Efficacy" Betty Reardon reflects on the state of peace education and offers a brilliant reaffirmation and further elaboration of the central importance and nature of a pedagogy of reflective inquiry for a comprehensive/critical peace education.[2] Betty Reardon is an internationally renowned peace scholar and peace educator. She has been instrumental in the establishment of peace education institutions and programs around the world. Her work has defined the fields of peace studies and peace education.[3]

---

[1] This text was first published as: Reardon, Betty A, and Dale T Snauwaert. "Reflective Pedagogy, Cosmopolitanism, and Critical Peace Education for Political Efficacy: A Discussion of Betty A. Reardon's Assessment of the Field." *In Factis Pax: Journal of Peace Education and Social Justice* 5, no. 1 (2011): 1–14; at: http://www.infactispax.org/journal/. Permission was granted by Dr. Dale Snauwaert, 12 March 2014.

[2] See Reardon, Betty A. "Meditating on the Barricades: Concerns, Cautions, and Possibilities for Peace Education for Political Efficacy." In *Critical Peace Education: Difficult Dialogues*, edited by Peter Pericles Trifonas and Bryan L. Wright. New York: Springer, 2013. The quotations and page numbers are from the unpublished manuscript July, 25, 2010.

[3] Reardon's Collected papers are housed at Ward M. Canaday Center for Special Collections, The University of Toledo Library; at: http://www.utoledo.edu/library/canaday/guidepages/education.html.

With Dale Snauwaert at the opening of the archive of Betty Reardon's work at the University of Toledo, 2009. *Source* Personal photo collection of the author

The purpose of this paper is to discuss her recent assessment and elaboration. In particular, the connection between cosmopolitanism and reflective pedagogy will be explored in greater detail, in addition to the posing of further questions for inquiry related to the relationship between dialogue, conceptual clarity, philosophical frameworks, diversity and reflective pedagogy.

13.1 Dale Snauwaert's Reflections

Reardon situates peace education within the broader issue of citizenship and argues that peace education should be fundamentally concerned with the development of the *political efficacy* of future citizens. She writes:

> Starting from the long held premise that peace education is education for responsible global citizenship, our task in general terms is educating toward political efficacy in the formation and pursuit of citizen action and public policy intended to move the world toward the achievement of a more just and less violent global order.[4]

[4] Reardon, "Meditating on the Barricades: Concerns, Cautions and Possibilities for Peace Education for Political Efficacy," 2.

Political efficacy is not necessarily a matter per se of *what* to think; it is more fundamentally about *how* to think. In other words, political efficacy is dependent upon "sound political thinking," "for inquiry into obstacles and possibilities for transformation should form the core of peace pedagogy, so as to provide learning in how to think and to act for political efficacy in peace politics…"[5] Learning how to think concerns conceptual clarity, thinking within conceptual frameworks, posing questions, rationality, and most importantly reflective inquiry.

From an ethical perspective, political efficacy is grounded in the normative framework of *cosmopolitanism,* defined by Reardon as the value of "universal moral inclusion"[6] grounded in respect for human dignity. She maintains that cosmopolitanism "best articulates the normative goals of our evolving field… the vision of universal moral inclusion that inspires the normative goals of peace education; a vision in which all human beings are accorded respect of their fundamental human dignity."[7] From this perspective, political efficacy is driven by the values of universal human dignity and moral inclusion.

Political efficacy thus involves "complex learning that requires pedagogies of multiple forms of reflective inquiry."[8] Peace learning and thus reflective practice is both cognitive and normative, pertaining to both the discernment of the sociopolitical world and value-based ethical assessment. Reardon's basic presupposition is that political efficacy, the capacity to engage in transformative political action, is contingent upon the cognitive, ethical, and self-reflective capacities of citizens. Transformative action is a reflective-practice. Being a reflective practice it requires both the capacity and space for authentic open reflective inquiry in dialogue with the diverse range of other citizens. It requires "authentic open inquiry." Reardon writes: "All peace learning at whatever academic level in whatever learning setting should be directed toward developing a range of reflective capacities relevant to political efficacy."[9]

Reardon articulates three forms of reflective inquiry: critical/analytic; moral/ethical; and contemplative/ruminative. *Critical/analytic reflection* pertains to the discernment of power, an understanding and critique of the functioning of social institutions, knowledge and analysis of the structural dimensions of social life, and the impact of power, institutions, and structures on the quality of life. Reardon writes: "It is more directly political than the other two as its primary inquiry is into the nature, functions and distribution of power, the political institutions and social structures through which it is mediated and the consequences of these circumstances to human lives and relationships."[10]

---

[5] ibid., 3.
[6] ibid., 3.
[7] ibid., 3.
[8] ibid., 3.
[9] ibid., 6.
[10] ibid., 8.

With Cora Weiss, President of the Hague Appeal for Peace at the El-Hibri Peace Education Prize Ceremony, 2013. *Source* Personal photo collection of the author

"*Moral/ethical reflection* addresses questions of fairness and moral inclusion with queries on issues of the goodness, distribution of advantage and harm, the justice and potential detriments and benefits of relationships, effects upon quality of life and the biosphere. Transformative moral/ethical reflection is guided by normative principles consistent with the values designated as the indicators of what is considered to be socially good and humanly enhancing."[11] Moral/ethical reflection involves the principled application of practical reason to the many moral and ethical issues inherent in the political and social realms. She makes an important distinction between the moral as precepts to guide life and the ethical, as principled practical reason. It is the latter that is most fundamental to political efficacy and the education of cosmopolitan citizens.

"*Contemplative/ruminative reflection* is a process consistent with the breadth of thought inspired by a cosmopolitan view. It is a wider sphere of reflection, which facilitates perception of the full scope of the complex systemic, dynamic interrelationships comprising our natural and humanly constructed environments. It makes

[11] ibid., 8.

space for affect and intuition as more complex forms of reason. It is the deeper thought through which persons gain the forms of self-awareness from which to develop capacities to lead not only humanly fulfilling lives, but even more to the point, to live personally, socially and politically so as to be agents of social and political transformation."[12] Contemplative reflection is thus conceived as critical self-examination regarding our internal motivations and moral capacities. It pertains to a reflection on what is meaningful and valuable. It is essential for ethical commitment and for the empathic moral response to the dignity of other persons.

Although Reardon does clearly posit the interconnection between the three forms of reflective inquiry and cosmopolitanism, arguing that they constitute capacities that make possible the transformative action necessary for the actualization of the cosmopolitan ideal, I believe that the relationship between cosmopolitanism runs even deeper than Reardon suggests. Reflective inquiry is not only a means to the actualization of cosmopolitanism; reflective inquiry is an *ethical requirement,* and thus a *constitutive element,* of cosmopolitanism. It can be argued that the cosmopolitan ideal of universal respect for human dignity and moral inclusion *itself necessitates* open reflective inquiry and in turn its reflective capacities, and that the three forms of reflective inquiry mirror the three dimensions of cosmopolitanism.

The ethical dimension of cosmopolitanism consists of universal respect for human dignity and moral inclusion. This ethic proclaims the equal inherent dignity and value of each and every human being as a human being. This value of universal moral equality in turn bestows moral *standing* to each person. Each person is a morally equal member of the human moral community and thus each person has a right to equal moral consideration. As a matter of basic justice, moral consideration includes **recognition** (recognition of all persons as moral equals, regardless of difference), **fairness** (impartial treatment and respect for persons), and **inclusion** (all persons have *equal standing* (membership) in the moral and political community). The ethical imperative of cosmopolitanism mandates that we see the other as a person; it demands that we transcend the objectification of persons in favor of the recognition of their: humanity. Thus, woven into this dimension is the ethical requirement of reflective inquiry into the moral standing of persons and the forces of objectification that deny them their humanity and rightful standing in the moral community.

The political dimension logically follows from the ethical. If all human beings are morally equal, then they possess a right to have their interests equally considered in the political process as well as the right to participate equally in that process. The rights to equal political consideration and equal political participation constitute political equality. The aim of political equality is the institutionalization of individual political empowerment. Critical/analytic reflection is a constitutive imperative of political equality and thus of cosmopolitanism, for the sustainable institutionalization of individual political empowerment is based upon individual awareness and knowledge of one's rights to consideration and participation and the internal capacities to effectively participate in the political process.

[12] ibid., 9–10.

The self-reflective, contemplative dimension of cosmopolitanism consists of the internal moral resources of the individual that provide the consciousness and capacity to be aware of and to ethically respond to the inherent dignity of every human being. Cosmopolitanism thus entails an internal disposition and capacity to respond to others empathetically with respect and care. It also entails a moral commitment to the ideals of human dignity and inclusion, which makes cosmopolitanism a deliberative choice. These dispositions emerge out of critical self-examination and contemplative reflection wherein their meaning and value are contemplated and affirmed by each individual citizen.[13]

In addition, if we take into consideration the almost incomprehensible scope of human diversity, the ideals of universal human dignity and moral inclusion, including the principles of recognition, inclusion, and fairness as well as equal political consideration and participation, require open impartial public deliberation.[14] It requires that everyone submit their values and ideas to open impartial scrutiny as a test of their objectivity, value, and validity. Given that our perspectives tend to be confined, exposing our positions to open impartial scrutiny is a means of transcending our positional confinement. This call for impartial scrutiny is central to Reardon's advocacy of reflective inquiry and her critique of the narrowness and partiality of the positioning of critical, reflective pedagogies as *ideologies* rather than as *methods* of inquiry and educational liberation.

My main point is that open reflective inquiry in general, and the three forms of reflective inquiry in particular, are constitutive elements of the cosmopolitan ethic. The cosmopolitan ethic is instantiated educationally through the pedagogical application of the three forms of reflection. From this perspective, peace education is the enactment of the cosmopolitan ethic. By enacting it pedagogically the school becomes the incubator, and the peace educator the midwife, of a cosmopolitan society.

Reardon offers a very insightful analysis of the nature of reflective inquiry. However, further questions into the nature of reflective inquiry can be posed as a means of further developing a reflective perspective:

1. What is the general methodological orientation of reflective inquiry? Is reflective inquiry a process of discovery, invention, or interpretation?
2. What is the place of dialogue in reflective inquiry? Is reflective inquiry dialogical?
3. Is mastery of conceptual frameworks necessary for conceptual clarity and critical thinking? Is a substantial degree of background knowledge necessary for reflective inquiry?

---

[13] See Snauwaert, Dale T. "Human Rights and Cosmopolitan Democratic Education." *Philosophical Studies in Education* 40 (2009): 94–103; Snauwaert, Dale T. "The Ethics and Ontology of Cosmopolitanism: Education for a Shared Humanity." *Current Issues in Comparative Education* 12 (2009): 14–22.

[14] See Nussbaum, Martha C. *Frontiers of Justice: Disabliity, Nationality, Species Membership*. Cambridge, Massachusetts: The Belknap Press of Harvard University Press, 2006; Rawls, John, and Erin Kelly. *Justice as Fairness : A Restatement*. Cambridge, Mass.: Harvard University Press, 2001; Sen, Amartya. *The Idea of Justice*. Cambridge, Massachusetts: The Belknap Press of Harvard University Press, 2009.

4. Can justice and peace be defined, and can reflective inquiry proceed, without the adoption of a political and moral philosophy? Can an exposure to a variety of philosophies be sufficient for reflective inquiry?

13.2 Reardon's Responses to Snauwaert's Queries on Reflective Inquiry

Dale Snauwaert has offered an excellent and incisive encapsulation of my proposals for reflective inquiry as an appropriate and effective pedagogy through which to pursue the political/social purposes of comprehensive critical peace education. This encapsulation prefaces some very significant challenges for the further explication and development of the proposals and arguments put forward in "Meditating on the Barricades: Concerns, Cautions and Possibilities for Peace Education for Political Efficacy". Snauwaert, an education philosopher has been a ground-breaker in articulating the moral and ethical dimensions of peace education and has situated the field within the philosophy of cosmopolitanism. His reflections deepening the inquiry into these dimensions offer a particularly provocative extension of the discussion I sought to open about current problems and possibilities in the pedagogies of peace education.

The following responses to his challenging queries attempt to bring further clarification and put a bit of meat on the bones of my propositions concerning reflective inquiry as peace pedagogy. The responses are represented in the order in which Professor Snauwaert posed questions as means to explore further the pedagogic characteristics of reflective inquiry, and are articulated in thematic fashion around the core concepts of his questions.

I need to note here that these responses—as are the assertions in the original essay—are subjectively based on my own experience as a practitioner supplemented by observations of current practice. Judgment on the degree to which my assertions and suggestions are transferable to the practice of others, is left to the readers.

13.2.1 Methodological Orientation: A Purposeful Interrogatory Process

The general methodological orientation of reflective inquiry is the nurture and development of the human curiosity and wonderment that is the font of learning. The starting point of authentic learning is not an instruction, but a question. The task of education is to guide the human attributes of curiosity and wonderment toward the achievement of the complementary, mutually reinforcing purposes of development of the self and of socially relevant knowledge and humanly enhancing skills and values. Reflective inquiry comprises a pedagogy of questions and queries as tools of learning facilitation. The art of this pedagogy is in the formation of the questions and queries that instigate reflective responses from learners. Instruction is designed to meet the needs of learners to develop skills for the interpretation of questions, to establish the relationship of the subject of the question to the social and learning environment in which a peace learning inquiry is pursued, and to illuminate particular dimensions of the subject of the inquiry or problem being addressed. The sequence and mode of instruction most effectively emerge from the learners' question, "What does this subject have to do with me, my life and the society in which I live?" In a peace learning inquiry that question will ultimately evolve to the query, "What has the subject to do with us as a community, our common welfare and the kind of society in which we would prefer to live?" The great need in the implementation of reflective pedagogy is to elicit and refine the capacities for such question formation and modes of posing those questions of teachers at all levels and of the learners whom they guide.

In that reflective inquiry can be pursued in analytic, ethical and contemplative modes, it is practiced through various thinking processes including discovery, invention, interpretation, explication and others. Reflection can lead to discovery in the sense of revealing elements of a subject of study not perceivable through surface observation. Reflection in the sense of careful and detailed thinking to fully examine all elements and aspects of a subject of study that can be 'seen' as through a kind of intellectual magnification is, in fact, an effective route to learning as discovery or as in deductive reasoning. Reflection toward discovery is elicited by questions specifically designed to reveal the less obvious aspects of the subject, questions rather than queries as per the distinctions made in the original essay—questions about specific aspects of the subject to which there are answers in the form of particular material attributes of the subject that can be observed by closer more thoughtful examination.

Reflective inquiry in the modes of invention and interpretation is more likely to be facilitated through queries, more open questions to which sufficient response is not one particular observable attribute or validated facts, but a range of responses revealing various possibilities in regard to how the subject might be dealt with (i.e. invention) or to its meaning to the larger realms to which the subject is or might be related (i.e. interpretation).

13.2.2 The Place of Dialogue: Communal Reflection Building Learning Communities

Reflective inquiry initiated by the posing of questions is deepened through the consideration of queries. In that it is in essence a process of thinking by interrogation, it is thus essentially dialogic, beginning with focusing on and encountering the subject of the inquiry as the entry point into the process of examination of what is to be further explored. In this respect, reflective inquiry begins with an inner process of confronting and questioning toward a basic understanding of the subject or issue. While it is possible for the process to remain inward and still be productive of learning, the practice of reflective inquiry as peace education—learning toward social and political change—must become outwardly dialogic in the form of a learning discourse through posing queries to elicit the individual reflections of all who comprise the learning community (or class). The social purposes of comprehensive critical peace education are best achieved through communally conducted reflective inquiry. Because it is a process of posing and considering questions, the instructional dimension—the intentional construction of learning experiences to achieve planned objectives—must be dialogical.[15] If it were simply questioning for comprehension rather than for the elicitation of multiple reflected responses, it might remain as retention of content, or in the absence of multiple views, easily slip into indoctrination, the antithesis of critical peace education. Were it to be left at the inward without the communal sharing, it might become meditative rather than ruminative, remaining personal, not becoming a social learning process, preparatory to the public political discourse for change.

Further, dialogue serves to develop conceptual clarity through communal explication of individual reflections, and contributes, as well, to honing the skills of articulation particularly necessary in the contentious discourse through which meaning is negotiated and peace and justice are pursued. In the sense of its application as intentional preparation for contentious discourse—as critical peace education pedagogy—reflective inquiry is dialogic in its confrontation of contradictions and disputations. Most essential in discussions of controversial and contentious social and political issues is to be cognizant of the need for reflected exchanges in lieu of the mutual vaulting of predigested, ideological positions. In fact, reflective inquiry is stressed as a possible antidote to the ideological reductionism that infects present political discourse.

One other aspect of the dialogic dimension of reflective inquiry is that dialogue is the process through which validation of arguments can be achieved by offering and testing of evidence, data, prior experience or related matters, and assessing its relevance to the problematic. Dialogue is the realm in which reasoning of the type Metcalfe advocated is the arbiter, the means through disputed differences are resolved. It is an outward manifestation of the reflective thinking Metcalf argued to be essential to the democratic process. The near total lack of reasoning and reasonable discourse in contemporary American politics impels me to advocate reflective inquiry as a common pedagogy in peace education.

13.2.3 Conceptual Frameworks: Tools for Shaping and Plotting the Inquiry

Conceptual frameworks are important to reflective inquiry as pedagogy. I hesitate to advocate that we strive for it as the measure of capacity to engage in reflective inquiry. Mastery, to me, means attaining the level of practice of the master (the

---

[15] I have written elsewhere about the functions of social purposes, educational goals and learning objectives in curriculum design, planning for the elicitation of intentional learning.

teacher/facilitator).[16] Within this concept of the term, there is an assumption that the master is the main—often sole—arbiter of the learning, and usually involves primary learning assessments being made by an agent or agents outside the learner, or even outside the learning community (i.e. education authorities). I hold that authentic assessment of learning, its quality, significance and relevance is most truly and usefully performed by the learner, not the teacher or those who have authorized her. We as educators have the responsibility to enable learners to develop skills of assessment and encourage them to so value learning that self-assessment becomes to them an integral part of the learning experience. In assessment, as well as in pedagogy, the formulation of questions and queries that are appropriately indicative of the desired learning and effective to the purposes of both learners and teachers is of prime importance.

This is not to say that educational authorities should not evaluate the learning that is acquired in our schools, but to note that such assessment would be primarily indicative of a degree of mastery as determined by an outside agent. These outside assessments are perfectly legitimate and often necessary. They do not however, substitute for autonomously assessed, personally integrated learning to which reflective inquiry as peace education aspires. The learning experiences that form the world views and citizenship capacities of learners comprise more than knowledge of government and organized politics and such that can be evaluated by authorities outside the learning selves of our students. Some—but not all—elements of the effective application of conceptual frameworks to reflective inquiry can be assessed by a teacher. A teacher can ascertain if learners are including all components of a framework and applying them appropriately to the problem at hand, but she is not likely to be able to adequately assess the degree to which the framework deepens and clarifies learners' conceptual understanding of the problematic. The best test of such comprehension is the communal conclusions and problem resolutions developed in consensus by the learning community. Comprehending the full significance of a framework to the illumination of a problematic is primarily a communal and dialogical process requiring the insights and reflections of all participants in an inquiry. There are areas in all learning situations that outside agents cannot apprehend. At later stages of judgment and action some indicators may be apparent, but they tend not to be of a nature that might be subject to the kind of surface assessment broadly applied in formal education.

Conceptual frameworks as constructions of thoughts and ideas that are often abstract and amorphous are instruments for defining and clarifying the core concepts relevant to the problematic that produces an inquiry. They illuminate the nature of and the relationships among components of a problematic. Thus, they are essential tools of reflective inquiry in peace education. Peace educators need to be

---

[16] The concept of mastery is one that originates in such achievements under the direction of an experienced practitioner. Certainly, it is a process with social merit that has a place in comprehensive critical peace education. It is not, however, appropriate to the open quality of reflective inquiry pedagogy.

alert to learners' comprehension of a concept as illustrated by how they use it in oral and written reflections. Indeed, they need to determine if students comprehend what a concept is. I have encountered significant lack of understanding among adult learners, not only of the learning uses of concepts, but even of how concepts function in thinking about peace and other social and political issues. Conceptual abstractions are in many ways the very essence of the peace education problematic, abstract ideas that can take various concrete forms (or be still without concrete form) and that serve many functions of meaning and description. Communal reflective inquiry can be used to clarify and determine a common meaning for concepts that comprise a framework for the study of a problematic or of proposals to respond to one. Indeed, in cases where the community has had sufficient experience of reflective inquiry, it can be used to communally construct the conceptual framework for study of the focus problem. This is a process through which a common vision of some of the potential features of the actualization of the concepts can be derived by the learning group. Peace building is a process of transforming the conceptual abstractions of our visions of peace into the material descriptions of the actual realization of the vision.

Frameworks make possible the use of holism, the means to a comprehensive view of any peace problematic. Frameworks serve both to delineate the problem and to discern patterns of relationships to be explored and analyzed through reflective inquiry. These functions apply to the understanding of the material nature of a problematic and to comprehension of proposed theoretical explications. I have found that learners sometimes confuse the functions of conceptual and theoretical frameworks, perhaps because there is little consideration given to theory at the level of general citizenship education; and—as noted in the original essay—where theory is addressed in university peace studies courses, it is often related to the consideration of the work of the recognized theorists, and not to theory making per se. All citizenship education should include experience with theory making, as preparation to be critically reflective in consideration of the rationales given for public policies. Political efficacy for change would capacitate citizens to formulate their own alternative theories, ones more likely to produce the peace directed policies we seek. One role for instruction can be in making these distinctions as part of the foundational substance that is provided as the content of an inquiry. In simplest terms, it can be postulated that conceptual frameworks work as descriptions of a problematic and theoretical frameworks as explications; the first is an attempt to describe *what* the subject comprises and *how* the components relate to each other; the second explains *why* it is as described and *how* the set of relationships came to be. Effective peace learning calls for practice in the use of conceptual and theoretical frameworks where and in the manner appropriate to the purposes of the inquiry, constructing knowledge that prepares us for effective political action for peace.

13.2.4 Background Knowledge: Substance Is Constitutive to Reflective Inquiry

The primary functions of frameworks in this pedagogy are the ordering and organization of knowledge, and providing a directional map for inquiry. Designating an order and delimiting a map as guiding functions for inquiry emphasizes the centrality of substance in critical reflection. The term "background knowledge" could be used to indicate the core substance or curricular content in the form of data of various kinds from sources such as student research, assigned readings, films, lectures, the web and prior discussions as guided by the initiator and/or facilitator of the inquiry—in schools, the teacher. This is instruction in the sense of building a basic, initial content into the common learning experience. Relevant knowledge produced by agents outside the learning community is always necessary, especially so when the community (or the class) itself has not identified the subject or the problem source of the core queries of the inquiry—usually the case with course syllabi. In instruction to initiate reflective inquiry, it should be stipulated that the knowledge provided is necessary but not sufficient to the inquiry. A core goal of the learning process is the creation of new knowledge, using, but going beyond the background provided. (This is another factor that influences my opinion on mastery.) As we would encourage learners to be independent theory makers, so too, we would guide them toward being autonomous builders of knowledge. In all peace education, we need to make clear that all the knowledge necessary for the making and building of peace is not yet available to us; that our task as peace learners and peace makers is to contribute to the building of the fundamental peace knowledge base, involving all existing fields of human knowledge and perhaps inventing new ones. Peace learning is a creative rather than a primarily receptive/retentive process.

Retention, however, is essential if knowledge building is to be a continuous process of adding to the store of peace information to which learners and their societies have ready access. Even in the age of info-tech, disciplined human memory has an important role to play in all social learning. The discipline to which I refer is a conscious process of mental review of what is known at a particular stage in a given inquiry, retrieving the relevant (a process of judgment making) and relating it to other knowledge, even to other inquiries—as a way of strengthening the retention capacity by identifying a previously integrated knowledge hook to hang it on. A similar function is served by applying information to another mental process or application to any thinking task. It is for this reason that I have taught through learning exercises that assess background knowledge through a task that requires its application rather than simply its recitation or repetition. These exercises put background knowledge through a process of review and retrieval that provides the essential substantive foundation for reflective inquiry. Knowledge, I have found, is best retained through the integration process of use, especially so when it is used to make new knowledge. Reflective inquiry emerges from a concept of learning that includes the building and as well as the acquisition of knowledge.

With Ambassador Anwarul Chowdhury, former UN Undersecretary General, Mrs Chowdhury and Olivier Urbain, Toda Institute, at book launch of "A Forum for Peace," 2014. *Source* Personal photo collection of the author

13.2.5 Justice and Peace: Defining Concepts, Describing Conditions, Honing Conceptual Tools

Defining the core and most cogent concepts for peace learning is both essential and problematic. Definitions make for the clarity needed to construct the framework of the discourse. However, they also may limit the degree of openness necessary to the creative forms of reflective inquiry that hold the possibility of producing the essential new learnings. Adding to this complexity is the widely held general perception of peace as being "a time between wars" or an indefinable and thereby an unsustainable or an unachievable abstraction. It raises the profound philosophically daunting issue of "what is it". Peace is—or will be—what we think it is. It is the destination toward which our values lead us. We will know it when we see it. If we are committed to seeing it, we need to be able to envision it. Visions of the unprecedented lend themselves more to description than to definition, i.e. "It would look like or be like this…".

From a common comprehension of the vision/description, a definition of the abstract concept we might agree is peace, can be derived, the derivation coming from the social values that are our ideas about the good. Defining the concepts of a discourse directed toward change, especially within a learning experience, is a process of negotiation toward an agreement on what the term will mean within the communal inquiry. Thus, we can propose for these purposes such conditional definitions as, "peace is a condition in which justice is assured and violence is abjured." (A definition, I have used at various times) While I find that the widely used terms "negative peace" as the absence of organized political violence and "positive peace" as the presence of social and economic justice—i.e. conditions that could prevent organized violence—has been a useful device in widening thinking about what might actually constitute peace, I find them to have been used sometimes in ways that are definitive in the sense of closing the inquiry into the conditions of peace I see as necessary to making it possible to abjure violence. So, my argument is that peace can and should be conditionally defined as a tool of the inquiry at hand and continually reviewed as the inquiry produces new insights and knowledge. It is in this way that peace may be understood as a dynamic and socially creative process,[17] that those convinced of the need for social transformation intuit it to be. Indeed, were we to have been in the habit of such constant review of the concept of democracy, we would probably not now be in the political circumstances that so threaten democracy as Dewey and Metcalf conceptualized it in their notions of education for democratic citizenship.

13.2.6 Open Inquiry: Formulation of Cogent Questions; Expectations for Replies

Direct questions call for definitive, descriptive *answers.* Queries call for conditional, speculative *responses.*[18] Verbs are crucial in the formation of questions. For example 'can' implies that something is or is not possible, "Can we do so and so?" The expected reply is an affirmation or negation of the possibility (usually one or the other) imbedded in the question, i.e. an answer which may or may not be elaborated or subject to further questioning. Questions require primarily recall, or at best, reasoned deduction, rather than careful reflection. Queries are formed to initiate individual and group reflection intended to produce multiple responses from which a communal inquiry can be further elaborated. Questions might become queries when we substitute 'can' with 'might' or 'could.' The expected replies are more likely to be reflective speculations that could suggest possibilities and provoke further queries and questions as both would be required for deepening the exploration of proposed possibilities. Queries are a way of putting the 'quest'

[17] John F. Kennedy in his commencement address at American University in June 1963 defined peace as, "a process, a way of solving problems."

[18] Query is a term borrowed from a Quaker tradition, the form in which issues of concern are put before a meeting, expecting all to share their reflections toward making communal decisions.

into questions and the 'search' into research. It is the questing after and searching for the learning that will best prepare us to be makers and builders of peace that actually. It is the questing and the search that 'opens' an inquiry.

Raising issues for reflection as queries rather than questions, I believe, helps to makes it possible for all members of the community to contribute to the inquiry, and to have their responses validated as indicative of individual thinking that is valued by the group. Limiting learning exchanges to definitive or 'closing' questions tends to perpetuate the atmosphere of hierarchical valuing of replies, offering affirmation only to those who present the "right answer," closing possibilities for further reflection for all who fail to produce the answer, not a situation that contributes to self-esteem and respect for the individual capacities of all in the community.

13.2.7 The Moral and Political Philosophies of Open Reflective Inquiry

Reflective inquiry as pedagogy is itself a political philosophy grounded in a set of ethical principles, functioning as a moral philosophy to guide our judgments of what comprises a social good. It is premised upon undertaking the responsibility to contribute to a form of education that will serve to advance the development of an authentically democratic political order committed to human equality, nonviolence as the core guideline of individual and social relationships, and respect for the integrity of Earth, the components of what I have earlier referred to as universal moral inclusion.

It assumes that all human beings who enjoy unimpaired mental capacities—whatever their ranking on the various limited assessments of human intelligence—are capable of moral agency on behalf of justice and the reflective inquiry into social good that comprises ethical judgment making. This is a philosophy which obliges education to strive toward releasing and developing that capacity in all learners, no matter what life roles they are being prepared for. It is the core of the political philosophy of that which I believe to be authentic democracy. It would suggest that all political philosophies be reviewed and assessed for their potential for guiding principles for judgments in peacemaking and peace building. The motivating argument for such study lies in the assertion that all political philosophies should be assessed primarily in terms of their compatibility with the *sine qua non* principle of what I *intuit* to be peace and what I assert to be the fundamental social purpose of peace education, contributing to the achievement of universal moral inclusion.

13.3 Snauwaert's Concluding Reflections

An intimate connection between cosmopolitanism and reflective pedagogy is at the heart of a comprehensive, critical peace education. From this perspective, reflective inquiry is not only a means to the actualization of cosmopolitanism; reflective inquiry is an *ethical requirement,* and thus a *constitutive element*, of cosmopolitanism. The political efficacy, including political knowledge and skill, required for transformative social and political agency is based upon complex peace learning. This learning is in turn facilitated by a pedagogy of reflective inquiry. Reardon's complex and insightful inquiry into the nature of reflective inquiry and its pedagogy points to the insight that a pedagogy of reflective inquiry central to a critical peace education must not only engage and develop the inward reflection of the student; it must constitute a social and political dialogue. The pedagogy of reflective inquiry that leads to political and social transformation mirrors the nature of public reason and democratic deliberation.[19] The classroom, as a democratic public space of freedom, is a site of open, impartial deliberation wherein the reflective responses, proposals, visions, and ideals of citizens, present and future, are subjected to open (fully inclusive and cosmopolitan), impartial scrutiny. The responses that 'survive' such scrutiny are authentically reflective and dialogical, and qualify as potential transformative propositions. Through this process students develop the capacities of public reason and become adept at democratic deliberation. This pedagogy enacts the processes and substantive issues of democratic public deliberation in the classroom. From this perspective, critical peace education is authentic democratic education.

[19] *Sen,* The Idea of Justice.

Chapter 14
Epilogue: The First Day of Hope

Retrospective Reflection on the Epilogue (1982)

Reading this "futures scenario" written shortly after the actual historic, "first day of hope," is somewhat bittersweet. June 12, 1982 was the glorious early summer day of an historic anti-nuclear demonstration. The celebratory, hopeful tone of the scenario is reminiscent of many actual high points experienced in my years in the peace movement and the evolution of peace education. It calls to memory not only the spirit that surrounded the convening of the United Nations Second Special Session on Disarmament, but the sense of the possibilities for transformative change forthcoming from a massive, coordinated campaign by global civil society, the kind of change we know to be possible, given the realization of convergent conditions made possible by popular will and citizen action. Both the will and the action, we believe, can be cultivated through the creative and courageous exercise of people power inspired by human imagination, informed by full understanding of the opposing realities and knowledge of the intended social transformations human society has experienced throughout history.

Those years of vigorous action in the disarmament movement were both frightening and hopeful ones for peace learning and peace politics. The hope was sweet but the bitterness of fear prevailed, and another historic opportunity was lost, as it was to be again with the possibilities opened a few years later with the winding down of the Cold War, wasted in short sighted continuation of the traditional competitive and conflictual international politics of the war system. The same politics of fear perpetuated the arms production and trade that pushed conflicts into violence, as only limited reduction in the numbers of (outdated) nuclear weapons were made. Hope was sorely needed in these years in which fears incited by the nuclear arms race, produced education efforts that gave a boost to

B.A. Reardon and D.T. Snauwaert, *Betty A. Reardon: A Pioneer in Education for Peace and Human Rights*, SpringerBriefs on Pioneers in Science and Practice 26,
DOI 10.1007/978-3-319-08967-6_14

peace studies and peace education. Much of that education, however, focused on the dangers and destructive capacity of nuclear weapons with little in the way of alternatives beyond study of conflict resolution (largely applied to the playground and classroom) and understanding "the other" primarily "the Russians." Few educators devoted attention to the possibilities of altering the international security system so as to strengthen and increase its capacities to prevent war, or change the fundamental structures of the relationships that encouraged the amassing of more and more destructive weapons.

Among the purposes of including this scenario in this special issue of The Teachers College Record *on education about the nuclear arms race was opening readers minds to consideration of more constructive, potentially transformative possibilities. Such an educational goal remains an important responsibility of peace education. Written at the request of Douglas Sloan, editor of* The Record, *it was based on a teaching technique devised in my days of curriculum development and teacher training on world order studies. I was asked to offer something brighter in outlook than other articles in the issue, which dealt largely with education concerning the destructive consequences, including the annihilation of human society, inherent in the raging nuclear arms race, suggesting how to teach toward envisioning positive changes in the world order. I drafted the scenario, not as a prediction of a probable future, but as an example of envisioning preferred futures. Imaging preferred futures, was one method through which students were helped to conceptualize alternatives to the war system by proposing new institutions and situations, coupled with informed speculation on the strategies, policies and events that held promise of achieving the envisioned alternative. We always face a need to spark learners' motivation to consider possibilities for positive change. To consider the possibilities they have to see them.*

To meet the challenge we called upon devices to release the imaginative and creative capacities that had been given short shrift by standard citizen education, even the critical thinking approach that had been practiced since the days of Dewey. A teaching methodology of imaging and assessing alternative possible futures was adapted from the world order approach to its normative and futures perspectives and purposes as a teaching device of proposing images of probable, possible, and preferred futures. Often the images were specified with plans or 'models' of the institutions, which would be make preferred social and political conditions possible. Sketching out such possibilities was undertaken to encourage speculation on how events in the present could be starting points for the positive changes toward which we hoped peacelearning would provide preparation to take social and political action. Following the adage that "Without a vision, the people will perish," we sought to empower peace students and citizens to envision the world they hoped for. Conducted, as is most peace education, as an inquiry rather than exposition, imaging is cultivated around core questions: What is the nature of the world you would prefer to live in? What institutional changes would that require? What political and social changes might bring forth those changes? What events could lead to the change? What must we do now to start such a chain of events? What do we need to learn to be able to do it?

Peace education has largely been an informed inquiry (substantive knowledge is essential) into cultivating hope. Hope informed by a positive, specified vision and awareness of the possibilities to work toward it, helped to lift us from the despair so easily succumbed to under the nuclear fear. We strive to hold on to it now under looming fears of the proliferating wars of insurgency conducted and responded to with various forms of terror; and the horrendous possibilities of ecological collapse. We need to take action to face down the fear and make "another world possible." The task of peace education is to elicit the learning that will enable us to invest our strongest endeavors in moving peace from a preference to a possibility to a probability, to "keep hope alive."

Betty A. Reardon
April, 2014

It was cool and clear in the stadium this morning.[1] The sunlight was so bright I felt as if I could see past and future as now I could see places other than this huge arena thousands of miles from the New York home from which I viewed the events leading to this formal inauguration of the World Disarmament Plan. How had all this been possible when less than a decade ago we had been so close to unprecedented destruction? When did it start to happen? What was the turning point? Where did the vision come from that gave this sense of déja vu? Only once before had I seen or experienced anything like today. As I scanned the stadium on my own side where the observers sat, the faces and garb reflecting the varieties of human diversity, so recently and so vigorously reclaimed from disappearance into the homogenization of the global military/industrial culture, I remembered the huge auditorium of the Medical Center in Mexico where the Women's Tribunal met in June 1975. And I thought of the great assembly in another part of Mexico City where the formal U.N. conference convened as I watched the delegates file into their section, many of them embracing, shaking hands, greeting each other with the enthusiasm of members of a winning team, with the energy of those revitalized by ultimate success in a long and arduous struggle. The official delegates were somewhat more decorous than we nongovernmental observers, members of a multiplicity of organizations and movements, many totally unaffiliated participants in the struggle. Most of us had contributed to "stalling traffic" in the large tunnel entrances, shouting, waving to each other, hugging, blowing kisses; no small number doing dances of joy as they sang their way to their places in the stand. Even the delegates seemed joyously celebrant. I saw again that same day in June when the official delegates to the World Conference for International Women's Year assembled for the inaugural session, the expansive bright hall festooned with the flags of the member states and the largely female assemblage comprising a glorious costume display, representing all the world's cultures.

---

[1] This text was initially published as: Reardon, Betty A. "The First Day of Hope." *Teachers College Record* 84, no. 1 (1982): 255–65. The permission to republish this text was granted by Gary Natriello, Executive Editor, *Teachers College Record*, 8 March 2014.

Maybe it began there on those hot and rainy days when our feet were constantly wet from waiting for the bus to take us for our nearly daily trips from the non-governmental tribune to the official U.N. conference to lobby the delegates.[2] We struggled to assure that some consideration of the legitimate concerns of women would be included in the politics-as-usual discourse of the nation-states. Ah, the startled look of the grey-garbed Chinese delegate as she emerged from the toilet stall to have a disarmament statement thrust at her! We were determined to focus attention on disarmament as the basic requirement for 'peace' without which we saw little hope for the two other themes of that international year that became a U.N. decade, 'equality' and 'development.'

Memory carried me, more comfortably than did the chartered Mexican buses, back to the tribune and the panel on disarmament where a Nobel Laureate received a standing ovation from the women when he told them the task was theirs. Without their persistent, global, and voluminous demand, he asserted, the male power structures of the nation-states would never disarm. "If you have to take to the streets, do it! And keep doing it until we've got an agreement for General and Complete Disarmament!" General and Complete Disarmament (GCD) was his watchword and the constantly articulated vision he and those who clearly perceived the true dangers to human security put forth as the only real hope for peace, and the fundamental need for survival. He also continuously pointed, as he did in his call to the women to articulate their demands forcefully and publicly, to the legitimate expression of popular sovereignty in public opinion, and to the potential for articulation and execution of the "will of the people" that lay in communications media free of the control of nation-states.

Maybe that is what really made the difference, the media. Certainly without it the great outpouring of revulsion at the thought of nuclear war and the rejection of further development of nuclear weapons would not have been so quickly perceived and responded to by the policymakers, especially the leaders of the nuclear states and most especially the superpowers. Yes, it was the media, and their coverage of the changes in strategic doctrine—the shift from deterrence to limited nuclear war policy, which the politicians did not expect the masses of people to notice or respond to, assuming they could continue to cover it over with arguments about national security and technical competence and all the smoke screens that for so long had kept the average person from confronting the fundamental security issues.

Surely that had an impact—the mistaken assumptions of a leadership out of touch with the people, in fact out of touch with reality. The shift startled and frightened even those of us in the peace movement, including the researchers who had closely followed arms issues and were always aware of the grave danger. It made the danger more imminent. We could see it, smell it, feel it, almost touch

[2] All events and individuals mentioned prior to 1982 are actual as are some of the persons described as participants in the ceremony in the stadium. All of the events described as occurring after 1983 are as possible as the nuclear detonation that ends the "Last Day of Civilization" Volume 84, Number 1, Fall 1982.

it. It was in our heads constantly, often crowding out all other thoughts, screaming "Do something! Act on your analysis! Live your commitment!" And that was part of it, too, the numbers of people beginning to live by their commitment to the reversal of militarization and the abolition of war. Some even willingly died for this goal, not as the innocent victims of militarism and repression to whose liberation they committed their lives, but as persons consciously embracing the ultimate risk for the sake of the ultimate value. But again, without the media would so many have known of them, a few American religious, a Dutch journalist, and the others? None of them had to be there with their lives on the line in the struggle. Nor in fact did all the others about whom we never learned because neither their lives nor their deaths were considered 'newsworthy.' Now people demanded to know.

Yes, it might be that public opinion can influence the media as much as the other way around, and even journalists can have commitments and be both acclaimed and reviled for them. I thought briefly of the Jonathan Schell phenomenon and the startling impact of his book on people who had never thought seriously about the problem of nuclear war[3]; the great stir in the media and conversation, the chastening effect, and then the denial, "Oh well, nothing new in it after all." "Very badly written, don't you think?" "Oh, yeah, typical *New Yorker* verbosity." "Hell, there simply can't be total devastation. Something, someone will survive to build anew." "Indeed, where there is life there is hope " Ah, but that possibility could not be fully denied. There could, in fact, be no reflective life left, arrogant as that may seem to roaches and rodents. That was it. It was really just the opposite. This time the hope was born out of the realization that there could be no life, out of the determination to prevent the death of the planet.

Yet none of this could have happened without the visions and the plans to make realities out of possibilities, without the strategies and policies to capitalize on the tiny flickering lights of hope in the developments running counter to the arms race and war during those very days when the trends toward global militarization were so virulent. Yesterday on the plane, in a seat separated from the others in my chapter of Educators for Social Responsibility (ESR),[4] who formed one of the many observer groups traveling to witness this culminating ceremony (though most of us know it is only the beginning), I reverted to my distant past as a student and teacher of history and jotted down a chronology of the political events that got us to today's affirmation ritual—a goal that had so often seemed at best quixotic, at worst impossible, even to those of us who kept insisting we could stop the arms race, that it was only a matter of "political will." I did not bother to record the long history of disarmament efforts from the mid-nineteenth century, so frequently reviewed with students, nor did I start with the international treaties of the nuclear age, all too often cited as proof of the effectiveness or inadequacies, depending on

[3] See Schell, Jonathan. *The Fate of the Earth*. New York: Alfred A Knopf, 1982.

[4] Educators for Social Responsibility (Box 1711, New Rochelle, NY 10802), was founded in Brookline, Massachusetts, in 1981 (see organizations cited by Sam Totten in "Activist Educators" in this issue of the *Record*, pp 199–209).

the perspective of the chronicler, of arms control agreements.[5] Instead, I pulled from the roots of history, read or remembered, some twentieth-century landmarks on the road toward the abolition of war, toward the popularization and realization of the notion of general and complete disarmament. My chronology, as copied here from the back of the travel preparation memo and schedule ESR had sent to our group, went like this:

1928	Kellogg Briand Pact—renounced war as an instrument of national policy—signed by fifty nations
1932	World Disarmament Conference meets in Geneva—recognized arms race as a cause of war
1945	U.N. Charter declares as its purpose putting an "end to the scourge of war". First resolution of the General Assembly prohibits the use of nuclear weapons
1945	Japan dissolves its military
1948	Costa Rica abolishes its army; transfers funds to education
1950–1963	U.N. peacekeeping actions undertaken
1975	International Women's Year (IWY) catalyzes international women's movement for disarmament
1978	U.N. First Special Session on Disarmament (SSD I) designates total elimination of national military forces as long-range goal of disarmament[6]
1979–1982	Shift in strategic doctrine discloses seriousness of possibility of nuclear war
1980	UNESCO convenes World Congress on Disarmament Education; European women present disarmament petition with thousands of signatures to Secretary General at Women's Mid-Decade Conference
1981–1982	Massive demonstrations for nuclear disarmament take place in Europe, Japan, Australia, North America. June 1982 convening of SSD II becomes focal point for coordinated worldwide popular movement for disarmament
1983	Launching of U.N. World Disarmament Campaign to educate and mobilize the general public in favor of disarmament[7]
1984–1986	U.N. Peacekeeping Force established as member states initiate reduction of arms and armed forces having adopted the Defense Weapons System.[8] Several small states emulate Costa Rica and

[5] For information on this subject consult the U.N. Centre for Disarmament, United Nations, New York, NY 10017.

[6] The text of the final document of SSD I is available from the UN Center for Disarmament.

[7] Information on the World Disarmament Campaign is also available from the U.N. Centre for Disarmament.

[8] For a description of such a system see Hollins, Harry, B. "A Defensive Weapons System." The Bulletin of the Atomic Scientists, 1982.

abolish their armies, transferring funds to education and development.Regional Development/Disarmament Councils established in all world regions to guide economic conversion of resources and production from the military to civilian sectors and to assure security through the fulfillment of human needs

1987 SSD III outlines a basic treaty for general and complete disarmament

1990 Final ratification of the World Treaty on General and Complete Disarmament. Massive worldwide celebration—international ceremony to mark its coming into force.

Long before yesterday's review, the events leading us here seemed clear to me. Even as they happened I would mark them off as landmarks on my mental map of the journey to disarmament. Still, I could not put my finger on what really made the difference. I kept looking around the stadium, searching out individual faces of people I knew had been important in the movement, and representative groups recognized as significant political forces or gadflies. I focused on the bright yellow robes of a Japanese Buddhist monk standing at one of the entrances to the playing field. He was holding a round single-skin drum of a type that had set the rhythm for another week in June. As more clergy began to cluster around him, preparing themselves to walk out onto the platform on the middle of the field where the opening religious observation was to take place, I heard again the pulse of those drums, blending into the guitars and crisp voices of the young Benedictines singing in the Cathedral of St John the Divine in New York City. Ten thousand people representing virtually every spiritual and religious tradition crammed the entire space of the huge nave. Hearing the mental replay of those sounds reawakened the strong feelings of human solidarity and the spiritual energy released in the cathedral that June day in 1982.

The world religions have played a vital role in the struggle. More than any other single force in the movement, they demonstrated the ability to transcend cultural, political, and ideological differences, and manifested the courage to articulate fundamental moral principles in the face of political pragmatism. Their convergence into a single world force for peace and disarmament had come from small, fragmentary beginnings. I thought for an instant of a church basement in Brooklyn where another saffron-robed monk from Japan had spoken, simply but with passion, to a group of no more than fifteen people less than a year before the gathering of the ten thousand. We sat then at folding tables of the kind found m church basements and school gyms across the United States. Beside me was a Colombian Catholic priest, and next to him the Lutheran pastor of the church. I had never seen that pastor before, but we knew each other and spoke to each other from a relationship of long standing and the closeness that comes from recognition of a common struggle. The priest I had known over the decade since a small seminar m Mexico had brought together a handful of educators from the United States and Latin America to explore the possibilities of cooperative efforts in peace education. It was these small meetings, these tentative connections and common endeavors, that built a worldwide network of persons of very different backgrounds and life circumstance who shared similar hopes, fears, and visions. Although infrequently together, they had forged a community of caring through which they gave each other support and courage. The courage to continue in the face of setback after setback was undoubtedly the essential ingredient in the whole recipe of the disarmament struggle.

That courage was evident when some in the religious establishment who saw the need to return to the prophetic role of religion began to articulate what many were beginning to intuit about the meaning of nuclear weapons, and about the international system that had produced them at so great a cost to the entire human family. As nations marched blindly from one stage of military preparedness to the next "advance in weapons technology," military values took precedence over humane norms. It was in the early 1980s that the churches spoke out most forcefully against the irrationality and evil of the weapons, of the arms race, of the militarization process, giving popular voice to the ethical choice only a few scientists and philosophers had recognized in the early years of the "atomic age."[9] The churches had been in the forefront, too, in organizing the massive demonstrations against nuclear weapons and war that had taken place in cities all over the world m the early 1980s.

As the clergy gathered, preparing to file onto the platform, I noticed a young woman wearing a clerical collar above a dark blue bib. The collar made her appearance no less 'feminine' than that of the older woman she was chatting with. Her companion wore a heavy cross and chain on a turtleneck sweater above a simple skirt. I took her to be a Catholic sister. Their presence in that gathering represented not only the significant merger between feminist politics and the peace movement that had confronted the conscience of the churches and the governments, but also the millions of women who had worked in their own communities to educate people to the dangers and the possibilities. I thought of the letter I had received about 10 years ago from a young friend in Oxford, England, the mother of an 8-year-old girl who wanted a future for her child, who had surprised even herself, never having spoken in public, by beginning to make public speeches, first in her own village, then in other small communities across England. Together with other mothers who began to instruct themselves as they stood in the play yard watching children whose chances of becoming adults diminished with each technological weaponry advance. She formed a national movement similar to that being organized by women all over the world. In her letter she had told me of the four women who met around a kitchen table in Copenhagen about a year before the U.N. Mid-Decade Women's Conference was to meet there in 1980, and how from that conversation began the European Women for Peace movement, a high point of which was presenting a peace petition to the secretary general of the United Nations. It was indeed the women who nurtured and cultivated the grass-roots peace

[9] Listings of such statements available from United Ministries in Education, c/o Church of the Brethren, 1451 Dundee Avenue, Elgin, Il 60120.

movement, standing on American street corners with Freeze[10] petitions, traveling across Europe m second-class night trains to meet with sisters in other cities without the benefit of formal translation or any of the professional and diplomatic support systems that facilitate international dialogue. Their support system was their own commitment to the future of their children. Their facilities were their own energies and their conviction that the struggle for women's equality and the struggle for world peace were one, an insight that for so long many in the movement, even those whose contribution was the analysis of the situation from which political strategies were derived, found hard to comprehend. Indeed, many still find it hard.

Yes, many of us in this struggle have had our blind spots to the way in which particular individual or group concerns related to the common goal. Certainly diversity and political divisions had often threatened to shatter the force we had begun to build, to dissipate the unity of efforts toward a universal objective. There were more political struggles than those between the superpowers and between the first and third worlds. Divisiveness within nations was spawned by the traditional political approaches to the problem, and was sometimes made worse by controversies among the researchers and scientists, many of whom claimed to have the "correct analysis" on which the political strategy for disarmament should be based. The peace research movement that emerged in Europe and the United States in the 1950s and 1960s certainly made an important contribution in spite of such differences as those between advocates of "arms control" and the advocates of 'disarmament.'

Looking over the delegates, I picked out researchers I had known through the years who had devoted so much of their energies not only to the research, but to trying to bring their findings to the attention of the political establishment. I remembered the way in which the peace research community had worked to increase the participation and the substantive role of nongovernmental organizations in the U.N. deliberations on disarmament. From the early 1980s they had begun to act as a kind of global lobby in the interest of humankind, interacting with those in the international talks who were operating from the traditional national-interest perspective. Surely it was this sophisticated and informed lobbying that convinced the practical politicians that policy could be made in "the human interest."[11] The tenacious efforts of some of these researchers and other nongovernmental organizations in and around the United Nations had significantly changed the course of deliberations. It was wonderful to see the People's Security[12] lobby as an official delegation to the international meeting that had drafted and was

[10] Nuclear Weapons Freeze Campaign Clearing House, 4144 Lmdell Blvd, Suite 404, St Louis, Mo 63108.

[11] See Johansen, Robert. *The National Interest and the Human Interest.* An Analysis of US Foreign Policy. Princeton, NJ: Princeton University Press, 1980.

[12] For a definition of the concept of People's Security see Sakamoto, Yoshikazu. "Report of the Secretary General." International Peace Research Association Newsletter, Fall, 1981.

now bringing into force this Treaty for General and Complete Disarmament. Many nongovernmental organizations were represented by such official delegations to this signature ceremony.

As the People's Security delegation filed into the stand, we observers jumped to our feet in a wild burst of applause, for they represented more than anything else "our victory," a victory we knew to be possible only in the kind of game where everybody wins. Among those we recognized in the delegation were the Japanese teacher from the Asian Regional ESR walking with the African, Latin American, and European educators whom we had elected to represent us officially at the ceremony. Walking together among the International Physicians against Nuclear War[13] were a neurosurgeon from the Soviet Union and a psychiatrist from the United States. The others I did not know but assumed they were from the social scientist, performing artist, and other professional groups that had begun to organize and build global networks for nuclear disarmament in the spring and summer of 1982 following the example of the churches and the physicians, just as we had in forming Educators for Social Responsibility.

For a while I believed it was really the formal educational efforts that had made the difference, helping people to see the need to change, the need expressed by President Kennedy for "mankind to put an end to war [before] war [puts] an end to mankind." Educators organizing in response to the nuclear threat had served as a catalyst to introduce peace studies into schools and all kinds of learning settings throughout the world. The work that had been developed since the early 1960s on the methods of teaching about alternatives to war, and the possibilities for nonviolent conflict resolution, began to be accepted even in some of the more conservative educational systems.[14] Even now I was sure that education was a very significant part of it, perhaps the most significant. That whole movement during the 1980s was an educative process in itself. People were trying to learn, struggling to instruct themselves in the issues related to weapons development, to national security, to means to end the arms race and possible alternatives to war. It may have been one of the most important learning experiences in human history. Indeed, I was very sure that what we had learned about the international system and how our efforts to make our nations more secure through more numerous and more powerful arms only made us more insecure was the most important of all lessons. Yet cognitive learning, understanding even so important a phenomenon as armed insecurity, simply did not explain it all. There was something more that had made the difference.

Among the People's Security delegation I also noted the American senator who had been one of those to introduce the Nuclear Freeze into the U.S. Senate. His presence there reminded me of the parallel development of education with political

[13] Physicians for Social Responsibility, P O Box 411, Planetarium Station, New York, NY 10024.

[14] See Reardon, Betty A. *Militarization, Security and Peace Education.* Valley Forge, PA: United Ministries in Education, 1982.

action and the way in which the citizens movement had influenced and in fact provided the direction for changing political policies. Yet I thought, too, of the nature of the early antinuclear efforts, particularly the Nuclear Freeze, which called for a halt to the way things were going and became a prelude to a new direction. But as the freeze was first proposed and discussed, in itself it did not propose or contain a specific positive direction. Those positive energies I recalled from the cathedral service did find a political vehicle when the antiwar movement joined the social justice movement, when the commitment to fulfilling human needs became as strong as the urgent desire to prevent human annihilation. It was that merger, which generated the really significant force, which kept us going through this last decade. It brought into the movement many who previously had not seen as their own the problem of preventing nuclear annihilation and devising alternatives to war. We began to see how these issues were inseparably related, just as the feminists came to understand that the militaristic values propelling the arms race were the very same values that kept women "in their place." So, too, the economically deprived, and the politically oppressed, began to comprehend the war system as a fundamental cause of their condition.[15] Most people came to see that system pushing us closer and closer to the last day of civilization.

The connection to economic equity, social justice, and human rights gave us something very positive to struggle for. While the researchers had been putting out annual reports showing the social costs of the arms race from the mid-seventies on, it was the budget cuts in human services coming simultaneously with increasing arms expenditures to almost incomprehensible proportions that helped us put things together. Anyone following world events was painfully aware of two significant trends: severe economic crisis and unemployment on a worldwide basis, accompanied by a rising tide of global militarization. Many countries were falling under the control of the military and virtually all were building large military establishments. Arms control negotiations were stalled as one technological 'advance' after another produced ever deadlier weaponry. It took years before an alternative international security system as the fundamental requirement for disarmament became clear to all. The freeze and the proposals of the Defensive Weapons System for cutting back on the big weapons helped to focus on the need for system change, and made more sweeping proposals possible. When the U.N. Second Special Session on Disarmament was convened in 1982, the general concern and growing fear brought it unprecedented public attention.

The event itself was no radical departure from the ordinary diplomatic trends and events. The opening session replicated the same atmosphere, the same procedures as innumerable other sessions. That day I sat in the section reserved for observers from nongovernmental organizations, excited and hopeful because the

---

[15] See Reardon, Betty A. "Militarism and Sexism Influences on Education for War." *Connexion*, 9,3, Fall, 1981; and Sivard, Ruth. *World Military and Social Expenditures*. Leesburg, VA: World Priorities, Inc., 1977–1981.

session was finally taking place. Looking out at the assembly at all the close-cropped male heads and dark suits I thought, "It's all the same. How can anything different come out of this?" Recalling that small core of hope overlaid by the lack of expectation of anything from the established political order, it finally came to me. It was the environment in which the session took place. It was what was happening outside the halls that began to turn the tide.

It was the women, the religious, the educators, the professionals, the researchers, those few politicians who began to understand, all of them reaching out to take strength from each other, acknowledging a belief in the possibility of a future, affirming that the human drama was not yet played out. It was that, the people taking responsibility for the future, recognizing that the structures in place were not adequate to the task. So they took it up themselves with no small degree of fear and yet with courage and even a sense of joy. That was the real turning point. For me it was marked from the particular day when the largest of all the growing number of demonstrations for nuclear disarmament took place as a gesture of solidarity and support to the delegates of the Second Special Session on Disarmament. Nearly a million people came into the streets of New York surrounding the United Nations and walked together to Central Park. The park that day was used for recreation, for celebration in a way in which it had never been before, in which perhaps no public park had ever been used. The music, the speeches, the cheers, were the initiation of this very ritual we observe today. As colorful as this crowd is, it pales by comparison with the crowd that took to the New York streets on June 12, 1982, when youngsters with the safety-pin earrings of the punk-rock generation and monks garbed in the robes of their religious orders walked together with the elderly and disabled in wheelchairs, businessmen in vests and ties, and mothers pushing baby strollers. They had come from all over the world, the young, the old, those with means, those with none, to walk together, to say with one voice, "We will live! We choose life for ourselves and our children. And we will remember how close we are at this moment of choice to the possibility of death."

June 12, 1982, was the first day of hope, a day of affirmation when we knew there was the possibility that it could be done, because of our own commitment and because of those who had risked and struggled before us. As the marchers walked by the platform near the entrance to the park on which a group of Japanese musicians sat surrounded by banners carrying the slogan "Never Again," we took up that chant, "Never again! Never again!" We knew we had to remember, to remember Hiroshima, to remember the victims of weaponry, war, and militarism. Last fall when the discussions were taking place about the venue for today's ceremony, almost the only point everyone agreed on right away was that the location should have profound significance to this commitment not to forget what we have done as well as what we almost did. It should be in one of the many places that now symbolize the dark side of ourselves, which came so close to destroying us Guernica, Auschwitz, Hiroshima, Nagasaki, Afghanistan, My Lai, Lebanon. It was finally decided that we would come to this stadium, that we would observe that remembrance and this promise here in this place where the throats of poets were crushed, where the hands of musicians were smashed and the voices of those who cried for justice were silenced by militarism so deaf to poetry and music, so fearful of justice, that it brought us so very close to the final silence and to losing the possibility of this beginning.

About the Authors

Betty A. Reardon is a feminist peace and human rights educator—activist with six decades in the development and dissemination of the field. The founder of the International Institute on Peace Education (IIPE) and the original peace education graduate specialization at Teachers College Columbia University, and one of the civil society originators of U.N. Security Council Resolution 1325 on Women, Peace and Security, she has worked in all world regions toward international cooperation among peace educators.
Widely published in peace education and gender issues, including *Comprehensive Peace Education,* Teachers College Press (1985), *Educating for Human Dignity*, University of Pennsylvania Press (1995), *Tolerance*: *The Threshold of Peace*, UNESCO (1997), and *Education for a Culture of Peace in a Gender Perspective*, UNESCO (2001), her publications are archived in the Ward M. Canaday Center for Special Collections at the University of Toledo Library.

Dale T. Snauwaert, Ph.D. is Professor of Philosophy of Education and Founding Director of the Center for Nonviolence and Democratic Education and Co-Director of the Graduate Certificate Program in the Foundations of Peace Education in the Department of Educational Foundations and Leadership, Judith Herb College of Education, The University of Toledo, USA. He is the Founding Editor of *In Factis Pax*: *Online Journal of Peace Education and Social Justice*. He is widely published on such topics as democratic theory, theories of social justice, the ethics of war and peace and the philosophy of peace education in such academic journals as the *Journal of Peace Education, Educational Theory*, *Peace Studies Journal*, *Philosophical Studies in Education.* He is the author of *Democracy, Education, and Governance: A Developmental Conception* (SUNY Press, 1993), and with Fuad Al-Daraweesh, *Human Rights Education Beyond Universalism and Relativism: A Relational Hermeneutic for Global Justice* (Palgrave McMillan, forthcoming).

B.A. Reardon and D.T. Snauwaert, *Betty A. Reardon: A Pioneer in Education for Peace and Human Rights*, SpringerBriefs on Pioneers in Science and Practice 26,
DOI 10.1007/978-3-319-08967-6

About the Book

Betty A. Reardon is a world-renowned leader of peace education and human rights. Her pioneering work has laid the foundation for a new cross-disciplinary integration of peace education and international human rights within a gender-conscious, global perspective. This collection demonstrating reflective inquiry and ongoing learning offers essential works on peace education and human rights (1967–2014) and it provides access to key works of Betty A. Reardon. These texts have been foundational to the field of peace education during the past five decades of her practical experience. The unique conceptualization of a holistic framework for organizing content and the practical and specific descriptions of pedagogies for the practice of critical peace education in schools and universities have made the work useful to peace educators worldwide. Several texts are already widely included in the basic courses in the field. The book includes a scientific biography and a bibliography of her publications.

List of contents: Part I: Biography and Bibliography—Part II: The Foundations 1963–1985: The World Law Fund—Transformations into Peace and Survival: Programs for the 1970s—Conclusions from The Knowledge Industry—Disarmament Education as World Oder Inquiry—Part III: The Formation 1985–2000: The Fundamental Purposes of Peace Education—Towards a Paradigm of peace—Learning our Way to a Human Future—Part IV: Framing for Futures 2001–2014: Human rights learning—Human Rights and the Renewal of the University—Reflective Pedagogy, Cosmopolitanism, and Critical Peace Education for Political Efficacy—Epilogue: The First Day of Hope.

A website on this book with additional information on Betty A. Reardon, including links to videos and a selection of the covers of her major books is at: http://afes-press-books.de/html/SpringerBriefs_PSP_Reardon.htm.

B.A. Reardon and D.T. Snauwaert, *Betty A. Reardon: A Pioneer in Education for Peace and Human Rights*, SpringerBriefs on Pioneers in Science and Practice 26,
DOI 10.1007/978-3-319-08967-6

MIX
Papier aus verantwortungsvollen Quellen
Paper from responsible sources
FSC® C105338

If you have any concerns about our products,
you can contact us on
ProductSafety@springernature.com

In case Publisher is established outside the EU,
the EU authorized representative is:
Springer Nature Customer Service Center GmbH
Europaplatz 3, 69115 Heidelberg, Germany

Printed by Libri Plureos GmbH
in Hamburg, Germany